Student and
Academic Affairs
Collaboration

THE
DIVINE
COMITY

NASPA
Student Affairs Administrators
in Higher Education

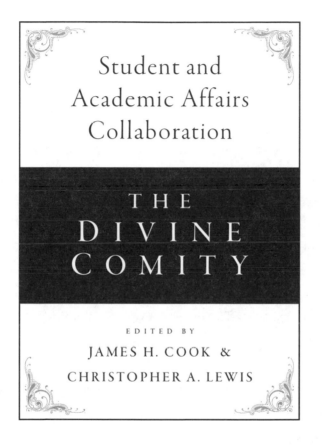

Student and Academic Affairs Collaboration

THE DIVINE COMITY

EDITED BY

JAMES H. COOK &
CHRISTOPHER A. LEWIS

NASPA
Student Affairs Administrators
in Higher Education

Student and Academic Affairs Collaboration: The Divine Comity

Additional copies may be purchased by contacting the NASPA publications department at 301-638-1749 or visiting http://www.naspa. org/publications.

ISBN 0-931654-49-1

TABLE OF CONTENTS

Student Affairs Philosophical Tenets and Assumptions
Cultural Differences between Academic and Student Affairs
The Rationale for Active Outreach and Collaboration
Developing Effective Outreach
Examples of Successful Practices
Tips for Student Affairs Practitioners
Conclusion
References

Structure and Culture: The Need for Both Formal and Informal
   Communication
Embedding the Values of Communication and Collaboration
   within the Culture
A Shared Focus for Communication and Collaboration
Conclusion
References

At the Crossroads of Civic Engagement and Engaged Learning
Mutuality, Reciprocity, and Partnership
The X-Factor: Dissonance and Transformation
Roles for Faculty, Student Affairs, and Senior Administration
Service-learning Best Practices
Conclusion
References

INTRODUCTION

Learning Reconsidered and Learning Reconsidered 2: What Now?

James H. Cook
and Christopher A. Lewis

L*earning Reconsidered* is an argument for the integrated use of all of higher education's resources in the education and preparation of the whole student. It is also an introduction to new ways of understanding and supporting learning and development as intertwined, inseparable elements of the student experience. It advocates for transformative education—a holistic process of learning that places the student at the center of the learning experience. (Keeling, 2004)

The publication of *Learning Reconsidered* (Keeling, 2004) reminded many in higher education of the critical importance of collaboration across the academy. Truly, no part of a university or college can be an island if it hopes to accomplish its role in the educational enterprise effectively.

Learning Reconsidered defined *learning* as "a comprehensive, holistic, transformative activity that integrates academic learning and student development" (p. 4). It went on to say that these are "processes that have often been considered separate, even independent of each other" (p. 4). The basic premise of *Learning Reconsidered* is that these processes *should not* be considered independent of each other.

If they are indeed viewed holistically, as a unified package of experiences one calls a college education, then what is implicit is a seamlessness (in practice, if not administratively) between academic and student affairs. In other words, a close, intentional, daily partnership between the two divisions tightly integrates academic learning and student development.

The *Student Learning Imperative* (ACPA, 1994) suggested the results for students of such a partnership: "students benefit from many and varied experiences during college and…learning and personal development are cumulative, mutually shaping processes that occur over an extended period of time in many different settings" (p. 3).

The key phrase in this passage is "cumulative, mutually shaping processes." What is required here are both hands working together at the potter's wheel—one complementing the other—to produce a work that is complete: balanced, maximized in its functionality, aesthetically developed, and strong enough for its intended use.

In direct reference to academic affairs–student affairs partnerships, *Learning Reconsidered* stated:

> The "powerful partnerships," jointly planned, combine knowledge acquisition and experiential learning to promote more complex outcomes. They include living–learning programs, career development, service learning, academic advising, cultural identity development, internships, study abroad, film festivals, honor code and academic integrity processes, campus media, culture festivals, and support services for students with disabilities. (p. 23)

These "powerful partnerships" are what *Divine Comity* is all about. Taking inspiration, theoretical direction, and conceptual cues from *Learning Reconsidered*, the originators of the *Divine Comity* project undertook to study the characteristics of effective student affairs–academic affairs partnerships. Research begun in Region III of NASPA–Student Affairs Administrators in Higher Education, was expanded to include the entire nation. As researchers received information about successful academic–student affairs partnerships, a pattern emerged. In fact, it was striking how quickly a *pronounced* pattern emerged. (But before more detail is given on the study's findings—the patterns or "nine circles"—a more specific description of the genesis of the *Divine Comity* project in the next section provides a contextual base upon which the "circles" will be layered in later chapters.)

As the editors and authors moved toward completion of this publication, *Learning Reconsidered 2* was published. *Learning Reconsidered 2* (Keeling, 2006) focuses on helping readers turn concepts in *Learning Reconsidered* into action on their campuses. The publication of this second volume is fortuitous in that *Divine Comity*, which benefits greatly from and adds to *Learning Reconsidered* and *Learning Reconsidered 2*, captures the theoretical spirit of the former and the application intent of the latter.

STUDENT AFFAIRS PROFESSIONALS WORKING WITH AND IN ACADEMIC AFFAIRS

Divine Comity is the outgrowth of a Student Affairs Professionals Working With and In Academic Affairs (SAPAA) Knowledge Community Best Practices project that started in Region III in February 2004. The object of this project was to collect best practices information from institutions in the region about effective student affairs–academic affairs collaborations/partnerships. After soliciting best practices submissions during the spring, the Region III SAPAA KC chair, James Cook, received materials from 24 universities. His intent was to prepare a best practices report for NASPA membership and conduct a presentation on results at a future NASPA conference.

Because the response was so strong and positive, James Cook, Christopher Lewis (past national SAPAA KC co-chair), and Kim O'Halloran (past national SAPAA co-chair) decided to expand the project nationally.

Prior to NASPA's 2004 Annual National Conference in Denver, Lewis broached the idea of condensing best practice materials and the lessons contained in them into a NASPA publication. After he spoke with NASPA Executive Director Gwendolyn Jordan Dungy about the project, NASPA expressed interest in such a publication. She was especially interested in making connections with the recently published *Learning Reconsidered*.

Throughout the writing of this publication, a fluid synchrony of give and take occurred. Cook and Lewis provided conceptual direction and an initiating framework, to which the team of authors added their passion, research, and experience. The editors are indebted to the team of writers not only for ably providing their appointed content, but also for making suggestions that went beyond their respective chapters and improved the whole of the work.

AND NOW FOR A LITTLE "HOUSEKEEPING"

The editors of *Divine Comity* wish to draw the reader's attention to a few formatting and content issues. This book is not intended to read as if it were written by one person. This is a collaborative effort among 16 authors; therefore there are 16 unique writing styles and perspectives on the book's central topic. The editors worked closely with the authors to make sure content matched the general topic, preordained subtopics, and the prescribed overall outline. They also partnered closely to construct a work with a flow of information that resulted in the conceptually whole treatment of the subject. Beyond that and American Psychological Association style, the editors left most stylistic issues to the discretion of the writers.

The reader will note some redundancy regarding the attention paid to the common characteristics of successful collaborative partnerships and barriers to the same. The editors sought to minimize this overlap, but in some cases deemed it necessary to establish flow and context in a particular chapter.

REFERENCES

American College Personnel Association. (1994). *The student learning imperative: Implications for student affairs*. Washington, DC: Author.

Keeling, R. P. (Ed.). (2004). *Learning reconsidered: A campus-wide focus on the student experience.* Washington, DC: National Association of Student Personnel Administrators and American College Personnel Association.

Keeling, R. P. (Ed.). (2006). *Learning reconsidered 2: A practical guide to implementing a campus-wide focus on the student experience.* Washington, DC: American College Personnel Association, Association of College and University Housing Officers–International, Association of College Unions International, National Academic Advising Association, National Association for Campus Activities, National Association of Student Personnel Administrators, and National Intramural-Recreational Sports Association.

CHAPTER ONE
Divine Comity: The Basics

James H. Cook,
Abby M. Ghering,
and Christopher A. Lewis

Thank you, Mr. Alighieri

When Dante Alighieri wrote his La Commedia di Dante Alighieri in the early 14th century (it wasn't titled La Divina Commedia (The Divine Comedy) until the mid-16th century—long after Dante was gone), he had no idea of how often and in how many different ways the story of his fictional travels through Hell, Purgatory, and Heaven would be read, examined, adapted, and applied.

Here it is applied again. When working on the original concept for *Divine Comity*, it occurred to the Dante fan on the editing team,

1

James Cook, that an interesting parallel exists between the structure of Dante's Heaven, Hell, and Purgatory—with each level's nine circles— and the nature of strong academic affairs–student affairs partnerships. Having arrived at the parallel in a moment of free association, and as a result of his penchant for wordplay (Divine "Comity"), and the recognition that indeed some days working in higher education are Heaven, some are Hell, and some are a little of both, Cook broached the connection to his partner, Christopher Lewis. After some discussion among the entire editing/writing team, it was decided to take the concept and run with it. The reader will notice allusion to circles (Figure 1.1) throughout the book.

The parallels go deeper than the circles, however. For purposes of explanation, the nature of the relationship discussed in this publication will be compared to Dante's travels through Heaven for a moment. This will better illuminate the extent to which Dante presciently addressed academic and student affairs relationships nearly 700 years ago—and didn't even realize it.

When Dante and his first guide, Virgil, reached the summit of Purgatory, Virgil bade Dante farewell. Virgil represented human reason and this was as far as human reason alone would allow someone to go. From that point, Dante was led into and through Heaven by the beautiful Beatrice. As they climbed ever higher, Dante encountered a progression of souls whose lives on earth had been lived in increasingly closer conformity to the ideal of heavenly perfection. Finally, when he and Beatrice reached the ninth Heaven (outer space), he was left alone amid the angelic chorus to experience the full glory of Paradise: Heaven completely realized was so awe-inspiring that Dante gasped, "O how scant is speech and how feeble to my conception!"

Assuming circles one and two exist already—the divisions of

academic affairs and student affairs—*Divine Comity* leads the reader through circles three through eight to a point where the ninth is achieved: a state of partnership that maximizes academic and student affairs' ability to have a positive impact on the lives of their students.

Figure 1.1. **Nine circles of academic and student affairs collaboration.**

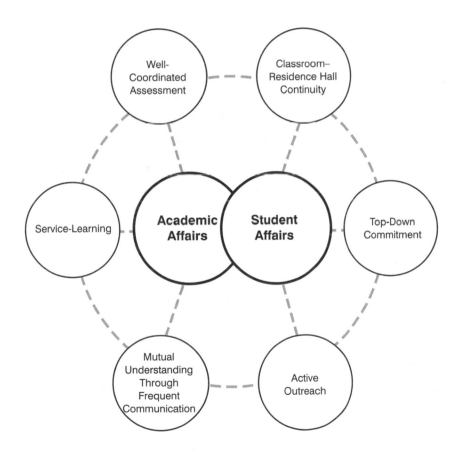

The ninth circle represents the relationship taken to its fullest potential. Good relationships can exist at lower circles, but without all of the *Divine Comity* practices in place, they cannot realize their potential to be the types of partners described by John-Steiner, Weber, and Minnis (1998): "...they plan, decide, and act jointly; they also *think together*, combining independent conceptual themes to create original frameworks" (p. 776).

Skeptics might ask if Beatrice, who symbolized faith and otherworldly truth, is symbolic of what it would take to fully develop the relationship *Divine Comity* promotes: supernatural assistance. Maybe so, but this "Beatrice," a team of able and experienced editors and authors, professionals who have extensive experience in academic and student affairs, offers the reader a natural path to partnership; a progression of circles very "this-worldly" in their practicality.

The definition of a comedy has changed since Dante's day. Back then it was any story that had a happy ending. We hope that *Divine Comity*, when applied, will live up to its comedic parallel.

PERSPECTIVE AND PASSION

The cornerstone to the type and quality of relationships that *Divine Comity* promotes between academic affairs and student affairs, the foundational element, is how personnel in the two divisions view the organization and to what extent their fundamental aspirations focus on learning as a personal and corporate activity essential to *causing* learning to occur among their students. Is the organization to them a "body"—a system—or do they see only the arm, leg, or head? Do they recognize and avail themselves of, or better yet *make*, the opportunities to learn from and with each other? Is the organization eager to learn?

In his book *The Fifth Discipline* (1990), Peter Senge suggested that the most effective organizations are learning organizations: places characterized by the synthesis of a systems perspective and a learning passion. According to Senge, they are places:

> ...where people continually expand their capacity to create the results they truly desire, where new and expansive patterns of thinking are nurtured, where collective aspiration is set free, and where people are continually learning to see the whole together. (p. 3)

What is "seeing the whole together?" It is more than the shared recognition of the big picture. The wholeness to which Senge refers is something deeper. It is at once caused by and causes systems thinking. Colleges and universities, like other large organizations, are single entities whose components are linked by a complex network of formal elements, such as reporting lines and common or interdependent functions; and informal elements, such as shared interests and agendas and psychological contracts.

Recognizing that institutions of higher education are complex systems and not simply aggregations of their parts is the first and most essential step in building successful and sustained academic affairs and student affairs partnerships. With regard to organizations in general, Senge (1990) said, "To understand the most challenging managerial issues requires seeing the whole system that generates the issues" (p. 66). He encourages managers to observe the "principle of the *system* [italics added] boundary" in which issues, not boundaries set by organizational structures, determine how interactions are examined and take place. From this one can conclude that while the divisions of academic affairs and student affairs should not necessarily lose their discrete identities, the content of what they do—if not the structural context—should become much more closely aligned and should be pursued more inter-dependently.

Senge (1990) said, "System thinking shows us that there is no outside; that you and the cause of your problems are part of a single system" (p. 67). Colleges and universities—academic affairs and student affairs divisions in particular—must operate as single systems with no "outsiders" if they are to educate successfully 21st-century students and deliver on the changing demands society places on them.

From Separation to Collaboration

There is a vast history of both collaboration and misunderstanding between faculty and student affairs professionals. Increasingly throughout the history of higher education in the United States, the gap between the roles of faculty and student affairs professionals has widened (Bloland, Stamatakos, & Rogers, 1994, 1996). According to Kellogg (1999), "As faculty found less time to focus on the social and professional development of their students, student affairs professionals emerged to fulfill that need" (p. 1).

This separation of responsibilities was further fueled in the early 20th century by the industrial phenomenon of specialization. The advent of scientific management—courtesy of Frederick Taylor and his time-motion studies—taken to its first great manifestation in Henry Ford's automobile assembly lines, brought on a revolution in organizational management. Organizations began to specialize, creating divisions such as marketing, finance, production, and research and development. Similarly, universities created departments of academic affairs, student affairs, finance and administration, development, and so forth.

All of us who have been to a family reunion and met with a

distant cousin we haven't seen in years can understand how time and distance can create a lack of familiarity that is momentarily awkward at best or has completely eroded the relationship at worst. The gap is one the two can either perpetuate or bridge. In many cases, academic affairs and student affairs have chosen, by intention or by simple neglect, to perpetuate the gap. Why have they made this choice, and what sustains it?

Kellogg provided the answer in her list of *wedges* that often separate the two divisions: "incorrect perceptions; lack of knowledge of each others' jobs; alienating and confusing jargon; increased specialization; and financial competition between the groups" (Knefelcamp, 1991; Kuh, Douglas, Lund, & Ramin Gyurmek, 1994; Love & Love, 1995). Kezar (2003) added organizational norms, embedded values, and hindering structures as contributors to the separation between academic affairs and student affairs. Countless permutations of these issues at institutions of higher education across the country create and perpetuate disconnects and misunderstandings that translate into a disjointed educational experience for which the student ultimately pays.

Each group can learn much from the other. Although traditionally students' social and emotional development are left to student affairs professionals and intellectual development reserved for faculty, it has recently become apparent that both the academic and student affairs sides of campus must work together if students are to learn and grow throughout their college experience (Bloland, Stamatakos, & Rogers, 1996; Kuh, 1996; Kuh, Douglas, Lund, & Ramin Gyurmek, 1994).

The *Student Learning Imperative* (American College Personnel Association, 1994) framed this dichotomy:

> Higher education traditionally has organized into "academic affairs" (learning, curriculum, classroom, cognitive development) and "student affairs" (co-curriculum, student activities, residential life, affective or personal development). However, this dichotomy has little relevance to post-college life, where the quality of one's job performance, family life, and community activities are all highly dependent on cognitive and affective skills. (p. 1)

By working together, academic and student affairs can bring "integration and coherence to a traditionally fragmented, compartmentalized, and often random approach to achieving important undergraduate education outcomes" (Schroeder, 1996, p. 2). What both student affairs professionals and faculty must understand is that though student affairs staffs are traditionally considered experts on who students are, faculty holds a different status as experts on what and how students learn. These differing roles and knowledge bases leave gaps where the weakness of one can be filled by the strengths of the other (Price, 1999).

By collaborating, both academic and student affairs professionals can learn to use effective learning approaches to create systems that link, align, and integrate a variety of resources, both on and off campus, to promote various learning outcomes (Schroeder, 2002).

DIVINE COMITY'S PRACTICAL INTENT

It is the editors' and authors' intent that *Divine Comity* be a practical work that the practitioner can use as a manual for developing or improving collaborative partnerships with faculty or student affairs personnel. In that spirit, *Divine Comity* is presented as a guide to creating better understanding between the divisions, building collaborative relationships, and improving service to students. More will be said about enhanced understanding between the two divisions in later chapters. For now, let us examine how these relationships can help us better serve our students.

Clearly, study of the promising practices that follow can help the reader understand the commonalities and differences between academic affairs and student affairs professionals and can serve as a guide to creating better relationships. But what is the anticipated end result of a successful academic affairs–student affairs relationship? The answer is simple: better service to students. *Learning Reconsidered* (2004) spoke directly to this issue:

> Presidents and senior officers in both academic and student affairs must adopt a partnership model that expects and rewards collaborations among all campus educators *for student learning* [italics added]. (p. 33)

According to Brady (1999):

> One of the best ways to make student learning come alive on campuses is to improve collaborations between student and academic affairs staffs. These collaborations need to go beyond relating out of class activities to the curriculum. They need to be true, substantive partnerships, across administrative lines, which serve to implement the goals of liberal education. (p. 14)

Several students who the authors interviewed expressed the importance of learning from both academic affairs and student affairs professionals. One student stated, "I could not have thrived, nor even survived, without support and mentoring from faculty *and* student affairs." With the impact that each group makes on students' lives, it is no wonder that collaborative efforts between the two groups benefit students tremendously. As Craig (2003) pointed out, "It makes sense that if you want to make things better for students, you pass the leadership charge to academic affairs and students affairs as equal partners, equally accountable" (p. 263).

One example of how academic affairs–student affairs collaborations benefit students is through Supplemental Instruction (SI) programs. At Denison University in Granville, Ohio, the Academic Support & Enrichment Center and First Year Program Office (both under the umbrella of student affairs) collaborated with the math department to pilot an SI program. SI uses a student leader to help students organize and understand course content for traditionally difficult courses. Institutions across the country support SI programs, many of which strengthen academic affairs–student affairs partnerships, and all of which benefit students. Another example of students benefiting from collaborations between academic affairs and student affairs is in the realm of career services. As J. Testani (personal communication, August 20, 2005) observed, "[Career services professionals] can collaborate with faculty to assist students in recognizing the merits of certain majors when a clear career path is not defined for them."

THE CIRCLES DEFINED

Circle Three: Top-down commitment—The relationship is intentional and a top priority for both the academic affairs and student affairs chief officers. At its very best, collaboration is a function of structural as well as cultural intentionality.

Circle Four: Active outreach—Both sides actively "reach across the aisle" in a constant and substantive effort to partner in the academic enterprise. Members of the academic affairs and student affairs communities constantly seek out opportunities to better serve students by working with the members of the other division in programmatic partnerships.

Circle Five: Frequent communication and mutual understanding—Information flows freely, frequently, and candidly between academic affairs and student affairs as an intentional means of fostering mutual trust and understanding. Academic affairs and student affairs seek to understand each other; to learn each other's language, roles, and priorities; and to appreciate each other's value in the academy.

(Note: Circles six through eight differ in orientation from circles three though five. The former focus on building a positive working culture between the divisions. Circles six and seven focus on the most frequent and successful types of programmatic collaborations between academic and student affairs. Circle eight highlights the importance of assessing the success of the partnership in educating and developing students.)

Circle Six: Service-learning focus—Academic affairs and student affairs work both inside and outside of the classroom to impart the value of service to students and offer them opportunities to serve the community. *Service* is a value central to the mission of both units. Academic

affairs seeks ways to incorporate service into the curriculum; student affairs gives service a prominent place
among its programs and schedules of activities.

Circle Seven: Classroom–residence hall continuity—
Academic affairs and student affairs work closely together to create a seamless living–learning environment.
Both divisions plan and implement intertwined services,
programs, and activities designed to bring down the artificial wall between the in-class and out-of-class learning
experiences—taking traditional classroom activities into
the broader classroom: residence halls and other living/
activity spaces, and involving the faculty in co-curricular
activities in the context of student affairs.

Circle Eight: Well-coordinated assessment—Academic
affairs and student affairs work closely with institutional
research or other assessment units to assess the impact
of their partnership on student education and development. Collaboration goes beyond the relationship and
the work to the results. Both divisions take a keen interest in what their collective work is doing to promote
student success.

Circle Nine: Successful collaboration—After the first
eight circles have been achieved, academic and student
affairs can work together to promote student success.
Chapter 13 examines this and provides a conceptual
framework for collaboration that may help student affairs practitioners organize their approaches to the practices in order to ensure effective campus action and assessment.

There are many excellent examples, across the country, of where the types of relationships and activities captured in the nine circles of collaboration are yielding positive results for students. Chapter 4 introduces 10 institutions with successful academic affairs–student affairs partnerships that typify the great things the two divisions can accomplish together.

REFERENCES

American College Personnel Association. (1994). *The student learning imperative: Implications for student affairs*. Washington, DC: Author.

Bloland, P. A., Stamatakos, L. C., & Rogers, R. R. (1994). *Reform in student affairs*: A critique of student development. Greensboro, NC: ERIC Counseling and Student Services Clearinghouse. (ERIC Document Reproduction service No. ED 366 862).

Bloland, P. A., Stamatakos, L. C., & Rogers, R.R. (1996). Redirecting the role of student affairs to focus on student learning. *Journal of College Student Development, 37*(2), 217–226.

Brady, S. M. (1999, Winter). Students at the center of education: A collaborative effort. *Liberal Education*, 14–21.

Craig, D. H. (2003). Not such strange bedfellows after all. *Journal of American College Health, 51*(6), 263–264.

Keeling R. P. (Ed.). (2004). *Learning reconsidered: A campus-wide focus on the student experience.* Washington, DC: National Association of Student Personnel Administrators and American College Personnel Association.

Kellogg, K. (1999). *Collaboration: Student affairs and academic affairs working together to promote student learning.* Washington, DC: The George Washington University, Graduate School of Education and Human Development. (ERIC Document Reproduction Service No. ED 432 940).

Kezar, A. (2003). Achieving student success: Strategies for creating partnerships between academic and student affairs. *NASPA Journal, 41*(1), 1–22.

Knefelcamp, L. L. (1991). *The seamless curriculum.* CIC Deans Institute: Is this good for our students? Washington, DC: Council for Independent Colleges.

Kuh, G. D. (1996). Guiding principles for creating seamless learning environments for undergraduates. *Journal of College Student Development, 37*(2), 135–148.

Kuh, G. D., Douglas, K. B., Lund, J. P., & Ramin Gyurmek, J. (1994). *Student learning.* ASHE-ERIC Higher Education Report, No. 8. Washington, DC: The George Washington University, Graduate School of Education and Human Development. (ERIC Document Reproduction Service No. ED 394 444).

Love, P. G., & Love, A. G. (1995). *Enhancing student learning: Intellectual, social, and emotional integration.* ASHE-ERIC Higher Education Report, No. 4. Washington, DC: The George Washington University, Graduate School of Education and Human Development. (ERIC Document Reproduction Service No. ED400 742).

Price, J. (1999, Fall). Merging with academic affairs: A promotion or demotion for student affairs? *New Directions for Student Affairs, 87,* 75–83.

Schroeder, C. C. (1996). Enhancing undergraduate education: An imperative for student affairs. *About Campus, 1*(4), 2–3.

Schroeder, C. C. (2002). *Collaboration and partnerships.* Retrieved November 12, 2002, from http://www.acpa.nche.edu/seniorscholars/trends/trends7.htm

CHAPTER TWO

Collaboration: Definitions and Barriers

James H. Cook,
Robert E. Eaker, Abby M. Ghering,
and Debra K. Sells

COLLABORATION DEFINED

I n his article "Proceed with caution: Uncommon wisdom about academic and student affairs partnerships," Peter Magolda (2005) observed that successful partnerships must be more than pseudo-collaborations. Magolda noted:

> The way collaboration most often works, particularly in highly complex and stratified organizations such as higher education institutions, is through hierarchies

based on possession of information and role specialization. Even the most egalitarian organizations exhibit individual differentiation in terms of political power and prestige. The extreme ideal of egalitarian exchange, while an espoused model for collaboration, is unlikely to represent an enacted model for collaboration. (p. 19)

Too frequently, a culture in which people communicate and *get along* is defined as a collaborative culture. Colleges and universities should strive to move beyond this culture of collaboration-lite and focus on developing true collaborative partnerships.

One way to think about moving toward a culture of collaborative partnerships is to differentiate among various levels of what is often referred to as collaboration. For example, in some cases what is called collaboration is really a culture of *informing*. Factual information regarding dates of events, changes in policies or procedures, or the addition of new programs is frequently announced across the organization. The staff will make such comments as, "We really do a good job of keeping everyone informed." Yet informing is not the same as collaborating.

Quite frequently, *communicating* is viewed as collaborating. A step beyond informing, communicating may involve face-to-face meetings in which information is shared and commented upon, but in-depth discussion, problem solving, and joint decision making are minimal. The staff might note, "We frequently communicate in a clear and concise manner."

Often a *cooperating* culture is mistaken for a collaborative culture. Areas may readily share information or even resources to assist in completing tasks or serving students. The emphasis is on getting along. The staff may say things like, "We cooperate with each other. In fact, we really like each other."

As Magolda pointed out, even what is called a collaborative culture may be less than the ideal. Shared planning and decision making, in the absence of shared goals and priorities, still fall short of the target. What is needed is a culture of *collaborative partnerships*—a culture in which all participants are viewed as equal partners who play equally important roles and have significant contributions to make. Glaser (2005) indicated:

> One of the great myths of organizational life is that territoriality is inevitable—that people, particularly under stress, will naturally retreat into their respective teams or departmental 'silos,' hunker down, and adopt an unhealthy WE/THEY attitude. The toxic belief that protecting one's turf is the norm and internal competition is actually good has caused much needless pain and kept many individuals and companies from achieving their full potential. (p. 64)

Instead, the goal should be the purposeful development of collaborative partnerships that are "meaningful, reciprocal and responsive" (Magolda, 2005, p. 21). John-Steiner, Weber, and Minnis (1998) took this definition a step further, stating:

> The principles in a true collaboration represent complementary domains of expertise. As collaborators, not only do they plan, decide, and act jointly; they also *think together*, combining independent conceptual schemes to create original frameworks. Also, in a true collaboration, there is a commitment to shared resources, power, and talent: no individual's point of view dominates, author-

ity for decisions and actions resides in the group, and work products reflect a blending of all participants' contributions. (p. 776)

BARRIERS TO THE CREATION OF A COLLABORATIVE CULTURE

If so many recognize the value of developing a collaborative culture, then why has developing it proven to be such a challenge for institutions of higher education? The answer is simple. After over half a century of research on the positive effects of collaborative cultures, higher education institutions remain, for the most part, a collection of independent kingdoms united by athletics and common parking lots. This situation is owing to a number of barriers, some structural and some cultural, that are perhaps unique to higher education.

Historically Distinct Roles

Academic and student affairs professionals maintain distinct roles on college and university campuses. Faculty have different expectations and reward systems than student affairs professionals; likewise, students tend to view the roles of each group differently. Historically, college and university academicians have been charged with cultivating students' intellect. In the past decade, there has been a substantial transition in emphasis from faculty *teaching* to student *learning*. The role of a student affairs practitioner has traditionally been to educate students during the time they spend outside the classroom. This role is also in transition. The complicated and specialized natures of their work have separated academic affairs and student affairs professionals (Brady, 1999). *Learning Reconsidered* (Keeling, 2004) recognized that:

> Every faculty member and student affairs professional
> who is involved in this approach to transformative edu-
> cation must have a sense of her or his role, or location
> on the map, and a broader sense of the roles of others
> and of the entire process. (p. 18)

Some student affairs professionals might lose focus on the intellectual development of students, emphasizing instead their social and
emotional development as members of the campus community. According to Brady (1999):

> It could equally be stated that [student affairs profes-
> sionals] are seldom invited, and perhaps are not wel-
> come, at the table where serious educational issues are
> discussed…Moreover, student affairs staffs have moved
> further away from the concept of whole student devel-
> opment and into specialized services and functions.
> Academic affairs staffs have separated the intellectual
> development of the student from other units of the cam-
> pus. (p. 19)

Without a clear understanding of the roles both entities should—
and do—play on our campuses, collaborations are unlikely.

A Habit of Isolation

The cultural history of higher education is, for the most part,
a history of individual scholars teaching classes, pursuing research,
and writing. While collaboration may be viewed as worthwhile in the
abstract, it is not historically the norm. The culture of professors working in isolation has extended to subparts of the institution. Academic

affairs, student affairs, athletics, and other units have traditionally worked largely in isolation.

Different "Languages" and Cultures

Academic and student affairs may or may not understand the other's language. Each group has an educational background that stresses different aspects of its work. Faculty members who teach are well versed in their subject areas, which are accompanied by a wealth of particular terms, concepts, and definitions. Even the completion of a terminal degree in a particular academic discipline may not guarantee that teaching faculty's curriculum has included a discussion of college students' development. On the other hand, most student affairs professionals have studied student development theory. As a result, they speak in terms consistent with the theories, definitions, and concepts of student development research, while faculty tend to speak the languages of their disciplines.

Thus, the two groups often have difficulty understanding each other's language. Sandeen (2004) pointed out that "some well-meaning efforts by student affairs personnel to become part of the campus educational program also have been thwarted by their own use of jargon, which has not been recognized or appreciated by their academic colleagues" (p. 29). Nevertheless, *Learning Reconsidered* (Keeling, 2004) made strides in promoting a common language when it defined and explained the concept of "student development education" (p. 12). Sharing concepts and definitions like this will help each group understand what the other is saying. The more often and the more intensely the two groups communicate, the more quickly a common language will emerge.

Kuh, Kinzie, Schuh & Whitt (2005) asserted that:

> "Culture" consists in part of tacit assumptions and be-
> liefs that influence both the substance of policies, pro-
> grams, and practices and how they are implemented.
> Culture also gives people a common language and val-
> ues. A strong, coherent institutional culture that features
> talent development, academic achievement, and respect
> for differences is congenial to student success. (p. 50)

Campus culture has a major impact on the lives of both academic
affairs and student affairs professionals. But each group might view
a given campus's culture differently. According to Donald H. Craig,
director of the Norris Health Center at the University of Wisconsin-
Milwaukee:

> The reward structures for faculty and student affairs
> staff are very different. Student Affairs staff are encour-
> aged to be generalists and to pursue collaborative, in-
> terdisciplinary initiatives. Faculty, on the other hand,
> are rewarded (i.e., promoted and tenured) for largely
> independent, discipline-based, scholarly work. Faculty
> are generally not rewarded for engaging in or contrib-
> uting to the broad student-affairs agenda of service to
> students. (p. 263)

With divergent reward structures and varying opinions of a
campus culture, the need for the two groups to communicate and seek
understanding is clear.

When the groups struggle to understand each other's roles, language, and culture, challenges emerge. One challenge that can result
from a misunderstanding of roles concerns the tendency of both groups

to be territorial about their areas of expertise. For example, the issue of student mental health has become increasingly important on campuses across the country. Sandeen (2004) argued that problems created by student stress and mental health demand more mutually supportive links between faculty members and student affairs staff. According to Sandeen:

> Student affairs staff should be expected to be on the cutting edge in handling such matters, but their academic colleagues also must be willing to engage in, and be drawn into, efforts to provide a caring campus environment through sound educational and support programs. At times, student affairs leaders have declared themselves the exclusive experts in such matters. By staking out what they viewed as their special professional turf, they sometimes have distanced themselves from their academic colleagues. (p. 32)

Combining strategies from both areas of expertise would transform this potential challenge into an opportunity to create a healthier campus for everyone.

Poor Communication

Academic affairs–student affairs collaborations are also challenged by poor communication. "More than a few joint efforts between academic and student affairs staff have failed because of poor communication or an inability to look beyond the traditional status differences between academic and student affairs personnel" (Sandeen, 2004, p. 30). Undefined learning outcomes or lack of structure make it difficult to convince one group to collaborate with another group. For example, a student affairs professional at a private, liberal arts institution noted

24

that it behooves student affairs to seek faculty buy-in when planning programs. According to Joseph Testani, assistant director in the Career Development Center at the University of Richmond (personal communication, August 20, 2005), "Much decision-making weight is given to faculty...[I]nitiatives from student development [affairs] should include some tie-in to the academic pursuits of students and the academic culture on campus." Frequently, the two sides of the house fail to communicate effectively to attain a shared goal.

Lack of Mutual Understanding

A common perception among student affairs professionals is that faculty members do not understand what student affairs professionals do. When asked about perceptions of academic affairs–student affairs collaborations on her campus, the former associate director of Academic Initiatives within University Housing at Eastern Kentucky University noted that, "While I think student affairs professionals get what faculty members do, I don't think they understand faculty culture" (H.G. Ryan, personal communication, July 26, 2005). On the other hand, Donald Craig (2003) asserted:

> To take the position that faculty, in general, don't care about our work is, in my opinion, an oversimplified and inaccurate generalization. Furthermore, and more damaging, it too easily becomes a self-fulfilling prophecy. We begin to behave like second-class citizens, assuming that partnerships and collaborative efforts with academic affairs associates are not a prospect. We do "our thing," they do theirs. The "we-they" mentality is counterproductive and often results in students being the real losers. (p. 263)

25

It is important to understand and analyze the perceptions and misperceptions each group has about the other. Perception is reality.

One of Steven Covey's *Seven Habits of Highly Effective People* (1989) was, "Seek first to understand, then to be understood" (Habit 5). Strong academic affairs–student affairs partnerships are typically characterized by a high degree of mutual understanding. By presenting certain promising practices, we wish to showcase the importance of mutual understanding between the two areas. If a high degree of understanding is present; if it is motivated by the intent to partner closely, frequently, and systematically; if it is built on shared values and goals; and if it utilizes common instrumentalities (creating a seamlessness in the content and context of the educational experience), then a highly positive and productive relationship can flourish. If one accepts the notion that the machine whose parts work most smoothly together is the most productive, then it is self-evident that a strong relationship must exist between academic affairs and student affairs for the kind of holistic learning espoused in *Learning Reconsidered* (Keeling, 2004) to flourish.

Lack of a Clear and Compelling Mission

Institutions of higher education are complex organizations. At any given time they are focused on a number of compelling (and in some cases, competing) initiatives. However, the research on highly effective organizations is clear. Effective organizations are characterized by a clear and compelling mission that is understood by everyone and around which policies, practices, and procedures are aligned. What is the central purpose of colleges and universities? Is it to provide a place for students to be taught? Is it to provide a place for professors to teach? Is it to provide a place for individual pursuits and personal autonomy? Institutions of higher education have not rallied around the notion that their central purpose is to ensure high levels of learning for students. If institutions of higher education could shift from a mission of *teaching* to a mission of *learning,* fundamentally different questions would be asked and fundamentally different cultures would be formed.

A Culture of Disjointed Incrementalism

Bureaucratic cultures are sometimes described by the term *disjointed incrementalism,* which describes piecemeal decision-making processes that are fundamentally disconnected from broader organizational goals or mission (Braybrooke & Lindblom, 1963). In larger organizations initiatives may be not only disjointed but actually in conflict with each other. Further, cultural change in bureaucratic organizations is rarely accomplished quickly, more often taking place in small increments over a long period of time. These two characteristics, *disjointed* and *incremental,* make deep cultural changes difficult to enact.

Lack of an Impetus for Change

Collaboration by invitation simply does not work. While developing a collaborative culture may be viewed as a worthwhile goal, in the day-to-day culture of colleges and universities, *autonomy* almost always trumps *collaboration.* Unless developing a collaborative culture is clearly articulated as a high-priority goal, the necessary structural and cultural shifts are unlikely to occur.

Inability to Model Best Practices

As noted earlier, the emphasis on creating collaborative cultures is not new. In fact, the importance of developing collaborative organizational cultures has been taught for years in colleges and university classrooms. Yet, despite the abundance of evidence regarding the benefits of developing collaborative cultures (and the virtual absence of evidence to the contrary), the norm for institutions of higher education continues to be one of autonomy and isolation. Jeffrey Pfeffer and Robert Sutton (2000) elaborated on the *knowing-doing gap* by describing the disconnect between knowledge and action as one of the "great mysteries in organizational management: why knowledge of what needs to be done frequently fails to result in action or behavior consistent with that knowledge" (p. 4).

CONCLUSION

A wide range of literature has described common challenges to collaboration. Kezar (2003) noted:

> The barriers described in the literature shed light on institutional problems and help to identify possible approaches for overcoming these obstacles. The following barriers to collaboration are most commonly identified: organizational fragmentation and division of labor, specialization among faculty, lack of common purpose or language, few shared values, history of separation, different priorities and expectations, cultural differences between academic and student affairs in terms of personality styles, and competing assumptions about what constitutes effective learning (American College Personnel Association, 1994; Blake, 1979; Kuh, 1996; Kuh, Douglas, Lund, & Ramin Gyurmek, 1994; Lamarid, 1999; Love & Love, 1995; Martin & Murphy, 2000). These studies point to existing cultural (lack of a common language or few shared values) and structural (divi-

sion of labor or specialization among faculty) aspects of campuses that appear to prevent collaboration and suggest strategies for change. (p. 3)

Current attempts at academic and student affairs collaborations run the gamut from simple efforts to inform to more complex efforts to cooperate in shared planning and decision making. However, true collaborations between academic and student affairs depend on a blending of areas of expertise and the sharing of resources, decision making, and effort to create new outcomes (John-Steiner, Weber, & Minnis, 1998).

While a number of barriers complicate collaborative ventures, the synergy that results when colleagues recognize the unique expertise and contributions available within both the academic and student affairs traditions is fantastic. That synergy is evident in the promising practices highlighted throughout this publication.

REFERENCES

American College Personnel Association. (1994). *The student learning imperative: Implications for student affairs*. Washington, DC: Author.

Blake, E. S. (1979). Classroom and context: An educational dialectic. *Academe, 65*, 280–292.

Brady, S. M. (1999, Winter). Students at the center of education: A collaborative effort. *Liberal Education*, 14–21.

Braybrooke, D., & Lindblom, C. E. (1963). *A Strategy of decision*. New York: Free Press of Glencoe.

Covey, S. (1989). *Seven habits of highly effective people* (1st ed.). New York: Free Press.

Craig, D. H. (2003). Not such strange bedfellows after all. *Journal of American College Health, 51*(6), 263–264.

Glaser, J. E. (2005). *Creating we*. Avon, MA: Platinum Press.

John-Steiner, V., Weber, R. J., & Minnis, M. (1998). The challenge of studying collaboration. *American Educational Research Journal, 35*(4), 773–783.

Keeling, R. P. (Ed.). (2004). *Learning reconsidered: A campus-wide focus on the student experience*. Washington, DC: National Association of Student Personnel Administrators and American College Personnel Association.

Kuh, G. D. (1996). Guiding principles for creating seamless learning environments for undergraduates. *Journal of College Student Development, 37*(2), 135–148.

Kuh, G. D., Douglas, K. B., Lund, J. P., & Ramin Gyurmek, J. (1994). *Student learning*. ASHE-ERIC Higher Education Report,

No. 8. Washington, DC: The George Washington University, Graduate School of Education and Human Development. (ERIC Document Reproduction Service No. ED 394 444).

Kuh, G. D., Kinzie, J., Schuh, J. H., & Whitt, E. J. (2005). Never let it rest. *Change, 37*(4), 44–52.

Lamarid, L. (1999). Putting Descartes before the horse: Opportunities for advancing the student affairs link with academic affairs. *College Student Affairs Journal, 19*(1), 24–34.

Love, P.G., & Love, A.G. (1995). *Enhancing student learning: Intellectual, social, and emotional integration.* ASHE-ERIC Higher Education Report, No. 4. Washington, DC: The George Washington University, Graduate School of Education and Human Development. (ERIC Document Reproduction Service No. ED 400 742).

Magolda, P. M. (2005). Proceed with caution: Uncommon wisdom about academic and student affairs partnerships. *About Campus, 9*(6), 16–21.

Martin, J., & Murphy, S. (2000). *Building a better bridge: Creating effective partnerships between academic and student affairs.* Washington, DC: National Association of Student Personnel Administrators.

Pfeffer, J., & Sutton, R. (2000). *The knowing doing gap.* Cambridge, MA: Harvard Business School Press.

Sandeen, A. (2004). Educating the whole student. *Change, 36*(3), 28–34.

CHAPTER THREE

The State of Student and Academic Affairs Partnerships: A National Perspective

Kim C. O'Halloran

Due to the loosely coupled nature of college and university organizations and the differences in the subcultures of academic and student affairs, collaboration does not emerge naturally (Brown, 1990). Since the early 20th century, the two groups have cooperated only on an ad hoc basis or in response to organizational mandate, rather than because of a shared interest in working together to achieve educational goals (Brown, 1990). In recent years, however such collaborations have become more common.

The increasing pressure on higher education to better prepare students for a complex, globalized world and to enhance educational outcomes forces leaders to consider new solutions to old concerns. These concerns present new opportunities to create seamless learning environments that connect in- and out-of-class experiences (Engstrom & Tinto, 2000). As higher education institutions struggle to address new challenges, collaboration between academic and student affairs personnel "may no longer be simply a desirable option, but, rather, an absolute necessity" (Schroeder, DiTiberio, & Kalsbeek, 1989, p. 19). For seamless learning to become a reality, academic and student affairs professionals must collaborate (Kellogg, 1999).

A review of research and literature on collaboration between academic and student affairs indicated that both groups valued collaboration as a means of enhancing student learning, and that collaboration was most often led by student affairs. While collaboration between academic and student affairs has been a frequent topic in the literature during the past decade, much of the literature is anecdotal in nature.

In addition, the research has been narrowly focused, limited to examining specific types of collaboration, the process of developing collaboration activities, and the factors that influence the success or failure of such partnerships. While studies have delved deeply into specific instances, there has been no comprehensive look into the definition of collaboration, the differences and similarities among types of collaboration, or their connection to various types of higher education institutions. This chapter will describe a recent study aimed at filling these gaps in the literature and developing a theory that explains collaboration between academic and student affairs on a larger scale (O'Halloran, 2005).

COLLABORATION TYPES

Much of the literature on collaboration between academic and student affairs focuses on examples of collaboration activities. The major examples of collaboration may be broken into academic support and co-curricular, orientation, service, residential, and policy and planning activities.

Academic support activities include those initiatives that most directly support a student's in-class experience (Aviles, 2000; Brady, 1999; Caple, 1996; Fried, 1995; Schroeder, 1999b). They include activities such as the assessment of student outcomes, academic warning and early intervention programs, professional development of faculty and student affairs around student learning, academic advising, course registration and scheduling, team teaching, placement testing, scholarship selection, and honors programs.

Co-curricular and orientation activities include initiatives that most likely take place outside of the classroom or combine in- and out-of-classroom activities, including health and wellness education, student organizations, student government, career planning, mentoring programs, orientation, and first-year experience courses (Bourassa & Kruger, 2001; Fried, 1995; King, 1993; Martin & Murphy, 2000). Activities also include freshman interest groups (FIGs), which are often cited as among the most successful collaboration activities (Schroeder, 1999b). FIGs consist of groups of students who are enrolled in a cluster of courses at the same time around a specific theme or topic. FIGs often include both in-class learning coordinated by faculty and out-of-class learning coordinated by student affairs.

Service activities typically center around two types—community service and service-learning (Engstrom & Tinto, 2000; Jacoby, 1999;

McDonald et al., 2000). Community service activities are identified primarily as volunteer experiences that stand alone; service-learning is defined as experiential education that allows students to combine service to a community with an intentional learning component in the classroom (Jacoby, 1999).

Collaboration around residential experiences is most commonly enacted through learning communities and residential colleges (Bourassa & Kruger, 2001; Engstrom & Tinto, 2000; Golde & Pribbenow, 2000; Hargrave, 2000; McDonald et al., 2000; Newton & Smith, 1996; Phelps, 1993; Schroeder, 1999a; Smith, 2003). In a residential setting, learning communities are interest groups of students centered on an academic theme, such as a major or an interdisciplinary topic (Bourassa & Kruger, 2001). Staff build residence life programs around such themes that complement the students' academic experience. Residential colleges take this experience a few steps further connecting academic courses with a residence life experience (Guarasci, 2001). In these settings, courses are often taught in residence halls; faculty may live in the residence and work closely with the residence life staff to coordinate seamless learning experiences.

Other examples of collaboration center on institutional governance and organization, and include policy development (Engstrom & Tinto, 2000, Fried, 1995; Schuh, 1999). For example, Schuh (1999) cites several principles demonstrating effective partnerships on a given campus, including policies requiring credit-bearing courses to have out-of-classroom activities as integral components. He argues that "the more evidence of these principles on a given campus, the greater the likelihood that effective partnerships have been formed between academic and student affairs" (p. 86).

A second type of collaboration in the area of governance includes the institutional planning function (Banta & Kuh, 1998; Bourassa & Kruger, 2001; Engstrom & Tinto, 2000; Kellogg, 1999; Martin & Murphy, 2000; Schuh, 1999; Smith, 1989; Westfall, 1999). For example, Banta and Kuh (1998) assert that the most promising type of collaboration is joint planning of curriculum and assessment, and student outcomes assessment in particular. They comment that this type of collaboration is most likely to be successful, as it provides the best chance for academic and student affairs to function as equal partners. Bourassa and Kruger (2001) pose a similar argument, stating that ongoing planning teams are more likely to lead to successful academic and student affairs collaboration than one-time partnership efforts.

REASONS FOR COLLABORATION

Collaboration between academic and student affairs may have benefits both for students and for the institution (Westfall, 1999). For example, the greater the collaboration between academic and student affairs, the greater the potential for a congruent and supportive learning environment throughout the institution (Newton & Smith, 1996). Such partnerships illustrate an approach that fosters inclusiveness, brings varying perspectives to bear on problems, and affirms shared educational values (American College Personnel Association & National Association of Student Personnel Administrators, 1997).

Higher education is being challenged to become more student-centered to improve student learning and educational attainment (Grace, 2000; Fuller & Haugabrook, 2001; Schroeder, 1999a). One way to energize student learning on campuses is to improve the collaboration between student and academic affairs staffs (Brady, 1999). A shift from an emphasis on teaching to an emphasis on learning has been a major factor in creating a climate in which collaboration emerges as a key method to achieve defined and measurable learning outcomes (Brady, 1999; Caple, 1996; Johnson & Cheatham, 1999). In fact, student learning has been the primary purpose for the development of academic and student affairs partnerships (Martin & Murphy, 2000; Schuh, 1999).

Administrators hope that collaboration will increase congruence with the institution's mission, improve retention, and enhance the total college experience for students (Kellogg, 1999). Many believe that increased collaboration will enhance learning by improving student understanding, sense of community, problem solving, and the quality of programs in which students participate (Sandeen, 2000). Collaborative partnerships make sense in addressing these outcomes, as most of these institutional issues are interdependent in nature and cross traditional organizational boundaries (Fuller and Haugabrook, 2001; Schroeder, 1999b).

On college campuses today, learning can be piecemeal for the student, as there is a lack of coordinated effort regarding student-centered learning and the student experience is often made up of disjointed parts (Blimling & Whitt, 1999; Schroeder, 1999b). The literature assumes that if the institutional components involved in learning are separated from one another, students' overall personal development as well as the quality of their academic experience will be impeded (Schuh, 1999; Schuh & Whitt, 1999). In fact, a substantial amount of a student's time in college is spent outside the classroom, and some researchers assert that some of the most effective forms of teaching take place outside of class (Banta & Kuh, 1998; DiGregorio, Diamond, & Passi, 1996; Price, 1999). A growing body of literature asserts that cognitive and affective development are keenly intertwined, and that in- and out-of-class experiences have remarkable effects on each other. As a result, partnerships between academic and student affairs that seamlessly connect (1) in- and out-of-class experiences, (2) cognitive and affective learning goals, and (3) intellectual, social, and emotional learning processes may be especially effective in promoting student success (Banta & Kuh, 1998; Blimling & Whitt, 1999; Brady, 1999; Engstrom & Tinto, 2000; Grace, 2002; Kellogg, 1999; Newton & Smith, 1996; Schroeder, 1999b; Schuh & Whitt, 1999).

In addition, waste and redundancy may exist where: services are duplicated across offices; students are uncertain of where to find a particular service; or contradictory messages are being sent to students (Bourassa & Kruger, 2001; Newton & Smith, 1996). Sharing human and financial resources, technology, and expertise may improve an institution's effectiveness (Grace, 2000).

RESEARCH ON THE IMPORTANCE OF COLLABORATION

Three empirical studies examined why collaboration is important. Abdullah (1998) examined how student affairs professionals could work with faculty to incorporate co-curricular credit activities into the classroom. The study focused on how collaboration provided an enhanced learning environment and how it may have impacted student development through a first-year experience course for credit at one institution. It was a qualitative case study of collaboration between academic and student affairs regarding a first-year experience course. The study found positive perceptions by the faculty, students, and the researcher regarding the ability of collaboration to enhance learning and development.

Hall and Sears (1997) examined the influence of structured curricular intervention on students' personal and social development in the classroom. Their study used a pre-test/post-test method to review the faculty role in students' personal and social identity development through classroom teaching and collaboration with student affairs. The study resulted in recommendations on how faculty and student affairs can work together to support education in each other's domains.

Kolins (1999) conducted a survey of chief student affairs officers (CSAOs) and chief academic officers (CAOs) at public two-year colleges. The study sought to identify collaborative practices between academic and student affairs by determining and comparing the perceptions of CSAOs and CAOs regarding their satisfaction with these practices and how important they are to student success. The results indicated that CSAO and CAO perceptions about collaboration were generally positive and that collaboration is important in enhancing student success. In addition, it found that CSAOs and CAOs view collaboration from different cultural perspectives, and that faculty set the tone for the components of collaboration.

THE CURRENT STATUS OF COLLABORATION: A QUANTITATIVE STUDY

As stated earlier, while collaboration between academic and student affairs has been a frequent topic in the literature during the past decade, much of the literature is anecdotal in nature. In addition, the research has been narrowly focused.

A 2004 study provided a national perspective on the status of collaboration at U.S. colleges and universities. The study sought to gain an understanding of what types of collaboration activities were taking place, the goals of initiating such activities, and the congruence between the two areas.

A survey was developed, tested, and distributed to CSAOs at 395 colleges and universities. Surveys were sent solely to CSAOs, as the literature indicated that collaboration activities were being initiated primarily by student affairs professionals, and thus CSAOs would best be able to answer questions regarding collaboration on their campuses. This survey included questions to ascertain the types of collaboration that were taking place on each campus.

The survey sample aimed to collect responses from institutions representing both public and private colleges and universities from each category of the Carnegie Classification. Because they are often under-represented in the research, additional Historically Black Colleges and Universities were added to the sample.

The survey received 195 responses (50% response rate). Response rates of 60% or better were obtained for all but three Carnegie categories. Only 19% of the Baccalaureate/Associate Institutions in the sample returned a completed survey. None of the Tribal Institutions or Specialized Institutions responded. While those return rates are disappointing, the researcher took all possible steps through repeat contact with sample members to ensure response. Many contacts from the Specialized Institutions indicated that the survey was not appropriate for their type of campus owing to a specialized or narrow mission. A future study should be undertaken to examine collaboration between academic and student affairs in Tribal Institutions to ensure that their role is incorporated into this dialogue. Though they are not a formal part of the Carnegie Classification, it was important to ensure that Historically Black Colleges and Universities and Hispanic Service Institutions were represented in the sample. Twelve of the 23 Historically Black Colleges and Universities and Hispanic Serving Institutions in the sample returned the survey (52%).

Respondents were asked to indicate which of 44 types of collaboration activities were taking place on their campus. They were also asked to rank in order of importance from 1 to 8 the reasons informing academic and student affairs collaboration on their campus: (1) Enhance Academic Performance, (2) Increase Retention or Persistence, (3) Increase Sense of Community on Campus, (4) Enhance Multicultural Understanding, (5) Develop Leadership Skills, (6) Connect Theory with Experience, (7) Decrease Waste or Redundancy, and (8) Other, with an area to explain the specific reason. This list of reasons was based on the most common reasons for collaboration found in the literature.

Results

The first question on the survey asked whether a specific type of collaboration activity is taking place on the participant's campus. The following activities took place to some degree on 75% or more of participant campuses where there is some type of collaboration between student and academic affairs:

* Student Outcomes Assessment

* Academic Warning/Early Intervention

* Student Activities/Groups

* Diversity Programs

* Career Planning/Placement

* Orientation

* First Year Experience/New Student Seminar

* Institutional Planning

* Standing Committee Membership

* Student Discipline

* Advisory Committees

* Search Committees

* Institutional Effectiveness/Evaluation

Participants also were asked to what degree such collaboration was taking place throughout their campus organization, as opposed to in limited interactions between individuals or departments. Collaboration activities taking place across the organization included the following:

* Distance Learning

* Academic Policy

* Development/Revision of General Education Curriculum

* Institutional Planning

* Standing Committee Membership

* Institutional Effectiveness/Evaluation.

The reasons for collaboration cited in the literature as most common include direct academic support and student learning types of activities.

Some of the findings were consistent with those in previous research. Collaboration is indeed taking place at a diverse array of colleges and universities across the country, regardless of institutional size, control, location, or type. Such collaboration exists throughout institutions, as opposed to limited partnerships between individuals.

In the survey responses, the two reasons most often cited for collaboration, to "enhance academic performance" and to "increase retention or persistence," made up 81% of the highest ranked responses, followed by "increase sense of community on campus" at 11%. There was no connection between an institution's most important reason for collaboration and the cluster in which the institution was placed.

The most common reasons cited for collaboration—enhancing academic performance, increasing retention or persistence, and increasing sense of community on campus—echoed the primary themes found in the literature to some degree. The reasons cited for engaging in academic and student affairs collaboration in this study centered on improving of student outcomes such as academic performance, retention rates, and graduation rates. The movement to bring learning beyond the strictly cognitive process to one that is dynamic and social is at the heart of collaboration, as both speak to meeting the needs of the whole student. The literature identified the primary reasons for collaboration as improving student learning and the environment for learning, as well as providing opportunities to enhance institutional efficiency and effectiveness and eliminate waste and redundancy. Thus, the three primary reasons for collaboration cited in this study are consistent with the national dialogue for improving undergraduate education.

However, there appears to be a disconnect between the reasons cited for engaging in collaboration and the types of collaboration activities actually taking place on a given campus. To what degree is the collaboration that is taking place meeting the reasons cited for undertaking collaboration activities? The most common collaboration activities taking place across campus organizations are predominantly policy and systems issues, including Distance Learning, Academic Policy, Development/Revision of General Education Curriculum, Institutional Planning, Standing Committee Membership, and Institutional Effectiveness/Evaluation. On the other hand, the primary reasons cited for engaging collaboration were enhancing academic performance, increasing retention or persistence, and increasing sense of community on campus.

As a result, there was little evidence that the types of collaboration analyzed as part of this study were directly related to institutional goals to connect in-class learning with out-of-class learning. In addition, activities that foster this type of connection, such as service-learning, were not as prevalent as other collaboration activities. Many of the collaborative activities were more likely to emphasize processes and policy, as opposed to activities that may more directly impact student learning. In addition, eliminating waste and redundancy, one reason cited in the literature for engaging in collaboration, was one of the lowest priorities among participants in this study.

RECOMMENDATIONS FOR PRACTICE AND RESEARCH

Just as it is worthwhile for student affairs professionals to connect research to their practice, it is useful in collaboration to connect actions to learning goals. Student affairs professionals must first examine institutional needs and learning goals for their students, and then design collaborative activities that foster those goals. If student needs and learning goals are not clear or current, collaboration may be utilized to measure and understand these goals prior to designing new initiatives or modifying existing ones.

Institutions may also find ways to connect policy and systems initiatives more directly to learning goals and measure the effect of such policies and systems. For example, it may be useful to examine academic warning and early intervention programs, academic advising, course registration and scheduling, or placement testing to determine how well they are identifying students who are not advancing appropriately. In addition, developing partnerships between student and academic affairs in assessment, planning, and policy development may lead to better research and more accurate goals, systems, and policies that support student learning.

As the learning needs and styles of our students change, so must our professional development initiatives. Professional development activities that provide meaningful connections between student and academic affairs allow for sharing of valuable information, and may result in the most comprehensive strategies to positively affect student learning.

Finally, even the best and most creative partnerships mean little without some understanding of their results. Colleges and universities need to develop mechanisms to measure the success of such partnerships in meeting their goals. Such goals may include those that are meant to improve student outcomes, such as learning, retention, or persistence to degree. They may also include organizational efficiency and communication.

In general, then, for collaboration between student and academic affairs to be more than a simple exercise, it must take place in an environment where needs are assessed, goals are developed to meet such needs, partnerships are created that directly address those goals, and mechanisms are designed to measure outcomes. By strategically connecting each of these steps, institutions can reap the rewards of collaboration activities between individuals and departments and across the organization.

REFERENCES

Abdullah, Z. (1998). Collaborative work in action: Creating a learning environment in the class with out-of-class activities. *Dissertation Abstracts International, 59*(11). ProQuest AAT 9912974.

American College Personnel Association and National Association of Student Personnel Administrators. (1997). Principles of good practice for student affairs. Washington, DC: Authors.

Aviles, C. B. (2000). *Successful collaboration between student affairs and academic affairs with a graduate follow-up survey.* Buffalo, NY: State University of New York, College at Buffalo, Social Work Department. (ERIC Document Reproduction Service No. ED 446 707).

Banta, T. W., & Kuh, G. D. (1998, March/April). A missing link in assessment: Collaboration between academic and student affairs professionals. *Change,* 40–46.

Blimling, G. S., & Whitt, E. J. (1999). Identifying the principles that guide student affairs practice. In G. S. Blimling & E. J. Whitt (Eds.), *Good practice in student affairs: Principles to foster student learning* (pp. 1–20). San Francisco: Jossey-Bass Publishers.

Bourassa, D. M., & Kruger, K. (2001). The national dialogue on academic and student affairs collaboration. *New Directions for Higher Education, 116,* 9–38.

Brady, S. M. (1999, Winter). Students at the center of education: A collaborative effort. *Liberal Education,* 14–21.

Brown, S. S. (1990). Strengthening ties to academic affairs. In M. J. Barr & M. L. Upcraft (Eds.), *New futures for student affairs: Building a vision for professional leadership and practice* (pp. 239–269). San Francisco: Jossey-Bass Publishers.

Caple, R. B. (1996). Student affairs professionals as learning consultants. In S. C. Ender, F. B. Newton, & R. B. Caple (Eds.), *Contributing to learning: The role of student affairs* (pp. 33–44). San Francisco: Jossey-Bass Publishers.

DiGregorio, K. D., Diamond, M. R., & Passi, C. E. (1996). *Partners in the wilderness: Building alliances with faculty to redefine learning.* Washington, DC: National Association of Student Personnel Administrators.

Engstrom, C. M., & Tinto, V. (2000). Developing partnerships with academic affairs to enhance student learning. In M. J. Barr, M. K. Desler, & Associates (Eds.), *The handbook of student affairs administration* (pp. 425–452). San Francisco: Jossey-Bass Publishers.

Fried, J. (1995). Border crossings in higher education: Faculty/student affairs collaboration. In J. Fried (Ed.), *Shifting paradigms in student affairs: Culture, context, teaching and learning* (pp. 171–188). Lanham, MD: University Press of America, Inc.

Fuller, T. M. A., & Haugabrook, A. K. (2001). Facilitative strategies in action. *New Directions for Higher Education, 116,* 75–87.

Golde, C. M., & Pribbenow, D. A. (2000). Understanding faculty involvement in residential learning communities. *Journal of College Student Development, 41*(1), 27–40.

Grace, T. (2000). The integrator: Linking curricular and cocurricular experiences. In J. L. Bess (Ed.), *Teaching alone, teaching together: Transforming the structure of teams for teaching* (pp. 151–172). San Francisco: Jossey-Bass Publishers.

Guarasci, R. (2001). Recentering learning: An interdisciplinary approach to academic and student affairs. *New Directions for Higher Education, 116,* 101–110.

Hall, S. E., & Sears, S. J. (1997). Promoting identity development in the classroom: A new role for academic faculty. *Journal on Excellence in College Teaching, 8*(3), 3–24.

Hargrave, A. L. (2000). Faculty and student affairs staff involvement in learning communities at five midwestern public universities. *Dissertation Abstracts International, 61*(2).

Jacoby, B. (1999). Partnerships for service learning. In J. H. Schuh & E. J. Whitt (Eds.), *Creating successful partnerships between academic and student affairs* (pp. 19–36). San Francisco: Jossey-Bass Publishers.

Johnson, C. S., & Cheatham, H. E. (Eds.). (1999). *Higher education trends for the next century: A research agenda for student success.* Washington, DC: American College Personnel Association.

Kellogg, K. (1999). *Collaboration: Student affairs and academic affairs working together to promote student learning.* Washington, DC: Office of Educational Research and Improvement.

King, N. S. (1993). Partnerships and collaboration for new student success. *College Student Affairs Journal, 13*(1), 44–47.

Kolins, C. A. (1999). An appraisal of collaboration: Assessing perceptions of chief academic and student affairs officers at public two-year colleges. *Dissertation Abstracts International, 60*(11).

Martin, J., & Murphy, S. (2000). *Building a better bridge: Creating effective partnerships between academic affairs and student affairs.* Washington, DC: National Association of Student Personnel Administrators. (ERIC Document Reproduction Service No. ED 443 074).

McDonald, W. M., Bacon, J. L., Brown, C. E., Carter, A. W., Littleton, R. A., Moore, B. L., Roper, L. D. & Tankersley, E. (2000). *Collaboration and community: Boyer's guiding principles.* Washing-

ton, DC: National Association of Student Personnel Administrators. (ERIC Document Reproduction Service No. ED 443
075).

Newton, F. B., & Smith, J. H. (1996). Principles and strategies for
enhancing student learning. In S. C. Ender, F. B. Newton, & R.
B. Caple (Eds.), *Contributing to learning: The role of student affairs*
(pp. 19–32). San Francisco: Jossey-Bass Publishers.

O'Halloran, K. C. (2005). A classification of Academic and Student Affairs collaboration in higher education from a Student
Affairs perspective. *Dissertation Abstracts International, 65*(11).

Phelps, C. E. (1993). The faculty fellow program at the University
of Arizona. *College Student Affairs Journal, 13*(1), 29–36.

Price, J. (1999). Merging with academic affairs: A promotion or
demotion for student affairs? In J. H. Schuh & E. J. Whitt
(Eds.), *Creating successful partnerships between academic and student
affairs* (pp. 75–83). San Francisco: Jossey-Bass Publishers.

Sandeen, C. A. (2000). Developing effective campus and community relationships. In M. J. Barr, M. K. Desler, & Associates
(Eds.), *The handbook of student affairs administration* (pp. 377–
392). San Francisco: Jossey-Bass Publishers.

Schroeder, C. C. (1999a). Forging educational partnerships that
advance student learning. In G. S. Blimling & E. J. Whitt
(Eds.), *Good practice in student affairs: Principles to foster student
learning* (pp. 133–156). San Francisco: Jossey-Bass Publishers.

Schroeder, C. C. (1999b). Partnerships: An imperative for enhancing student learning and institutional effectiveness. In J. H.
Schuh & E. J. Whitt (Eds.), *Creating successful partnerships
between academic and student affairs* (pp. 5–18). San Francisco:
Jossey-Bass Publishers.

Schroeder, C. C., DiTiberio, J. K., & Kalsbeek, D. H. (1989). Bridging the gap between faculty and students: Opportunities and obligations for student affairs. *NASPA Journal, 26*(1), 14–20.

Schuh, J. H. (1999). Guiding principles for evaluating student and academic affairs partnerships. In J. H. Schuh & E. J. Whitt (Eds.), *Creating successful partnerships between academic and student affairs* (pp. 85–92). San Francisco: Jossey-Bass Publishers.

Schuh, J. H. & Whitt, E. J. (1999). Editors' notes. In J. H. Schuh & E. J. Whitt (Eds.), *Creating successful partnerships between academic and student affairs* (pp. 1–3). San Francisco: Jossey-Bass Publishers.

Smith, B. L. (2003). Learning communities and liberal education. *Academe, 89*(1), 14–18.

Westfall, S. B. (1999). Partnerships to connect in- and out-of-class experiences. In J. H. Schuh & E. J. Whitt (Eds.), *Creating successful partnerships between academic and student affairs* (pp. 51–61). San Francisco: Jossey-Bass Publishers.

CHAPTER FOUR

Circles One and Two: Promising Practices in Academic and Student Affairs Collaboration

James H. Cook
and Abby M. Ghering

This chapter will present and discuss a number of promising practices in academic affairs–student affairs collaborations. These practices are a valuable guide to understanding the nature of these partnerships. Many differences exist between faculty and student affairs professionals; understanding each entity's roles, culture, and language is integral. Anticipating challenges in collaboration and being aware of perceptions and misperceptions of each group also aids in understanding the common aspects of the practices highlighted in this chapter.

TEN PROMISING PRACTICES

At the outset of the research that led to this publication, promising practices in academic affairs–student affairs collaboration were solicited from universities and colleges across the country. Researchers asked the institutions to provide the following information:

1. The nature of the working relationship between academic affairs and student affairs

2. The factors to which they attributed the positive working relationship

3. How they arrived at a close working relationship (history)

4. The future of the relationship (How did they see it progressing from that point into the future?)

5. What they had learned through the relationship (regarding how good academic affairs–student affairs relationships are developed and maintained, pitfalls to avoid, etc.)

We examined the responses for commonalities. What we found were nine common characteristics—either explicitly in evidence or implied—of effective collaboration between the two divisions—hence the "nine circles."

The practices showcased in this chapter represent excellent examples of how effective collaboration can be between academic affairs and student affairs. These are relationships and programs that evince the best of what *Divine Comity* is trying to promote for the future. They provide a standard toward which we encourage all institutions of higher education to strive.

54

ANNE ARUNDEL COMMUNITY COLLEGE

Arnold, Maryland

Program: Black Student Success Team

The Black Student Success Team (BSST) is composed of faculty, administrators, and professional staff. The BSST is designed to help African American students integrate academically and socially into their college careers at Anne Arundel Community College (AACC). The program focuses on improving study habits, mentoring, social networking, and academic performance monitoring. An outgrowth of the BSST is AACC's Summer Bridge Program, which helps new African American students integrate academically and socially during the summer before their first long semester at AACC. The Summer Bridge Program involves faculty and staff from 12 departments in AACC's three divisions. According to program administrators, "The retention rate for Bridge program participants is impressive, given the developmental needs of some of the students. Two of the initial 15 Bridge participants have graduated and transferred. Nineteen of the 23 students enrolled in the summer 2002 program have been retained, and 20 of the 26 students enrolled in 2003 summer program have been retained. Since the Summer Bridge Program's founding, it has become a part of AACC's Student Achievement and Success program (SASP). SASP provides academic support services to an average of 200 new, under-prepared students each academic year."

CENTRAL MICHIGAN UNIVERSITY (SAPAA KNOWLEDGE COMMUNITY PROMISING PRACTICES AWARD WINNER, 2006)

Mount Pleasant, Michigan
Program: Leadership Institute

The Leadership Institute encompasses a five-tiered system of leadership training and development: The Leader Education And Development (LEAD) Model. The five tiers are Aspiring Leaders Program for incoming Central Michigan University (CMU) freshmen seeking involvement; Emerging Leaders Programs for freshmen and sophomores active in a registered student organization; Transitional Leaders Programs for sophomores and juniors on an executive board; Advanced Leaders Programs for sophomores, juniors, and seniors; and Capstone Leaders programs for juniors and seniors with extensive leadership experience. The Leadership Institute provides information and leadership development opportunities through workshops, seminars, academic courses, and experiential challenges. It is a collaboration of student affairs and academic affairs in many aspects, and has resulted in Central Michigan becoming the first public institution in Michigan to offer a minor in leadership

DEPAUL UNIVERSITY (SAPAA KNOWLEDGE COMMUNITY PROMISING PRACTICES AWARD WINNER, 2005)

Chicago, Illinois
Program: The Chicago Quarter

The Chicago Quarter introduces first-year students to the academic experience of college and assists them in making a successful transition to college life, the DePaul community, and the city of Chicago. The Chicago Quarter, which includes 30 Discover Chicago courses and

55 Explore Chicago courses, is required of all first-year students entering DePaul.

In addition to the academic content, 10 hours are added to each course for the "Common Hour." During the Common Hour, staff professionals and student leaders facilitate discussion about issues relevant to students' personal and intellectual transition to university life.

Courses in the Chicago Quarter are team taught by faculty, students, and staff professionals. Faculty, students, and staff work together on multiple levels, from constructing appropriate teaching teams, preparing team members to teach, and facilitating team conflicts to developing course materials, sharing teaching responsibilities, and grading.

ELON UNIVERSITY

Elon, North Carolina
Program: Academic–Student Affairs Partnerships

Academic–student affairs partnerships at Elon are characterized by a joint approach to internship, study abroad, service-learning, leadership, and undergraduate research programs. Together, these programs are known as "Elon Experiences." Academic affairs and student affairs also collaborate closely on Elon's General Studies Program, which includes an experiential learning requirement.

Other areas of collaboration include monthly joint academic affairs–student affairs deans' meetings, residential-based learning communities, Elon Experiences transcripts for program participants (chronicle participation in study abroad, volunteer service, internships/co-ops, leadership, and undergraduate research programs), substance abuse programming, and the Faculty Fellows Program, whereby faculty are given release time to work with student life's service-learning and leadership programs.

INDIANA UNIVERSITY–PURDUE UNIVERSITY INDIANAPOLIS (SAPAA KNOWLEDGE COMMUNITY PROMISING PRACTICES AWARD WINNER, 2006)

Indianapolis, Indiana

Program: First Year Students Learn & Achieve Socially Here (FLASH)

FLASH is designed and administered by student affairs but relies heavily on participation by academic affairs. Its purpose is to integrate first-year students socially and academically into college life. FLASH consists of (1) pre-admission, (2) new student orientation, (3) first semester, and (4) second semester. During each of these stages, student affairs staff work closely with partners in academic affairs to promote the curricular and co-curricular experiences and to prepare students to succeed once they enroll.

MINNESOTA STATE UNIVERSITY, MANKATO (SAPAA KNOWLEDGE COMMUNITY PROMISING PRACTICES AWARD WINNER, 2006)

Mankato, Minnesota

Program: Service-Learning Program

The Service-Learning Program is woven tightly into the academic curriculum, with more than 50 professors using service-learning as a pedagogy that ties classroom learning to real-world service experiences in the community. The program, which began with grants in the mid-1990s from the AmeriCorps National Service Program and the National Jumpstart Literacy Program, has expanded to include New

Student Project Program, Make a Difference Day, Earth Day, Hunger and Homelessness Awareness Week, National Children's Book Week (over 5,800 books collected), Youth Activity Fair, Alternative Spring Break Trips, The Sound of Reading Literacy Project, and Dr. Seuss' Birthday/Literary Event. The Service-learning Program partnered with the community to raise $8,841 for victims of the tsunami that hit Southeast Asia in 2004.

MANSFIELD UNIVERSITY OF PENNSYLVANIA

Mansfield, Pennsylvania
Programs: Faculty in Residence Program, Frederick Douglass Collaborative, and the Student Learning Forum

Through the Faculty in Residence Program, faculty members enter the residence halls and present on topics that are not related to what they teach. They are encouraged to discuss hobbies or areas of intellectual interest outside of their faculty roles. This program enables students to become acquainted with the faculty as "real people" outside the classroom.

The Frederick Douglass Collaborative closely involves academic and student affairs in student leadership programs, research, visiting scholars programs, and a lecture series. Mansfield University intends to expand the Collaborative to include living–learning communities and joint support programs for underprepared students.

The Student Learning Forum is a cross-divisional group appointed by the president and charged with improving the university's living–learning environment. It is currently developing a transcripted certificate program in leadership.

59

STONY BROOK UNIVERSITY (SAPAA KNOWLEDGE COMMUNITY PROMISING PRACTICES AWARD WINNER, 2006)

Stony Brook, New York
Programs: Undergraduate Colleges

All incoming freshmen are assigned to one of six undergraduate colleges: Arts, Culture, and Humanities; Global Studies; Human Development; Information and Technology Studies; Leadership and Service; or Science and Society. Academic and social life revolves around the themes established by the names of each college. Each college is led by a faculty director. The staff comprises a college advisor, who provides academic guidance and support, and the quad director and residence hall directors, who provide social support and student life activities. All residents take a shared freshman seminar in the fall and another in the spring.

SYRACUSE UNIVERSITY (SAPAA KNOWLEDGE COMMUNITY PROMISING PRACTICES AWARD WINNER, 2005)

Syracuse, New York
Program: Office of Learning Communities

The Office of Learning Communities administers two programs. Residential learning communities are partnerships between academic affairs and student affairs and integrate academic and co-curricular components to promote, enhance, and support students' academic, personal, and professional growth and success. Nonresidential learning communities are intrafaculty partnerships that integrate academic courses and experiences to promote, enhance, and support students' academic, personal, and professional growth and success.

The University of Arizona

Tucson, Arizona

Program: Maximum Educational Results in Two Semesters (MERITS)

The MERITS Program is a two-semester, goal-oriented program designed to help first-year students make a smooth transition to the University of Arizona. The program is founded on the concept that students should be most responsible for their own success. The program promotes this philosophy by providing periodic, individual student–peer advisor meetings, weekly workshops on topics related to academic and social success in college, and activities such as educational mixers with faculty and Food-4-Thought sessions that connect students to faculty and campus resources. Also offered are free tutoring and opportunities for students to compete for book scholarships and tuition waivers as incentives for program participation. The MERITS Program is housed within the Department of Multicultural Programs and Services, whose mission is to increase the numbers of historically underserved graduates and to prepare all students to be culturally aware participants of the 21st century.

CHAPTER FIVE
Circle Three:
Top-Down Commitment

Tomás D. Morales

P residential leadership style and how presidents build their
leadership teams influence how members of their teams work
together (Bensimon & Neumann, 1993). Leadership teams
that collaborate with each other and foster collaborative partnerships
throughout the organization are those that trust each other. Trust
is manifested by openness and honesty among team members. Collaborative presidential team members are those who are comfortable
arguing and debating issues and ideas with each other and who view
constructive conflict as positive. For example, the literature describing

presidential leadership in higher education often describes a comfort level and tendency of presidents to assume a "traditional" and "directive" leadership role, as opposed to adopting "two-way communication or social exchange processes of mutual influence or to identify leadership as facilitating rather than directing the work of highly educated professionals"(Bensimon, Birnbaum, & Neumann, 1989, p. iv).

Effective senior executive teams exhibit commitment to the mission of the organization, are accountable to each other, and are intentional about achieving the results identified by the team, even if it means sacrificing the individual needs of a team member or those of the division they lead (Lencioni, 2002).

Collaboration between members of a senior executive team cannot be legislated or imposed. Shared authority and responsibility strengthen interdependence while creating interactive synergy among team members (Bensimon & Neumann, 1993). Collaborative-centered leadership creates a comfort level and acceptability of different perspectives by capitalizing on differences for the good of the team. A president who fosters this type of team behavior is skilled in bringing together a group of diverse minds that reflect a variety of points of views. This team-centered approach results in a leadership team that works as a whole, is able to master new knowledge, and is committed to innovation, problem solving, and productivity (Bensimon & Neumann, 1993). Executive teams that exhibit these characteristics are those that have strong relationships between academic and student affairs.

Creating Organizational Change

Building a leadership team that values and promotes a strong partnership between academic affairs and student affairs requires a commitment to organizational change and is often a departure from how leadership teams in higher education have traditionally functioned. For example, student affairs has often been associated with the delivery of services to support the bureaucratic relationship between the student and the institution, such as supervising students who live in residence halls, administering and delivering financial aid, orienting of new students, administering campus life, adjudicating student behavior, and orchestrating student activities. Academic affairs, on the other hand, has traditionally been responsible for the delivery of instruction, research, curriculum design, and upholding academic standards. Forging a more collaborative academic and student affairs partnership requires creating a common language and developing new social and professional relationships between senior academic and student affairs officers, which in turn would change how these senior administrators perform and are evaluated (Huber & Glick, 1993). Their performance should be measured by their ability to meet institutional mission, vision, and goals as well as to achieve the learning outcomes identified by their institution.

The challenge for the president, academic affairs officer, and student affairs officer in leading organizational change is to convince their followers that a viable partnership between these two critically important divisions is central to advancing learning. The faculty, academic administrators, and student affairs professionals may not share that belief. James O'Toole, in his book *Leading Change: Overcoming the Ideology of Comfort and the Tyranny of Custom*, suggested "a sine qua non of effective leadership is the ability to overcome resistance to change among followers" (O'Toole, 1995, p. 158). Institutions of higher education are steeped in tradition and tend to resist change. Leaders often struggle to "overcome this chronic and inevitable pattern of resistance" (O'Toole,

1995, p. 14). O'Toole believed the only way to overcome resistance to change is "by building an alternative system of belief and allowing others to adopt it as their own" (O'Toole, 1995, p. 14).

Changing institutional culture and campus value systems requires strong "values-based leadership" (O'Toole, 1995, p. 14). The research teams that studied "Good to Great" corporate organizations identified the importance of a chief executive officer who sought a departure from top-down management. Effective presidential leadership engages the entire campus community in a dialogue and debate regarding a shared vision and the importance of collaboration resembling the leadership of the exemplary firms described in *Good to Great* (Collins, 2001).

THE ROLE OF THE PRESIDENT

Regional accreditation requirements and other internal and external forces will influence a strong partnership between academic and student affairs. Such partnerships support the centrality of learning and the institution's need to measure learning outcomes both in and outside the classroom, as well as to demonstrate that it is serving the public by encouraging civic engagement on the part of the campus community.

In an article titled "Presidential Leadership: Moral Leadership in the New Millennium," Robert A. Corrigan, president of San Francisco State University, introduced a new paradigm in presidential leadership. He described a presidency that is able to mobilize the intellectual capital of the institution to serve the public good by bringing together "extraordinary faculty, great students, an enormous research capability, and support personnel with skills" (Corrigan, 2002, p. 2). A strong partnership between academic and student affairs divisions will enable them to work together to improve K–12 education, rebuild decaying urban neighborhoods, and facilitate civic engagement by faculty, students, and staff.

Portland State University, the University of Southern California, Southwest Missouri State University, the University of Rhode Island, the University of Pennsylvania, and California State University, Fresno are examples of institutions led by morally centered presidents who have a common vision to serve the public, whose leadership is grounded in a sense of what is right and wrong, and who embrace the challenges facing the region that the institution serves (Corrigan, 2002). The type of leadership described by Corrigan is strongly committed not only to creating strong academic and student affairs partnerships but to mobilizing the entire leadership team to address student learning, both in and outside the classroom, as well as the needs of the institution's neighboring communities.

The late Frank Newman, former director of Brown University's Futures Project: Policy for Higher Education in a Changing World, with his colleagues Lara Couturier and Jamie Scurry in their recently published book *The Future of Higher Education: Rhetoric, Reality, and the Risks of the Market,* asked a fundamental question: "[W]ho is responsible for student learning?"(Newman, Couturier, & Scurry, 2004, p. 135). The answer to this question will drive institutions to create and sustain strong partnerships between academic and student affairs. A prerequisite to creating learning-focused institutions includes six characteristics that require a strong partnership between academic and student affairs: (1) "clearly defined outcomes for student learning;" (2) "student participation in a diverse array of learning experiences;" (3) "systemic assessment and documentation of student learning;" (4) "emphasis on student learning in the recruitment, orientation, deployment, evaluation, and reward of faculty and administrators;" (5) "institutional and individual reflection about learning outcomes leading to action aimed at improvement" and (6) "focus on learning consistently reflected in key institutional documents, policies, collegial effort, and leadership behavior" (Newman, Couturier, & Scurry, 2004, pp. 139–140).

Supporting and Assessing Student Learning

The Council for Higher Education Accreditation and several regional accrediting agencies call for the development of a culture of evidence to verify the assessment of learning outcomes both in and outside the classroom (Newman, Couturier, & Scurry, 2004). For example, the Western Association of Schools and Colleges (WASC) (2001) Accrediting Commission for Senior Colleges and Universities Standards of Accreditation states under Standard 1, Criteria for Review 1.3, that "the institution's leadership creates and sustains a leadership system at all levels that is marked by high performance, appropriate responsibility, and accountability" (p. 17). Standard 1, Criteria 1.5, states, "Consistent with its purposes and character, the institution demonstrates an appropriate response to the increasing diversity in society through its policies, its educational and co-curricular programs, and its administrative and organizational practices" (p. 18). To meet this standard, presidential leadership teams must be collaborative, including a strong partnership between academic and student affairs.

In WASC Standard 2, "Achieving Educational Objectives Through Core Functions" under the subheading "Teaching and Learning," Criteria for Review 2.3 states:

> The institution's expectations for learning and student attainment are clearly reflected in its academic programs

and policies. These include the organization and content of the institution's curricula; admissions and graduation policies; the organization and delivery of advisement; the use of its library and information resources;
and (where applicable) experience in the wider learning
environment provided by the campus and/or co- curriculum. (p. 21)

The importance of creating and sustaining a strong partnership
between academic and student affairs is evident if institutions are to
meet Standard 2 under the subheading "Support for Student Learning," Criteria for Review 2.11, which states, "Consistent with its purposes, the institution develops and implements co-curricular programs
that are integrated with its academic goals and programs, and supports
student professional and personal development" (p. 23), and Criteria
2.13, which states, "Student support services—including financial aid,
registration, advising, career counseling, computer labs, and library and
information services—are designed to meet the needs of the specific
types of students the institution serves and the curricula it offers" (p.
23). In examining the regional accrediting agencies, one finds similar
expectations that institutions create the kind of organizational structure and leadership culture in which the senior academic and student
affairs officers are working closely to create a learning-centered collegial
environment.

In his opening keynote presentation at the American Association
of State Colleges and Universities (AASCU) provost summer meeting,
Peter Ewell, vice president of the National Center for Higher Education Management Systems, gave a preview of the AASCU graduation
rate outcomes study released in fall 2005. The report, *Student Success in
State Colleges and Universities: A Matter of Culture and Leadership* (Ameri-

can Association of State Colleges and Universities, 2003), examined best practices at 11 AASCU institutions. Even though the institutions studied were diverse in character, they were very successful in achieving high graduation rates. Ewell's presentation described the cultural and organizational characteristics of these institutions, which were largely focused on student success and learning and not solely on improving their graduation rates. These characteristics included a campus culture of high expectation, a sense of belonging, and an environment in which members of the campus community understood the institution's purpose and place. These institutions had the "scaffolding" infrastructure to ensure that students were able to meet high expectations (Ewell, 2005).

The leadership of these institutions was shared, pervasive, and empowering and modeled the core values of the institution. The organizational leadership was described as including cross-functional work teams, eliminating silos, and having unusual levels of trust among members of the leadership team and a strong partnership between academic affairs and student affairs (Ewell, 2005).

The persistent call from external stakeholders for accountability, increased graduation rates, evidence of learning outcomes, and prepared graduates will result in the type of presidential leadership that will encourage a strong collaborative partnership between academic and student affairs. In *Student Success in College: Creating Conditions That Matter* (Kuh, Kinzie, Schuh, Whitt, & Associates, 2005), presidential leadership was examined extensively. Each of the institutions studied in the Documenting Effective Educational Practice (DEEP) project was led by a president who was committed to creating a campus environment in which student success and a quality undergraduate experience were the centerpieces of the administration (Kuh et al., 2005).

EXAMINING SHARED INSTITUTIONAL LEADERSHIP

In examining presidential and institutional leadership, common themes began to emerge that showed why DEEP schools performed exceptionally well in facilitating student success. Members of the president's leadership team, academic deans, and faculty shared institutional leadership. Traditional boundaries between academic affairs and student affairs were nonexistent. The faculty and administrative leadership publicly announced their commitment to undergraduate education. DEEP schools had a distributed system of formal and informal leadership structure dedicated to student success. Throughout these institutions, programs and services jointly administered and led by faculty, academic, and student affairs administrators were pervasive (Kuh et al., 2005).

Kuh (1996) observed that creating a meaningful collegiate undergraduate experience requires academic and student affairs to work closely together. Kuh's model speaks to the importance of creating and agreeing to a common language and shared vision as a prerequisite to connecting curriculum and co-curriculum activities. He points out the importance of leveraging the human and fiscal resources needed to create an effective learning environment both in and outside the classroom (Kuh, 1996). During the past decade, the number of academic and student affairs collaborations has increased (Bourassa & Kruger, 2001). Many of the historical and cultural barriers between faculty and student affairs educators are being replaced with a renewed emphasis on partnering to enhance learning. These collaborations have resulted in an increase in service-learning, first-year and senior-year experience programs, faculty residential life programs, the development of learning communities, and an overall shared commitment to student success.

There are many examples of collaborative efforts between academic and student affairs. Wagner College in New York City has developed freshman and senior program-learning communities linking clusters of courses with experimental learning opportunities by placing students at selected sites throughout the city. The Senior Learning Community serves as a capstone course in the major, combining an internship placement and research project. The Wagner Plan is jointly administered by academic and student affairs to connect learning communities and experiential fieldwork (Tagg, 2003).

The University of Texas El Paso (UTEP), under President Diana Natalicio, has developed several programs that bring academic and student affairs together to support student learning. UTEP created the Entering Student Program (ESP), a campus collaborative effort to support entering students by integrating academic-based content programs, a student leadership institute, academic support services, and orientation and advising programs employing both faculty and student affairs professionals (Kuh et al., 2005). This confluence of programs creates for "students the scaffolding they need to support their growth as learners" (Tagg, 2003, p. 321).

At Miami University in Oxford, Ohio, senior academic and student affairs administrators created a shared vision of what a quality undergraduate experience should be. A collaborative approach was used to develop a comprehensive First-Year Experience and Choice Matters program emphasizing "intellectual growth and challenge" (Kuh et al., 2005, p. 165) in the undergraduate experience.

Student services staff at Alvernia College in Reading, Pennsylvania, have created co-curricular learning outcomes and consider themselves partners in the development of a community of learners. Annually, Alvernia documents partnerships with academic affairs and other campus offices and community programs (Kuh et al., 2005).

Presidential, senior administrative, and faculty leadership is critically important in creating the partnership between academic and student affairs. Creating and sustaining learning-centered campuses committed to student success will require a tripartite of academic affairs, student affairs, and students.

REFERENCES

American Association of State Colleges and Universities. (2005, September). *Student success in state colleges and universities: A matter of culture and leadership.* Washington, DC: Author.

Bensimon, E. M., Birnbaum, R., & Neumann, A. (1989). *Making sense of administrative leadership: The 'L' word in higher education.* ASHE-ERIC Higher Education Report No. 1. Washington, DC: School of Education and Human Development, The George Washington University. (ERIC Document Reproduction service No. ED 316074).

Bensimon, E. M., & Neumann, A. (1993). *Redesigning collegiate leadership: Teams and teamwork in higher education.* Baltimore: The Johns Hopkins University Press.

Bourassa, D. M., & Kruger, K. (2001). The national dialogue on academic and student affairs collaboration. *New Directions for Higher Education, 116,* 9–38.

Collins, J. (2001). *Good to great: Why some companies make the leap... and others don't.* New York: HarperCollins Publishers, Inc.

Corrigan, R. A. (2002). Presidential leadership: Moral leadership in the new millennium. *Liberal Education, 88*(4), 6–13.

Ewell, P. (2005, July). *Student success in state colleges and universities: A matter of culture and leadership.* Paper presented at the Provost Summer Meeting of the American Association of State Colleges and Universities. Snowbird, UT.

Huber, G. P., & Glick, W. H. (1993). *Organizational change and redesign: Ideas and insights for improving performance.* New York: Oxford University Press.

Kuh, G. D. (1996). Guiding principles for creating seamless learning environments for undergraduates. *Journal of College Student Development, 37*(2), 135–146.

Kuh, G. D., Kinzie, J., Schuh, J. H., Whitt, E. J., & Associates. (2005). *Student success in college: Creating conditions that matter.* San Francisco: Jossey-Bass.

Lencioni, P. (2002). *The five dysfunctions of a team: A leadership fable.* San Francisco: Jossey-Bass.

Newman, F., Couturier, L., & Scurry, J. (2004). *The future of higher education: Rhetoric, reality, and the risks of the market.* San Francisco: Jossey-Bass.

O' Toole, J. (1995). *Leading change: Overcoming the ideology of comfort and the tyranny of custom.* San Francisco: Jossey-Bass.

Tagg, J. (2003). *The learning paradigm college.* Bolton, MA: Anker Company, Inc.

Western Association of Schools and Colleges. (2001, January). *Handbook of accreditation standards: Addressing core commitments to institutional capacity and educational effectiveness.* Alameda, CA: Author.

CHAPTER SIX
Circle Four: Active Outreach

Robert Caruso

I ntegrative, holistic learning...transformative education...deep
learning...seamless learning...intentional learning. These are just
some of the terms often associated with effective student learning in higher education. *Learning Reconsidered: A Campus-Wide Focus on
the Student Experience* (Keeling, 2004) is "an argument for the integrated
use of all of higher education's resources in the education and preparation of the whole student" (p. 3). As the authors stated, in order to
reach the goal of transformative education,

> every aspect of the student experience must be examined
> and a new configuration of learning processes and out-
> comes created. All of the resources of the campus must
> be brought to bear on the students' learning process and
> learning must be reconsidered. (p. 11)

The authors further indicated that, in order to achieve holistic, integrated learning outcomes, student affairs administrators must be prepared to make substantive changes in the nature and assessment of their work (p. 14). In bringing together human and other institutional resources to support the learning process, it is vital that faculty and administrators collaborate to maximize the benefits to students. Shared student learning outcomes must be the superordinate goal that unites their activities, and active outreach to enlist one another's support must be a priority. Learning experiences must be identified and enhanced across all organizational boundaries—wherever and whenever student learning has an opportunity to flourish.

Jacobson (2004) stated that "the number of students graduating from high school in the United States will continue to rise steadily over the coming years, reaching a peak of 3.2 million in 2008–09, according to the Western Interstate Commission for Higher Education along with the College Board and ACT, Inc." (p. A28). As Hoover (2002) added in a *Chronicle of Higher Education* article, the proportion of high school graduates going directly to college increased to more than 60% in the late 1990s from about 50% over 20 years ago.

Distance learners are also becoming an increasingly important student constituent in colleges and universities. Schwitzer, Ancis, and Brown (2000) affirmed the continuing impact of distance learners by stating:

Certainly high school seniors who go on to pursue "four critical years" of traditional learning and developmental experiences in conventional college campuses will continue to be a major segment of the higher education market in the United States; however, there is already widespread evidence of what the National Education Association (NEA) called an "exploding"...distance learning trend. (p. 3)

Finally, in the *Critical Issues Task Force Report* (American College Personnel Association, 2001), association leaders identified academic and learning concerns as one of the critical issues facing today's college students.

Essentially, the charges posed in the publications above to the higher education community make the case for active outreach from student affairs professionals, including provosts, vice presidents, deans, department heads, and faculty members, in order to achieve the integrated student outcomes at the core of transformative education. The challenge for student affairs administrators continues to be how to work actively with academic affairs colleagues to help create an integrated learning environment incorporating the curriculum and co-curriculum that both traditional and nontraditional students deserve and need (Caruso, 2004). This chapter explores the topic of active outreach as one of the many important components of effective collaboration between student affairs professionals and their colleagues in academia. It includes some discussion of cultural differences between student affairs and academic affairs, cautions about undertaking partnerships, the rationale for and process of developing partnerships, discussion of representative successful practices, and tips for practitioners.

STUDENT AFFAIRS PHILOSOPHICAL TENETS AND ASSUMPTIONS

According to Young (2003), there are many values associated with student affairs practice that revolve around human dignity or individuation. "Individuals are whole, unique, and responsible; their experience is the measure of their education and the source of student affairs programs" (pp. 98–99). There are also, however, "contextual values" that include community, equality, justice, caring and caring-based ethics, and service and services (p. 100).

Thus, student affairs practitioners must be prepared to address not only individual student concerns and growth challenges but also students' need for community within the context of an institution. The wide range of roles student affairs professionals play requires that they engage in active outreach on a regular basis. These roles, as enumerated by many authors (e.g., Banning, 1978; Brown, 1972; Knock, 1990; Miller & Prince, 1976) include student development educator, diagnostician, consultant, environmental manager, programmer, researcher, and campus ecologist.

Several assumptions about student learning have guided the student affairs profession for many years. In some way, each of them has a connection to the need for improved collaboration among student affairs professionals, faculty, and academic affairs administrators. As described in *Points of View: A Perspective on Student Affairs*, which traced the history and philosophy of the student affairs profession (National Association of Student Personnel Administrators, 1987, pp. 12–14), these key assumptions include the following: the academic mission of the institution is preeminent; student involvement enhances learning; out-of-class environments affect learning; a supportive and friendly community life helps students learn; the freedom to doubt and question must be guaranteed; and effective citizenship should be taught.

A more recent conceptualization of student learning from the National Panel Report of the Association of American Colleges and Universities (2002, p. xi) "calls for higher education to help college students become *intentional learners* [italics added] who can adapt to new environments, integrate knowledge from different sources, and continue learning throughout their lives." The panel went on to state that "these intentional learners should also become empowered through the mastery of intellectual and practical skills, informed by knowledge about the natural and social worlds and about forms of inquiry basic to these studies, and responsible for their personal actions and for civic values" (p. xi). So-called "deep learning" (Association of American Colleges and Universities, 2002; Weigel, 2002) is strengthened by activities that connect the curriculum and the co-curriculum, offer students experiential opportunities to test learning assumptions, and encourage students to engage the world beyond the campus. Deep learning enhances both student development and active student involvement in academic life.

CULTURAL DIFFERENCES BETWEEN ACADEMIC AND STUDENT AFFAIRS

Love, Kuh, MacKay, and Hardy (1993) pointed out that there are some legitimate cultural differences that tend to divide faculty members and student affairs professionals and that represent somewhat different concepts of the place of faculty and student affairs professionals within the higher education environment. According to the authors, key faculty values include the creation and dissemination of knowledge as the primary goal of higher education, professional autonomy and academic freedom to achieve this goal, collegiality as expressed through self-governance, and thinking and reflecting over doing. By contrast, student affairs values emphasize holistic student development, collaboration over autonomy, acceptance of structure and a differentiated hierarchy, and doing.

The classic teaching-research-service triad upon which faculty members are evaluated is a different set of standards from a student affairs evaluation process, which typically may include such factors as leadership, judgment, organizational awareness, appreciation of diversity, and communication competencies. There is very little in student affairs that approximates the tenure, promotion, and reappointment process. Student affairs professionals generally have year-to-year appointments and are subject to at least an annual evaluation process.

As Love et al. (1993) described, the degree to which part-time and adjunct faculty are employed is often foreign to student affairs professionals. While there are certainly part-time members of student affairs staffs, their numbers do not approach the growing numbers of adjuncts needed to support academic programs. In some instances, entire programs are largely supported by part-time or adjunct faculty. The latter generally are not well connected to the institution and principally perform a utilitarian function, filling in as needed for full-time faculty. This situation makes it very difficult for student affairs professionals to incorporate academic part-timers into partnerships and collaborative activities where the need for contact time and consistency is paramount.

Finally, there is essentially no undergraduate correlate to a graduate program in college student affairs. Many faculty members find that situation difficult to understand and occasionally question the quality and the relevance of such training. Love et al. (1993) concluded that "taking into account the cultures of faculty and student affairs enriches understanding of both groups which increases the likelihood that student affairs and faculty can work together to create conditions that enhance student learning and development" (pp. 52–53).

Given the cultural differences between academic and student affairs, some writers (e.g., Magolda, 2005) argue that student affairs professionals must proceed cautiously as they consider engaging their faculty counterparts in collaborative activities. Moreover, Magolda asserts that before any of the administrative or logistical portions of collaboration are discussed, overarching moral questions must be asked such as, "Will the creation of this partnership be good for students and partners? How does collaboration fit with the partners' teaching and learning beliefs?" (p. 17). Student affairs professionals must be poised to highlight their expertise as educators as much as their administrative savvy. Magolda concludes (p. 21) that collaboration is best not only when it is "meaningful, reciprocal, and responsive" but also when partners openly acknowledge differences and address conflict as a normal part of the collaborative process.

THE RATIONALE FOR ACTIVE OUTREACH AND COLLABORATION

Certainly, there are many reasons why active outreach is important, and it may be useful to practitioners to offer a summary. Ardaiolo (1993), Fried (2005), Hirsch & Burack (2001), Keeling (2004), and Smith (1988) have collectively delineated the following reasons for collaboration: assessment of student learning; impact of technology on the teaching and learning processes; changing student populations; diversity issues; student mental health issues; enrollment management, including recruitment, orientation, and retention issues; changes in general education; increased emphasis on civic engagement, service-learning, and leadership development; quality of the undergraduate educational experience; and compliance with and accountability for new laws and evolving standards of practice. Specific types of collaboration that may be suggested include one-on-one personal and electronic student affairs–faculty contacts, use of general education or liberal studies learning outcomes in the planning process within student affairs, joint work groups and task forces, jointly developed virtual learning communities for distance learners, and organizational restructuring.

Martin and Murphy (1997) offer a faculty perspective on classroom challenges that can provide a foundation for active outreach with student affairs professionals: the growing number of part-time students seeking self-paced learning, disappearing elements of traditional campus life, decreasing student skill levels, expanding part-time faculty culture, and a graying professoriate. According to these authors, among the partnerships that these factors suggest are those related to student and faculty support in such areas as student time management, academic skills development, decision making, services for adult learners, learning communities, classroom behavior management, and orientation programs for part-time faculty.

How can student affairs administrators respond? Among the many possibilities are new faculty orientation sessions and related "how-to" brochures on management of student disciplinary problems in the classroom, mental health referrals, refinement of the academic integrity procedures using the expertise of the judicial affairs office, and joint workshops with the faculty development center on a variety of learning-oriented topics.

DEVELOPING EFFECTIVE OUTREACH

What drives strong relationships between academic affairs and student affairs? How do these relationships begin? What does the active outreach process look like? Livingston and Croft (2005) categorized three major types of interventions that could be useful to student affairs practitioners in framing and deciding on the best approaches to collaborate with academic affairs: organizational structures, curricular innovations, and programmatic activities. Ardaiolo (1993) asserted that both structural and personal means can work well in building partnerships. Structural means are advantageous when "there are clear responsibility and authority for student affairs professionals' performing things considered academic, especially those borderline functions which could be in either area depending on a campus's unique culture or current state of political affairs" (p. 4). Personal means work best when student affairs professionals "seek out opportunities usually through issues or controversy for an entrée into building relationships with academic affairs" (p. 4). Clearly, demonstrated competence in conducting certain activities that might be considered "academic" and assertiveness in transforming campus issues into collaborative opportunities can often be very productive means of advancing student affairs professionals' credibility and visibility with faculty and administrators.

Engstrom and Tinto (2000) described a three-phase continuum of involvement approaches: serving as *information* clearinghouses in which student affairs professionals share information with faculty and others; working *cooperatively* with faculty in which traditional student affairs and faculty roles are maintained and operationalized, albeit in the context of joint, worthwhile activities; and working *collaboratively* with faculty in a context in which:

...all group members are perceived and recognized as holding important knowledge and experiences that can contribute to the group's learning process. The responsibilities and roles of participants are in constant negotiation; authority is shared and shifts continually based on the knowledge and experiences of group members. (pp. 435–436)

EXAMPLES OF SUCCESSFUL PRACTICES

Institutions committed to bringing together the finest assets of student affairs and academic affairs must obviously begin with some plan of action. Several institutions have vigorously approached the how and the why of partnership building, and their approaches are worthy of discussion.

Using College and University Advisory Committees

The Students Utilizing Community College to Expand Educational Dreams (SUCCEED) program at Paradise Valley Community College (PVCC) in Phoenix, Arizona, is an English as a second language (ESL) high school bridge program that focuses on high school juniors and seniors to address a high drop-out rate among first-generation Hispanic students. SUCCEED provides the opportunity for these students to enroll in college courses at PVCC to ease the transition from high school to college. The students enroll in a block program of six college credits each semester of the first year and six credits of their choice the following year (P. Dale, personal communication, June 30, July 5, July 7, 2005).

Perhaps the most important factor in sustaining the SUCCEED program is that it is coordinated by a collaborative academic and student affairs team of business division faculty, counselors, financial aid staff, and the SUCCEED coordinator. A community diversity committee identified the low high school completion rates and low levels of community college attendance of ESL students as community concerns. Academic and student affairs provide the foundation for program development to meet these community needs.

The goal of Columbia College's (Columbia, Missouri) Unity in the Community (UC) program is to create a community that embraces all members of its population and provides support and resources when necessary. A group of students, faculty, and staff came together as an advisory group to create the program in fall 2004. UC has provided opportunities for interaction between academic and student affairs in two ways: The work that is done on the UC Committee allows for in-depth dialog about issues affecting the campus population, and faculty and staff expertise is used to facilitate many of the UC programs (K. Kinyon, personal communication, June 23, 27, 2005).

Establishing Community–University Partnership Opportunities

Wayne State University in Detroit, Michigan, has developed an unusual approach to the alternative spring break programs now becoming common on many campuses. As an urban university, it is Wayne State's mission and duty to give back to the city and help it grow. The Detroit Orientation Institute is a center within the Provost's Office that focuses on orienting new business and civic leaders to the city of Detroit. The Dean of Students Office and the Project Volunteer student organization partner with the Detroit Orientation Institute to offer Alternative Spring Break-Detroit (D. Strauss, personal communication, June 28, July 5, July 6, 2005). The program has helped Detroit's urban renewal initiative by engaging students with the city.

87

Refocusing the Context for Collaboration

Texas A&M University in College Station, Texas, has taken a positive step toward active outreach. According to the vice president for student affairs:

> We've enjoyed substantial recent success by reframing the collaboration challenge as one of *integration* [italics added]. The message has been to apply what is learned from in-class activities to what is learned/practiced in out-of-class activities, and then to return that experience to the classroom discussion, forming a continuous loop. We've asked all units in student affairs to look at their programs and activities, and ask the question "how does this extend in-class learning, and what will a student take from our activities/programs back to their classrooms?" We've also encouraged discussions with students and particularly student leaders on that point, and it's proven to be more than simply rhetoric...students are coming back to class and talking with faculty about how they applied things from class to their co-curricular activities! The particularly exciting thing is that faculty are hearing that and starting to appreciate that outside activities are a complement versus competition with classroom learning. (D. Bresciani, personal communication, July 13, 2005)

Bresciani goes on to point out that the student center has probably made the most progress by restructuring many unconnected activities around the integration theme and tying them more closely to both classroom and contemporary university priorities for learning so as to provide a progression of experiences—all linked to courses and curricula on campus.

Publishing an Agreement between Student Affairs and Academic Affairs

The University of Cincinnati has developed a student affairs–academic affairs agreement called "A Statement of Shared Responsibility: Creating a Learning Oriented Campus." According to the vice president for student affairs, the partnership is partially based on Tinto's work on student integration into both the academic and social environments and "is a result of a series of discussions between Academic Affairs and Student Affairs regarding collaborative programs and initiatives that was ultimately formalized in our first planning retreat. There are many similar programs between the two divisions that provide multiple opportunities for joint collaborations" (M. Livingston, personal communication, July 26, 27, 2005). A copy of the agreement appears in Appendix A.

Creating Faculty Appointments within Student Affairs

At the State University of New York at Geneseo, the use of faculty members to carry out traditional student affairs functions extended an already positive relationship between student affairs and academic affairs. Customarily at Geneseo, a full-time faculty member has filled the position of assistant dean of the college in the academic affairs area for a three-year term. After three years, other faculty members are given the opportunity to fulfill this administrative role, which concerns such issues as academic advisement and academic standards (R. Bonfiglio, personal communication, June 24, 2005). With the departure of the coordinator of new student orientation, the vice president for student affairs proposed to the provost that the model of a short-term faculty appointment be used to staff this position. Because of the relationship that had been cultivated with academic affairs, especially with regard to orientation, the proposal was favorably received. The position was retitled associate dean of students for new student orientation and first-year programs.

With this change in staffing, the vice president reports that the college has improved its capacity to realize some of its goals related to the first-year experience, including enhanced attention to the challenging nature of the academic experience at Geneseo, a common summer reading program for new students, and an expanded first-year student peer mentoring program. Academic affairs continues to pay the associate dean's salary, and student affairs has been responsible for the compensation of the adjunct instructors hired to teach the courses formerly taught by the associate dean, resulting in substantial savings for student affairs.

Restructuring to Create Mergers

At the University of Colorado at Boulder, the most effective outreach was accomplished by merging student affairs with academic affairs. Today, student affairs is seen as a collaborator with the provost and the academic deans. As part of the merger, the associate vice chancellor for undergraduate education and the executive director of enrollment management were placed under student affairs. Adding these programs to the student affairs portfolio gave student affairs credibility with faculty (R. Stump, personal communication, June 12, July 6, 2005). The two areas have developed a common mission and common student learning outcomes. Rapport has also been enhanced through readings and related discussions, as well as regular sharing of student affairs issues and problems.

The vice president for student affairs and formerly vice provost and dean of students at Michigan Technological University in Houghton, Michigan, also benefits from previous direct involvement in the academic arena. Quality time in the academic area gave him some of the breadth of experience and cooperation skills that have allowed his division not only to continue those relationships with faculty in his new role but also to broaden his scope of responsibility to include enrollment management, marketing, and alumni relations (L. Cook, personal communication, June 15, 2005).

In 2004, the University of Arkansas in Fayetteville, Arkansas, created a new position: associate vice chancellor (AVC) for institutional diversity and education. The AVC is a senior administrator/scholar who reports to *both* the provost/vice chancellor for academic affairs and the vice chancellor for student affairs. The AVC conducts scholarly work relevant to diversity and multicultural issues; provides guidance on matters related to the curriculum and its reflection of diversity/multicultural issues; works with academic units to develop diversity plans for each college; articulates a vision and provides leadership and direction to the implementation of the university's Diversity Plan; and provides visionary leadership to the Multicultural Center (J. Brazzell, personal communication, June 21, 2005).

Using Other Organizational Structures

Winthrop University in Rock Hill, South Carolina, has developed a vibrant University College (UC) model that combines units from both academic affairs and student affairs.

> University College brings together existing and planned programs focused on increasing student achievement and engagement across the university. The College co-

ordinates and guides programs from both academic affairs and student affairs, honing their focus across disciplines to ensure that every Winthrop student, regardless of their ultimate degree goal, has a common academic foundation as they commence their course of major study. (University College, 2005, para. 1)

University College brings together Winthrop's revised General Education program, ACAD 101 (Principles of the Learning Academy), the Honors program, and the activities and opportunities available through the International Center. The Teaching and Learning Center, which provides professional development opportunities for faculty and works with faculty who are new to Winthrop, is also a key component. An overarching focus for all of the dynamic elements of University College is enhancing the freshman-year experience and student retention. (University College, 2005, paras. 1–2)

According to the vice president for student life, students do not formally matriculate through UC, but the college functions as the focus for many academically related matters as they affect new students. UC is overseen by the dean of University College, who reports to the vice president for academic affairs. The latter formally evaluates his staff but considers the UC dean's input in their tasks completed as part of the UC umbrella. These methods allow all of academic affairs, UC, and student life to claim equal shares in the outcomes of UC (F. Ardaiolo, personal communication, July 6, 31, 2005).

Incorporating Active Outreach into Strategic Plans

West Chester University of Pennsylvania's Plan for Excellence includes five transformations: student success (the defining characteristic of the plan), diversity, human capital, resourcefulness, and responsiveness (D. Devestern, personal communication, June 16, July 14, 2005).

With the new strategic plan in place, there has been increased emphasis on cross-divisional efforts as critical to accomplishing its goals. Expectations to cooperate, collaborate, and integrate both areas are found in the strategic plan and in the annual goals and objectives statements for each division. The unifying areas included in the student success transformation are retention issues, student involvement/engagement in campus life, general education curriculum and developing skills, connecting theoretical and applied knowledge (e.g., service-learning), assessment, and academic and career advising.

Employing Continuous Quality Improvement

West Shore Community College in Scottville, Michigan, used the goal of at-risk student success as a basis for adopting the Academic Quality Improvement Program (AQIP), the North Central accreditation model. It was adopted because it promoted annual continuous improvement and focused on measurable results. West Shore was one of the first 40 to 50 colleges to join the accreditation model, which requires colleges to create measurable action projects and to produce annual progress reports (K. Pollack, personal communication, June 17, 2005).

The vision and strategic plan associated with the project focused on student success, the new AQIP accreditation process with a specific student-oriented action project, and the implementation of a faculty–staff team approach to address at-risk students. Activities include a year-long, student-friendly course schedule; a "D, W, F" grade report that collects grade statistics for all college courses over a five-year period in order to identify high-risk courses; changes in developmental math and English classes, expanded supplemental instruction, and an intensive mentoring program.

Encouraging Academic Classes to Study Student Affairs Issues

The University of Kansas Medical Center in Kansas City, Kansas, conducted a major Student Health Center Needs Assessment Survey to determine the level of services that students desired in the student health center and student willingness to approve a fee increase. During the construction of the survey, the project team collaborated with a faculty member from the Health Policy and Management (HP&M) department. His cost management class reviewed the survey and provided valuable feedback before it was administered (C. Mcicrs, personal communication, July 1, 7, 2005). This initial partnership has opened up other opportunities for collaboration. All of the health care providers in the Student Health Center are part-time, so they have little time for administrative duties related to improving operational effectiveness. Future plans include student projects related to reviewing office protocols, reviewing health policies such as immunization compliance, and assisting in the selection of a new student health information management system.

Creating a Committee on Student Learning

At Western Carolina University in Cullowhee, North Carolina, the director of service-learning, a member of the student affairs division, and the director of the Faculty Center for Teaching and Learning formed a partnership based on student affairs' and academic affairs' interest in the overarching goal of student learning. This committee is considered so important that it has its own brochure. The primary purpose of the committee, co-chaired by the two leaders, is to "promote the integrated use of university resources for the holistic development of students" (Western Carolina University, 2005).

The committee coordinates programs and makes recommendations to senior administration designed to create a holistic learning environment. Members use *Learning Reconsidered* recommendations as a basis for facilitating their implementation; coordinate the selection process for the Integration of Learning Award, which honors faculty members who work with student affairs on jointly developed programs with jointly developed learning outcomes; offer audio and teleconferences on the partnership theme; and plan roundtable discussions on topics related to active outreach and collaboration. The Year of Significant Student Learning initiative sharpened the focus on the university's primary mission of teaching and learning. Specific programs and events highlighted factors and features of student learning wherever it occurs—inside or outside the classroom, throughout and across the university experience (G. Bowen, personal communication, July 15, 2005).

Examining the Student Experience Itself

Alfred University's (Alfred, New York) Career Development Center class called Passport to Career Success: A Personal and Professional Development Series looked specifically at students' experience and found that they felt unprepared for job interviews and career fairs despite the workshops and conventional training the Center had provided for them (K. Woughter, personal communication, June 13, July 6, 2005). The center developed a goal statement around the need for better preparation, complete with assessment measures, and involved faculty and staff at the ground level during the planning phase for the class. The idea was taken to the dean of the College of Business, who supported it by offering space in his curriculum and eventually enrolling 75 students in a class that continues to flourish.

TIPS FOR STUDENT AFFAIRS PRACTITIONERS

Acknowledging the cultural and institutional differences between student affairs and academic affairs the author wishes to offer some advice to student affairs practitioners.

1. Do not interpret active outreach as providing funding to academic affairs for particular initiatives. While funding will continue to be important, money should not be the primary basis for a partnership. Include it as one of many factors.

2. Do not be only the logistics person on every partnership with academic affairs. Yes, student affairs professionals have unusual administrative and organizational skills, but they have much more. While it is certainly acceptable to move a project along with these skills, student affairs professionals should be committed to identifying themselves as educators.

3. Despite the issue raised in item #2, recognize that the "60/40" workload rule may come into play often. New professionals in particular often expect that a partnership means that everything must be done on a 50/50 basis as a project develops. That is simply unrealistic. Faculty members have their own set of demands and interests and may have to defer to student affairs professionals to frame the basic elements of an activity. Do that and quickly move beyond it to get at core issues that will really sustain the partnership.

4. Use obvious opportunities to make quick and inexpensive connections. New faculty orientation programs, faculty development center activities, joint department head meetings with academic affairs, new academic majors, and presentations at deans' councils are only a few of the many opportunities. Build on these encounters so that short-term opportunities can beget long-term benefits.

5. Be a spokesperson for active student involvement in academic life. Yes, that is a twist for many student affairs administrators accustomed to championing only the value of the co-curricular program. Be assertive in recognizing the importance of internships, field experiences, service-learning, cooperative education experiences, academic honor societies connected to specific majors, honors college involvement, and participation in undergraduate research and creative opportunities with faculty. In essence, be an advocate for the "life of the mind" and be a facilitator of student involvement in such activities.

6. Teach! Whether it is an undergraduate course, freshman experience opportunity, or a graduate course in a college student personnel curriculum, take advantage of opportunities to teach. They provide a fresh perspective on student life issues, cast you in the role of educator, and establish credibility as a basis for partnership building.

7. Employ faculty members when feasible. For example, Western Carolina University's Health Center employs a nutritionist on a shared basis with her home depart-

ment of Health Sciences. Look for opportunities involving "faculty fellows" to support specific programs and "faculty members-in-residence" to enrich the residential life program if you have one.

8. Ask students to identify key faculty who have influenced them as a basis for possible academic partnerships. Ask students key questions such as: What faculty members were most involved in your lives? Who paid attention to missed classes and poor class performance? What professors have challenged their boundaries? (K. Kinyon, personal communication, June 27, 2005).

9. Remember that true partnerships consist at a minimum of joint planning, joint implementation, and joint assessment. Make sure that you agree on the learning outcomes you hope to achieve. Whether you use focus groups, reflection sessions, written surveys, or e-mail questions, look to your liberal studies or general education learning outcomes as guideposts. Consider the learning outcomes identified by the Council for the Advancement of Standards in Higher Education.

10. Consider joint research, joint publications, and joint professional presentations as opportunities to build bridges and initiate partnerships.

11. Place faculty members on advisory committees used to guide individual offices in student affairs (e.g., student union, intramural sports). Do this when the committee is formed, not as an afterthought. Consider faculty to be an important stakeholder in program improvement.

12. Recognize faculty for their outreach with your division. Stipends, honoraria, recognition banquets, and faculty awards are only some of the many ways to recognize their efforts to integrate teaching with the activities of the student affairs division in order to achieve jointly developed learning outcomes.

13. Share your collaborative work with students. Help them see the connections you are trying to make between the curriculum and the co-curriculum. Collaboration can breed the same type of cooperation among students. They, too, can become advocates for active outreach across campus constituencies.

14. Finally, as the authors of *Learning Reconsidered* suggest, try to *map* where learning opportunities can take place on your campus. Look at the intersections between academic and student affairs as a basis for initiating conversations about partnerships. For example, consider establishing student affairs liaisons to each of your academic colleges to explore common ground or developing a list of classes in which experiential learning opportunities in student affairs can enhance instruction and support student development. And do not overlook the creative ideas that can flow from informal one-on-one meetings, working lunches, and "food for thought" e-mails.

CONCLUSION

Magolda's (2005) adjectives "meaningful, reciprocal, and responsive" (p. 21) sum up the key characteristics that contribute to active outreach and successful partnerships between academic and student affairs. Active outreach is not a trend or passing fancy; it places student affairs professionals at the very heart of the academy with their academic colleagues. Active outreach reinforces the values and learning assumptions upon which the student affairs profession was founded. Practitioners have a variety of methods available to them to initiate partnerships. Now more than ever, student affairs professionals have an opportunity to affect the quality of student life and learning as well as the vitality of our institutions of higher education.

REFERENCES

American College Personnel Association (2001). *Critical issues task force report*. Washington, DC: Author.

Ardaiolo, F. (1993). Involving faculty with student affairs: some personal pointers. *The College Student Affairs Journal, 13,* 24–28.

Association of American Colleges and Universities. (2002). *Greater expectations: A new vision for learning as a nation goes to college.* Washington, DC: Author.

Banning, J. (Ed.). (1978). *Campus ecology: A perspective for student affairs*. Portland, OR: National Association of Student Personnel Administrators.

Brown, R. (1972). *Student development in tomorrow's higher education–A return to the academy*. Washington, DC: American College Personnel Association.

Caruso, R. (2004, August/September). Now more than ever: Student affairs' important role in enhancing the quality of student life and student learning. *NCommunicator. Newsletter for the North Carolina College Personnel Association, VII, 7.*

Engstrom, C., & Tinto, V. (2000). Developing partnerships with academic affairs to enhance student learning. In M. Barr, M. Desler, & Associates (Eds.), *The handbook of student affairs administration* (4th ed.) (pp. 425–452). San Francisco: Jossey-Bass.

Fried, J. (2005, May 2). Student mental health and *Learning Reconsidered:* A very powerful partnership. *NetResults.* Retrieved January 10, 2007, from http://www.naspa.org/membership/mem/nr/article.cfm?id=1495

Hirsch, D., & Burack, C. (2001). Finding points of contact for collaborative work. In A. Kezar, D. Hirsch, & C. Burack (Eds.),

Understanding the role of academic and student affairs collaboration in creating a successful learning environment (pp. 53–62). New Directions for Higher Education, No. 116. San Francisco: Jossey-Bass.

Hoover, E. (2002, November 29). The changing environment for college admissions. *The Chronicle of Higher Education,* A30.

Jacobson, J. (2004, February 6). In baby boomlet, number of new high-school graduates is projected to rise. *The Chronicle of Higher Education,* A28.

Keeling, R. P. (Ed.). (2004). *Learning reconsidered: A campus-wide focus on the student experience.* Washington, DC: National Association of Student Personnel Administrators and American College Personnel Association.

Knock, G. (1990). Development of student services in higher education. In M. Barr and L. Keating & Associates (Eds.), *Developing effective student services programs* (pp. 15–42). San Francisco: Jossey-Bass.

Livingston, M., and Croft, L. (2005, June). *Building bridges between academic affairs and student affairs.* Audio conference. Madison, WI: Magna Publications, Inc.

Love, P., Kuh, G., Mackay, K., & Hardy, C. (1993). Side by side: Faculty and student affairs cultures. In G. Kuh (Ed.), Cultural perspectives in student affairs work (pp. 37–59). New York: Brunner-Routledge.

Magolda, P. (2005, January–February). Proceed with caution: Uncommon wisdom about academic and student affairs partnerships. *About Campus*, pp. 16–21.

Martin, J., & and Murphy, S. (1997). *Building a better bridge: Creating effective partnerships between academic affairs and student affairs.*

Washington, DC: National Association of Student Personnel Administrators.

Miller, T., & Prince, J. (1976). *The future of student affairs: A guide to student development for tomorrow's higher education*. San Francisco: Jossey-Bass.

National Association of Student Personnel Administrators. (1987). *Points of view: A perspective on student affairs*. Washington, DC: Author.

Schwitzer, A., Ancis, J., & Brown, N. (2000). *Promoting student learning and student development at a distance*. Bluc Ridgc Summit, PA: Rowman and Littlefield.

Smith, D. (1988). A window of opportunity for intra-institutional collaboration. *NASPA Journal, 26*(1), 8–13.

University College. (2005). Winthrop University College. Retrieved August 1, 2005, from http://www.winthrop.edu/universitycollege

Weigel, V. (2002). *Deep learning for a digital age: Technology's untapped potential to enrich higher education*. San Francisco: Jossey-Bass.

Western Carolina University. (2005). *Committee on Student Learning* [brochure]. Cullowhee, NC: Author.

Young, R. (2003). Philosophies and values guiding the student affairs profession. In S. Komives and D. Woodard, Jr. (Eds.), *Student services: A handbook for the profession* (4th ed.) (pp. 89–106). San Francisco: Jossey-Bass.

CHAPTER SEVEN

Circle Five:
Mutual Understanding
through Frequent Communication

Robert E. Eaker
and Debra K. Sells

The academic culture of most institutions of higher education can best be described as a collection of separate and distinct niches of academic learning (departments, degrees, majors, courses, etc.). Students are better served in a culture where learning is viewed as a broad, complex, and integrated endeavor. Successful collaboration between academic affairs and student affairs is based on the development of mutual understanding between the two divisions, and nothing is more critical to the development of that understanding than frequent communication. It is impossible to develop a culture of interdivisional understanding against a backdrop of isolation. If institutions of higher education are serious about *learning* as their core purpose and if learning is defined as a "comprehensive, holistic, transformative activity that integrates academic learning and student development," (Keeling, 2004, p. 2), creating and supporting high-quality communication—both formal and informal—between academic affairs and student affairs is particularly critical.

The call for frequent communication and the development of mutual understanding within a collaborative culture is not a particularly novel idea. Generally acknowledged as foundational documents of the student affairs profession, both the 1937 *Student Personnel Point of View* (American Council on Education, 1983a) and the 1949 statement by the same name (American Council on Education, 1983b) reference the need for cooperation among the teaching and administrative staff, and for coordination between curricular and co-curricular programs.

Subsequent reports such as *Seven Principles for Good Practice in Undergraduate Education* (Chickering & Gamson, 1987), *An American Imperative* (Wingspread Group on Higher Education, 1993), *The Student Learning Imperative: Implications for Student Affairs* (American College Personnel Association, 1994), *Principles of Good Practice for Student Affairs* (American College Personnel Association & National Association of Student Personnel Administrators, 1997), and *Powerful Partnerships: A Shared Responsibility for Learning* (American Association of Higher Education, American College Personnel Association, & National Association of Student Personnel Administrators, 1998) emphasized the need for collaboration between academic and student affairs to support student learning. More recently, *Learning Reconsidered: A Campus-wide Focus on the Student Experience* (Keeling, 2004) called for an understanding of the interconnectedness of student learning that would, if implemented, necessitate high-quality formal and informal communication to support collaborative relationships and meaningful partnerships between academic and student affairs.

STRUCTURE AND CULTURE: THE NEED FOR BOTH FORMAL AND INFORMAL COMMUNICATION

Establishing true collaborative partnerships between academic affairs and student affairs requires both formal and informal communication that is frequent and meaningful. Formal communication is reflected in the structural aspect of organizations. Structural initiatives are typically found in an organization's policies, rules, regulations, organizational charts, job descriptions, and improvement initiatives. Formal initiatives within the organizational structure such as holding regularly scheduled joint meetings, redefining role responsibilities, undertaking joint initiatives and, most important, making the quality of collaboration a key part of the administrator evaluation process can improve the frequency and quality of communication between the divisions.

Informal communication, on the other hand, is usually reflected in organizational culture—the assumptions, beliefs, expectations, and habits that constitute day-to-day norms. Both the formal communication reflected in organizational structure and the informal communications reflected in organizational culture require attention and leadership. In most institutions, however, there is a heavy reliance on formal structures and much less attention paid to informal communications. Unfortunately, a focus on structure alone is never enough. If effective collaboration between academic and student affairs is to be truly valued, the importance of frequent and meaningful informal communication must be reinforced consistently and repeatedly until it becomes firmly embedded within the informal culture as well as the formal structure.

EMBEDDING THE VALUES OF COMMUNICATION AND COLLABORATION WITHIN THE CULTURE

Key organizational values, such as the importance of cross-divisional communication and collaboration, become embedded within organizational culture through numerous activities, the most important of which are planning, modeling, monitoring, celebrating, confronting, and resource allocation (Dufour & Eaker, 1998, pp. 107–114).

The very process of *planning* for the implementation of improved communication strategies sends a clear signal regarding the importance of those values. If communication between academic and student affairs is really important, specific strategies will be developed to ensure that communication between divisions is pursued. Planning support will be provided for staff and work teams to pursue tactics for improving communication and collaboration. On the other hand, it is not uncommon for organizations to espouse ideals but never develop specific plans for their realization. When this happens, members of the organization recognize that the idea was not genuinely valued in the first place.

The same is true of *modeling*. Those in leadership positions, such as vice presidents and deans, must model the behavior that is expected of others, including efforts to maintain frequent communication and mutual understanding between student and academic affairs. Faculty and staff will note the congruence—or incongruence—between the stated values and behavior of their senior management. Division heads must demonstrate their commitment to improved communication in

108

tangible ways; faculty and staff must be able to observe their vice presidents communicating effectively and working collaboratively to achieve institutional goals.

It has long been said that what gets measured is what gets done. Leaders monitor and check on those things they value most. Therefore efforts to create effective communication channels and collaborative relationships must be assessed and corrective adjustments undertaken when needed. Annual reports, performance evaluations, and strategic planning documents must reflect institutional expectations for improved communication and collaboration between student affairs and academic affairs. When important values are regularly monitored and are subject to ongoing feedback, personnel understand that the organization is serious about those ideas.

Celebration goes hand-in-hand with *monitoring*. In order to embed communication and collaboration between academic and student affairs as significant values within the culture, leaders must recognize and celebrate the best of these practices. Effective organizations not only build cultures by monitoring performance; they also publicly acknowledge and celebrate specific behaviors. Types of recognition and celebration may run the gamut from structured awards processes to special mention of successful collaborative efforts in university publications or important speeches.

In order to fully embed the value of effective communication between academic and student affairs within the organizational culture, leaders must be willing to *confront* behavior that is incongruent with this priority. Nothing destroys a leader's credibility faster than unwillingness to correct an obvious problem. The willingness to address behavior or plans that may hinder efforts toward improving communication reinforces the importance of this goal to everyone within the organization.

Ultimately, organizational resources such as time, energy, and dollars flow to those things that have the highest value. Personnel quickly recognize the true values of any organization each time a budget is prepared. Are *resources allocated* in such a way as to support enhanced communication and collaborative efforts between academic affairs and student affairs? Or are resources instead allocated in support of more hidden agendas, such as minimizing conflict or maintaining the status quo? Resources alone will not guarantee success, but the lack of resources will almost always ensure failure.

Together, these activities—planning, modeling, monitoring, celebrating, confronting, and allocating resource—communicate the dominant values of any organization. If frequent communication, high-quality collaboration, and mutual understanding are valued, they must be reflected in these behaviors.

A Shared Focus for Communication and Collaboration

Often people are urged to collaborate with their colleagues without a clear direction or purpose for their efforts. Lack of effective communication between divisions and departments will have a negative impact on collaborative efforts. Staffs are likely to focus on differences between their departments' missions rather than on their shared goals. Consider this quote from *Learning Reconsidered*: "Regardless of our past accomplishments or disappointments, we are all, as colleagues and educators, now accountable to students and society for identifying and achieving essential student outcomes and for making transformative education possible and accessible for all students" (Keeling, 2004, p. 1).

Unfortunately, divisions within most institutions still have not united around a shared understanding that the core purpose of both academic and student affairs is to ensure high levels of learning for students. A shared understanding of this core purpose is fundamental to effective communication between divisions. A shift away from a disjointed focus on teaching to a shared institutional mission of ensuring student learning would result in fundamentally different questions that would, in turn, guide the academic enterprise at all levels and across all divisions. Dufour, Dufour, and Eaker (2005) proposed the following four essential questions to be addressed by all parties attempting to create an environment devoted to supporting student learning. These questions are equally applicable to those working in student affairs and academic affairs, and they provide a common vocabulary and shared direction.

What Are Students Expected to Learn?

Academic and student affairs partners must engage in meaningful dialogue regarding essential learning outcomes for both the curriculum and for co-curricular efforts. Partners must communicate not only as to what learning is essential, but where those learning areas will be addressed, noting opportunities through both the in-class and out-of-class experience. *Learning Reconsidered* notes, "It is quite realistic to consider the entire campus as a learning community in which student learning experiences can be mapped throughout the environment to deepen the quality of learning" (Keeling, 2004, p. 13).

How Will We Know What Students Have Learned?

Once partners define *what* students are expected to learn, this is the obvious next question. Individual professors evaluate the levels of learning for individual students in their courses. However, broader questions related to student learning should be addressed and improvement initiatives undertaken by student affairs and academic affairs acting in collaboration. *Learning Reconsidered* notes:

> Student affairs must lead broad, collaborative institutional efforts to assess overall student learning and to track, document, and evaluate the role of diverse learning experiences in achieving comprehensive college learning outcomes. Assessment should be a way of life—part of the institutional culture. (Keeling, 2004, p. 26)

Of course, assessment can be used for more than merely determining what students have or have not learned. Stiggins (2002) made an important distinction between "assessment *of* learning" and "assessment *for* learning." In the latter case, assessment results create the basis for communication regarding shared decisions about ways to improve student learning.

How Do We Respond When Students Experience Difficulty?

A collaborative analysis of assessment results can provide important clues to the kind of support students need. Effective collaborations between academic affairs and student affairs require frequent communication in order to develop specific plans to assist students. Collaborative partners develop plans for tutoring, academic learning centers (such as math centers and writing centers), and other initiatives for academic support. The goal is to move from a culture of "It's my job to teach and it's the students' job to learn" to a culture where collaborative student affairs–academic affairs partnerships focus on identifying ways to support students in their learning, both in and out of the classroom.

How Can We Deepen the Learning Levels of Students who are Already Successful?

Ultimately, the goal must be more than simple acquisition of knowledge. Students should be expected to learn at high levels. It is important for collaborative partnerships not only to help students who need additional support, but also to stretch the learning levels of all students. After all, the goal of developing collaborative partnerships is to stretch the hopes, aspirations, and performance levels of students—and all others within the academic community as well.

CONCLUSION

While the push for more frequent and meaningful communication and collaboration is not new, renewed attention to its importance in higher education emerged with the publication of *Learning Reconsidered*. The premise is that if institutions of higher education are serious about a kind of learning that is "a comprehensive, holistic, transformative activity that integrates academic learning and student development" (Keeling, 2004, p. 2), then meaningful communication between academic affairs and student affairs is essential and must become the cornerstone of both the formal and informal organizational structure.

Although the importance of communication and collaborative within the organization has been generally acknowledged for years, implementing such practices in institutions of higher education has proven to be problematic at best. However, a number of colleges and universities have developed programs and practices that provide a how-to guide for those committed to creating effective student affairs–academic affairs partnerships. These practices provide evidence that universities can move beyond a culture of departmentalization and isolation. Key institutional questions to be asked include the following:

*   Do we have a plan to increase the frequency of communication and the level of mutual understanding between academic affairs and student affairs?

*   Are behaviors that lead to frequent communication and mutual understanding modeled by the highest levels of the administration?

*   Are the quantity and quality of collaborative efforts monitored, with appropriate adjustments made as needed?

*   Are successes related to increasing communication and collaboration between academic affairs and student affairs recognized publicly and celebrated in meaningful ways?

*   Are behaviors and activities that hinder communication and collaboration confronted?

*   Are resources of time, staff, and dollars allocated in such a way as to support increased communication and collaboration between academic and student affairs?

The focus of academic affairs–student affairs partnerships must go beyond merely getting along. A shared focus on improving student learning is essential. Therefore, such partnerships must work interdependently to achieve common learning goals and to accept common responsibility for achieving those goals.

REFERENCES

American Association of Higher Education, American College Personnel Association, & National Association of Student Personnel Administrators. (1998). *Powerful partnerships: A shared responsibility for learning.* Washington, DC: Authors.

American College Personnel Association. (1994). *The student learning imperative: Implications for student affairs.* Alexandria, VA: Author.

American College Personnel Association & National Association of Student Personnel Administrators. (1997). *Principles of good practice for student affairs.* Washington, DC: Authors.

American Council on Education. (1983a). The student personnel point of view: A report of a conference on the philosophy and development of student personnel work in colleges and universities. In G. L. Saddlemire & A. L. Rentz (Eds.), *Student affairs—A profession's heritage: Significant articles, authors, issues and documents* (pp. 74–87). American College Personnel Association Media Publication No. 25. Carbondale: Southern Illinois University Press. (Original work published 1937).

American Council on Education. (1983b). The student personnel point of view. In G. L. Saddlemire & A. L. Rentz (Eds.), *Student affairs—A profession's heritage: Significant articles, authors, issues and documents* (pp. 122–140). American College Personnel Association Media Publication No. 25. Carbondale: Southern Illinois University Press. (Original work published 1949).

Chickering, A., & Gamson, Z. (1987). Seven principles of good practice in undergraduate education. *AAHE Bulletin, 39,* 3–7.

Dufour, R. & Eaker, R. (1998). *Professional Learning Communities at Work.* Bloomington, IN: National Educational Service.

Dufour, R., Dufour, R. & Eaker, R. (Eds.). (2005). *On common ground: the power of professional learning communities.* Bloomington, IN: National Educational Service.

Keeling, R. P. (Ed.). (2004). *Learning reconsidered: A campus-wide focus on the student experience.* Washington, DC: National Association of Student Personnel Administrators and American College Personnel Association.

Stiggins, R. (2002, June). Assessment crisis: The absence of assessment for learning. *Phi Delta Kappan*, 258–265.

Wingspread Group on Higher Education. (1993). *An American imperative: Higher expectations for higher education.* Racine, WI: Johnson Foundation.

CHAPTER EIGHT

Circle Six:
Service-learning as Crossroads

Jeff P. Stein

What would Solomon say about the turf wars in today's kingdom of higher education? Like the authors of *Learning Reconsidered* (Keeling, 2004), he would urge movement beyond artificial borders in the seamless, or holistic, fabric of student learning. Unlike the biblical story of two mothers arguing over ownership of a child, pedagogies like service-learning have developed as dynamic new amalgams requiring the best practices of both academic and student affairs. Service-learning, in particular, requires reciprocal and mutual collaboration among students, academic affairs, student affairs, *and* community partners. From its origins, service-learning's outcomes and methodologies have inhabited an intersection of the cognitive and affective, of experience and knowledge, of the civic and disciplinary, of curricular and co-curricular. The transformative education at the heart of both *Learning Reconsidered* and service-learning requires academic affairs and student affairs to shift their paradigms of partnership and pedagogy.

Service-learning is, therefore, a hybrid, a new offspring created by joining multiple "parents" or rather, partners in the process of transforming learning by harnessing disciplines, students, and community. In her own hybrid text, *Borderlands: La Frontera*, Gloria Anzaldua (1987) described borders as artificial lines where two or more cultures, languages, or cultures come in contact. Anzaldua's border theory forces the realization that despite efforts to delineate distinct cultures on each side of the higher education fence, placing a fence in the ground does not ultimately change the landscape of the two countries. In fact, service-learning, at its best, works from the understanding that we cannot separate what is seamless—whether it is student learning, the academy, or civic community. Service-learning comes from the foundational understanding that, as stated in *Learning Reconsidered*, "learning and development as intertwined, inseparable elements of...transformative education" (Keeling, 2004, p. 3). And while it remains easy to assume academic affairs or student affairs can be the most effective practitioners, service-learning and its outcomes are not so easily demarcated. It is the students and community partners who suffer when student and academic affairs attempt to argue before Solomon that students and their learning belong to only one side of the higher education house. Neither group has the time or expertise to negotiate all the relationships with community partners, all the reflection by students, all the research, all the conferences and resources, or all the curricular integration. More important, at its core, service-learning as a pedagogy is about challenging and transforming our traditional notions of separation between community and university, teachers and learners, the powerful and the oppressed. It is counterproductive to act as though the lines between students, faculty, staff, and community partners actually define separate zones of learning or engagement. Service-learning shows us a much larger and more effective learning landscape that transforms and enriches all parties involved.

For these reasons, service-learning, the unique combination of service in the community with reflection and course material, inhabits an inimitable location in higher education, a point of convergence for partners, as well as a rare melding of hands-on, real-world experience, civic involvement, and classroom learning. Pedagogically, service-learning brings together more partners, methods, modes of reflection, and texts than perhaps any method of learning today. Multiple players function as teachers and learners, bringing assets and needs. Through a wide range of courses, study abroad opportunities, community scholars programs, capstone courses, community-based research, living–learning communities, and more, students across the country are connecting experience to knowledge, developing their values systems (Delve, Mintz & Stewart, 1990), exploring their own skills as well as their role in society, and developing awareness through service-learning.

What exactly is meant by *service* and *learning*? Though a national debate continues and conference sessions are consistently sidetracked by discussions on appropriate terminology, the term "community service" has often been used to refer to a rich array of co-curricular experiences including community service living–learning communities, service break trips and weekends, neighborhood clean-ups, and

119

community service clubs and organizations. Such community service experiences, although outside academic classes, are opportunities to learn about self and community, and they often include best practices that bring them to the level of "integrated learning experiences" (Keeling, 2004, p. 16). Few service programs leave learning to chance anymore. Instead, they rely heavily on intentional incorporation of the cycle of preparation-action-reflection in order to incorporate learning into all service experiences. Therefore, many use the terms "service" and "learning" to refer to both curricular- and co-curricular-based models. Over the past decade, student affairs departments and service offices/programs have become quite skillful at designing intentional learning-centered civil rights tours, urban plunges, and community-based student staff experiences. Community service and civic learning centers have focused on student engagement and learning by designing programs with learning objectives in mind at the outset, incorporating intentional reflections into every experience, leveraging partnerships with community agencies and faculty, and focusing on student leadership. Student leadership has developed beyond mere participation to taking on program coordination roles, leading group reflection activities, and communicating directly with community partners and faculty. Therefore, it impedes the collaborative nature of service-learning to distinguish between "service-learning" for course-based endeavors and "community service" for all co-curricular service programs. Based on Robert Sigmon's "Service and Learning Typology" (1994), many in the field make the conscious choice to use the term "service-learning" for programs and courses that balance their focus between service and learning (see Appendix B).

AT THE CROSSROADS OF CIVIC ENGAGEMENT AND ENGAGED LEARNING

Service-learning represents a crossroads in higher education not only in terms of its collaborative methods but also in terms of its origins. Timing cannot be overlooked in the rise of this crossbreed of experiential and civic learning. Service-learning began to bloom in both popularity and in research just in time to meet growing concerns about higher education becoming overly isolated or elitist and theoretical. Commenting on the dynamic positioning of service-learning, Barbara Jacoby (2003) wrote, "Service Learning is located squarely at the intersection of two powerful movements: the intentional orientation of undergraduate education toward active learning and the call for the civic renewal of higher education—the engaged campus" (p. xvii). Service-learning responded to and grew from concerns about both the impractical and isolated nature of higher education.

Nationally, we have a long history of altruism, service to others, and community involvement. But early in the 20th century, leaders like Jane Addams and John Dewey, concerned about young people's lack of connection to and awareness of their communities, pushed for students to get involved in their communities. Dewey (1916) focused on "learning by doing," what he called democratic education, which later became community service. The work of Dewey and others became the precursor to service-learning. The idea was that students and community would learn from each other, begin to understand connections between them, and learn how to increase "knowledge for the betterment of their shared physical and social space" (Enos & Morton, 2003, p. 21). Over time, community service came to be focused on experiences not connected to particular academic courses.

121

During the latter half of the 20th century, multiple commissions, reports, and consortiums addressed four main concerns with higher education: (1) elitist, ivory tower educational means and ends, (2) outdated teaching methods focused on teaching as opposed to learning, (3) complete disengagement from the communities and community issues surrounding higher education institutions, and (4) textbook learning with seemingly few practical applications or implications (Boyer Commission, 1998; Wingspread Group, 1993).

Yet perhaps even more important than concerns related to the isolation of colleges and universities from real-world problems was a growing sense that students and teachers alike had become unable, uninterested, and unwilling to engage in or care about local issues and politics. As Battistoni (2002) writes in *Civic Engagement Across the Curriculum*, "With mounting evidence of disengagement, especially among young people, from American politics and public life, there is an ever deepening feeling that our educational institutions are leaving students unprepared for a life of engaged, democratic citizenship" (p. 1). No longer a nation of brothers and sisters banding together to stand against adversity, Americans were described as "passive and disengaged," without confidence in our ability to rally together to "make a difference" by the National Commission on Civic Renewal (1998). The title of its report, *A Nation of Spectators: How Civic Disengagement Weakens America and What We Can Do about It*, conveyed this concern about national apathy.

As claims of national apathy and disengagement merged with concerns about passive, theory-based, ineffective teaching, both the scholarship of engagement *and* service-based learning emerged. As a result, academic affairs and student affairs were brought together, just as service-learning came to the forefront of the American higher education scene. The field of community service experienced further metamorphosis through the pedagogy of service-learning, which combined academic courses and disciplinary knowledge with direct service experiences in the community. Citizenship, democratic education, civic life beyond the classroom, and community engagement all became high priorities. For example, the Wingspread Group challenged educators to make students more aware of their local communities and local community needs and to encourage students to become more active, vocal, and thoughtful about their roles as citizens. During the 1980s, campuses across the country worked across divisions to focus on civic efforts as they formed Campus Compact, the Campus Outreach Opportunity League, and the National Society for Experiential Education to connect experiential education with the growth in service-learning (Battistoni, 2002). Even our language changed, with key phrases like "engaged learning," "student engagement," "civic engagement," and "seamless learning" becoming popular in academics and student affairs. This national analysis resulted in an integration and democratization of resources, access, pedagogy, and structural organization in higher education (Keeling, 2004). In the past two years, for example, the Carnegie Foundation has begun convening institutions focused on civic education to assist in the process of creating a new Carnegie classification for civically engaged campuses.

In other words, during the 20th century the focus of higher education's involvement with community and service completely changed. As Battistoni (2002) explained, "The ultimate aim has shifted from promoting community service to institutionalizing service-learning, and now to fostering civic engagement in a diverse democracy" (p. v). Service-learning and civic education have come to the fore and called for the joint expertise of both academic affairs and student affairs.

123

In service-learning, we have found a unique method for confronting traditionally dualistic thinking in education and forcing academic and student affairs to see education as a joint venture that links "cognitive and affective learning...conceptual and experiential learning," and the expertise of all educators in the process toward "seamless" or "holistic" education (Kezar & Rhoades, 2001, p. 153). In other words, this pedagogy is designed to leverage and ultimately achieve the type of learning the authors of *Learning Reconsidered* describe as a "comprehensive, holistic, transformative activity that integrates *academic learning* and *student development*" (Keeling, 2004, p. 4). Service-learning makes the world its textbook while harnessing reflection around the combination of academic knowledge and community issues and resources. Structured service in the community allows students to put knowledge into practice and perspective, but it also brings that knowledge and classroom experience to life. The goal is to structure learning in ways that are as inclusive and synthesized as the ways we actually learn in order to maximize both in-class and out-of-class experiences (Terenzini & Pascarella, 1994).

That is exactly where partnerships between academic and student affairs can play a major role. For this dynamic, emerging pedagogy is no panacea. No form of experiential education is. Rather, at all levels, effective service-learning requires leadership and facilitation from both sides of the academy. Faculty expertise in disciplinary issues and integration of in-and out-of classroom knowledge is paramount. Additionally, effective service-learning harnesses student affairs expertise in coordinating service site logistics, maintaining regular contact with community partners, matching appropriate courses and partners, and exploring students' personal and skill development in areas ranging from diversity to communication to social position to leadership.

MUTUALITY, RECIPROCITY, AND PARTNERSHIP

Service-learning's methodologies also focus on intentional intersections. At its core, service-learning, whether curricular or co-curricular, focuses on three key methods or principles: (1) democratic partnerships, (2) mutuality, and (3) reciprocity. For service-learning to work at any level, it must unite "different community and campus stakeholders together to meet community need and invigorate social change" (Ward, 1996, p. 62) through a *mutually* beneficial process based on joint goals and regular communication. Service-learning, then, is based in a postmodern academy that understands what *Learning Reconsidered* describes as the need for collaboration across campus—"linking the best efforts of educators across the institution to support student learning" (Keeling, 2004, p. 14)—and even moves beyond the campus walls to include community partners in this multidirectional process. Charity-based projects focused solely on the needs or deficits of the community represent only the simplistic end of the community service spectrum. Where service-learning excels is in bringing students, faculty, staff, and agencies together to develop and define *mutual* goals, needs, and desired outcomes—to build ongoing, collaborative projects that defy notions of the academy reaching out its rich resources to "lift up" the downtrodden community, or "other."

Effective service-learning requires reciprocal relationships. Instead of the community merely serving as a laboratory for students to enter, observe, and learn from, all players teach, learn, define needs, and gain from the process. Community agencies and their clients actually teach students and faculty as much, if not more, than students and faculty teach them—the teaching is *reciprocal*. Students learn about themselves, community issues, and their own roles as citizens as they teach or assist the community (Battistoni, 2002). Reciprocity requires a level of

125

respect for multidirectional collaborative work with community partners. All parties must be teachers and learners gaining from *and* striving toward mutually agreed-upon goals. This reciprocal nature distinguishes service-learning from community service and other forms of experiential education, as well as from inappropriate forms of paternalism.

The idea of reciprocity can also be seen in the outcomes of service-learning. On campus, academic affairs and student affairs have fought over the domain of these outcomes. But service-learning refuses to rest solely on either side of the academy. Researchers have repeatedly identified a wide range of learning outcomes for service-learning (Astin & Sax, 1998; Astin, Vogelgesang, Ikeda, & Yee, 2000; Eyler & Giles, 1999). After researching two national longitudinal studies, Eyler and Giles (1999) delineated 11 complex service-learning outcomes (see Appendix C). Similarly, Astin and the HERI (Higher Education Research Institute) group, through a national longitudinal study of 22,236 college undergraduates, described service-learning's outcomes on students' cognitive and psychosocial development. Their qualitative findings have been split into four types of outcomes related to increases in personal efficacy, awareness of societal and world issues, personal values, and successful engagement in the academic experience (Astin et al., 2000). After extensive review of national studies, some have pointed out that the future of service-learning may be damaged by a narrow understanding of its workings and outcomes. Kezar (2002) argued that "narrow notions of cognition [and student cognitive development] and traditional philosophies of outcomes assessment limit our understanding" of service-learning outcomes (p. 15). While some may choose service-learning for its impact on either civic-mindedness or disciplinary learning, we cannot filter out either the cognitive or psychosocial outcomes. The point of service-learning, as well as its outcomes, supports both academic affairs and student affairs initiatives and goals. Despite efforts to prefer certain outcomes, research continues to suggest that service-learning meets a broad range of outcomes, from higher grades and disciplined learning to increased belonging, civic awareness, and leadership.

Additionally, core concepts of reciprocity and mutuality mean that students are learning from real-world partnerships, as opposed to random placements at community agencies. Students have entered into dynamic multidirectional and multifaceted relationships. Therefore, students are more active participants in the multidirectional flow of information, skills, and knowledge. Students are learning about agencies, partnerships, course-based knowledge, their own skills in real-world situations, and how their coursework is applied outside the classroom walls. This, in turn, means that students are developing and learning in a more holistic fashion from both traditionally academic *and* traditionally student affairs learning situations, locations, teaching methods, and programs.

As a pedagogical approach, service-learning involves integrating formerly disparate academic and student affairs goals and mediates the different cultures and languages of the two (Blake, 1979; Engstrom & Tinto, 2000). Repeatedly, those who research and write about service-learning and service-learning partnerships (Engstrom, 2003; Engstrom & Tinto, 1997; Jacoby, 1999, 2003; Ward, 1996) state that "student learning experiences are enhanced when the expertise of both academic affairs and student affairs is tapped" (Engstrom, 2003, p. 65). This idea rests at the heart of *Learning Reconsidered* (Keeling, 2004) in the authors' clear understanding that academic learning and psychosocial development can no longer be viewed as distinct processes taught by distinct campus entities. Unfortunately, professionals on both sides of the divide are more comfortable with democratic notions of partnerships with the community than they are with sharing power with their own campus colleagues. As stated earlier, mutuality requires that all partners participate equally. Therefore, the external university–community partnerships in service-learning serve as models for academic affairs–student affairs partnerships *within* the university. Using Deweyan philosophy, Kezar and Rhoads (2001) pointed out that successful implementation of service-learning requires involving "all groups—faculty, student affairs, and community agencies—[as] equal partners" (p. 160). For service-learning to exist as a successful integrated learning experience, then, it is not difficult to appreciate that academic and student affairs partnerships must be strong in order to draw on the skills from both professions.

Part of the unique power of service-learning rests in its ability to shift our thinking and relationships from single interactions to actual collaborations between partners. Engstrom and Tinto (1997) noted that "Increasingly, service learning provides exemplary opportunities for collaborative activities between academic and student affairs in which both parties can make significant contributions to the educational process" (p. 10). Engstrom (2003) went further by delineating three actual models of academic–student affairs collaboration: the "clearinghouse model," the "cooperation model," and the "collaboration model" (p. 71). The goal is to move from the service-learning office as a point of information and resources in the clearinghouse model, to a mutual yet still limited relationship based on nonreciprocal or equivalent goals in the cooperation model, to a truly transformative relationship in which all parties participate as teachers and learners in the collaboration model. Collaborative partnerships, from the outset, balance multiple equal partners and goals in what Jacoby (2003) has called "democratic partnerships" that not only achieve balance between community and university needs but also reflect the same level of reciprocity and mutuality between on-campus partners as well (p. xviii).

Perhaps the most important reason for service-learning to combine academic and student affairs methodologies is the cycle of preparation, action, integration, and continual and varied reflection (similar to the two steps of "immersion in a complex experience that illustrates phenomena that are connected to the subject" and "active processing or reflection" described in *Learning Reconsidered* (Keeling, 2004, p. 13). Collaboration on this cycle across academics and student affairs makes service-learning an integrated learning experience. Whether it be a study-abroad course incorporating service-learning projects, a social justice living–learning community including classes and staff advising, or a service-learning college writing course, including this cycle requires expertise in psychosocial development as well as discipline-based critical and analytical thinking skills. Experience is not enough; context is necessary. Therefore, students must prepare for service experiences by exploring their own backgrounds, skills, and experiences—"the active context of students' lives" (Keeling, 2004, p. 13)—and the realities of the communities they are about to enter. Throughout the experience, students need opportunities to reflect on their own experiences, make connections to course material, and put their experiences into the context of the larger world around them. Faculty must fully integrate service experiences (and the knowledge gained through these experiences) into the flow of the course. Faculty must structure opportunities for students to put their knowledge into practice. Student affairs staff must regularly supply faculty with information and activities to assist in the development of assignments and activities. These activities should lead to preparation, integration, and reflection, whether the activities are journal assignments, simulations, facts on local communities, videos, articles, discussions, or writing prompts. Service-learning cannot be taught the same way a textbook or novel is taught. With assistance from both parties, the preparation-reflection process pushes students beyond settling on simplistic conclusions or avoiding the messy cognitive dissonance that experiential education creates so easily.

THE X-FACTOR: DISSONANCE AND TRANSFORMATION

Beyond the collaborative origins and methodologies, a clear understanding of effective service-learning pedagogy requires an awareness of what could be called the "X Factor." Unlike traditional one-sided pedagogies, including lectures and textbooks, service-learning requires openness—by all parties—to the unknown, to the messy, and to change. Service-learning is based on the notion that it is possible to get more from a textbook or lecture by pairing it with a real-world experience void of defined outcomes. When students enter community agencies, faculty members relinquish some control of the learning experience. Partnering with the community suggests the community has something to teach. One aspect of giving up control relates to the expertise of community partners and the unknown elements of the real-world experience. Partnering with the community requires the assistance of professionals who work daily with the community, regularly read service-learning journals and texts, and possess training and expertise on student developmental processes. For it is through the unknown and the messy dissonance that students learn the most. Kolb (1984) and other experiential learning theorists have made it clear that humans are not wired to automatically learn from experience. Service-learning forces faculty to give up the control of knowing exactly what will happen when students leave the classroom for experiences in the real world. Faculty members then become responsible for assisting students in working through the process of mining the experience, their frustrations, and the tensions between beliefs and experiences for that essential course-based knowledge.

Perhaps the best way to describe the X-Factor in service-learning is to discuss the shift it requires faculty to make in working within a transformative rather than transactional model of education. Enos and Morton (2003) made this central distinction by analyzing the "scope of commitment" and involvement in partnerships (p. 25). Their discussion rests within the framework of developing stronger and more democratic partnerships with the community. But their analysis of transaction vs. transformation goes far beyond partnership relationships. For it is not just our relationships with community agencies that have been reduced to mere exchanges of tit for tat; rather, as the indictments of 20th-century education point out, at its worst the higher education playing field has often been reduced to a paid transaction between students and faculty: here's the money, now hand over the information, or better yet, the certification or guarantee of knowledge. The engaged learning movement is centered in pedagogical methods to move beyond the transactions of faculty "bestowing" knowledge and students regurgitating it. Service-learning, as a model of the educational shift in *Learning Reconsidered* (Keeling, 2004), requires faculty and students to step out of well-defined roles of one-time transactions toward the potential for less-defined transformations through experience and reflection. This type of transformation occurs on a much broader educational canvas that places students within the larger societal framework and "places the student's reflective processes at the core of the learning experience" (Keeling, 2004, p. 10). And, as *Learning Reconsidered* points out, it is no secret that engaged learners have increased retention, growth and development, satisfaction, and learning.

In other words, the X-Factor in service-learning is related to the lack of prescription and control present in service-learning, yet it supplies the most potential for learning. The involvement and flexibility required of partners in this process is particularly high, because it is impossible to perfectly predict what will happen when students get involved in the community. Perhaps more important, the shift also occurs in the actual *location* of the learning itself. For service-learning to work, all parties must be willing to dive into the cognitive dissonance and potential transformation that all parties experience. The objective in service-learning is transformation and change. Enos and Morton (2003) raised the key question when they asked how open partners are to changes that will be suggested in the process. Are these one-time courses or projects that require a great deal of work but result in minimal analysis of structures and systems? Or are partners willing to take the opportunity provided by service-learning to "reimagine their roles and missions in communities?" (p. 39). We are standing at the crossroads; how far are we willing to go into the democratic process? Are we still attempting to separate disciplinary teaching and learning by prescribed parties, or are we willing to re-examine community, teaching, learning, and partnership through service-learning?

ROLES FOR FACULTY, STUDENT AFFAIRS, AND SENIOR ADMINISTRATION

With a clear understanding of the importance of partnerships in service-learning, we can proceed to a discussion of best practices, appropriate roles for key players on campus, hurdles to expect, and examples from successful campus collaborations.

Faculty Roles

Faculty members remain focused on course construction, research, disciplinary expertise, and academic rigor. But the transformative student learning described in *Learning Reconsidered* does not come without shifting paradigms. Faculty must re-examine and even reconceptualize courses and syllabi in order to fully understand the role of service and service-learning within the learning objectives of the course. Faculty must explore the most effective methods for integrating service experiences and course material. Additionally, faculty must consider regular methods of recording, exploring, analyzing, and contextualizing student experiences.

Most of all, as with any form of experiential learning, faculty must open the door for the experience to become part of the learning of the course. This shift requires relinquishing some level of control to students, community partners, and the hands-on experience itself. Faculty members, therefore, must keep an eye out for unexpected learning opportunities, for the X-Factor described earlier. These learning opportunities are easily missed when student complaints about service experiences, their discomfort, and their dissonance are overlooked or handed off to student affairs staff. Yet students' cognitive dissonance about their expectations, frustrations, and prior beliefs often represents the richest opportunity for learning. Faculty must be prepared to "push" on this dissonance, to help students explore their discomfort and connect it to the larger context of their course.

Essentially, it remains important to keep in mind that transformative education is an individualized and personal process situated close to each student's unique re-assimilation of prior knowledge and beliefs, course materials, and service experiences, and faculty members' ability to harness all three. For most faculty members, working within this

133

new paradigm requires adjustment. Constructing service-learning syllabi, deciding on the number of hours for service projects, working with community partners, integrating service into courses, and letting go of a more linear learning process take experimentation. This process is not a simple matter of cutting and pasting, removing one paper assignment and adding in service hours. Most first-time service-learning faculty members, in fact, starting with a stronger dedication to traditional academic assignments and a long list of learning objectives, start small with a manageable project and assignment. These initial efforts often locate service-learning at the margins of a course. Over time, faculty work toward more fully integrating courses as they find that students learn more about the discipline through integrated hands-on experience. Paralleling the increased integration of service-learning is faculty's increased communication and contact with community partners and student affairs staff.

Faculty members must be able to explain their courses to community partners and student affairs staff in order to fully develop the service-learning component. Student affairs staffs are often educated in methods for integrating course content and service components. Timing is perhaps the key issue, because faculty members should come forward early in the planning process to develop necessary relationships, explore options, and determine logistical issues. Similarly, in co-curricular service-learning opportunities, faculty members must bring disciplinary expertise to the table and allow students, community partners, and student affairs staff to bring other forms of knowledge.

Typical hurdles for faculty members include lack of communication with agency partners or student affairs staff, failure to fully integrate service-learning experiences into courses, lack of focus on the experience and its connection to the discipline, and insufficient time spent on preparation and reflection. Strategies for getting past these hurdles include considering learning objectives for both the course and for the service-learning component and how those objectives will be connected. It can also be helpful for faculty to explore desired types of projects or placements (e.g., serving directly with a community of need, serving as consultants for an organizational challenge, creating products for an agency). And most important, in terms of collaboration, faculty can explore ways student affairs staff can assist with service-learning courses (e.g., logistical support, agency placements, presentations to students about service-learning, facilitating preparation/integration/reflection activities, course/service assessment, finding resources such as sample syllabi and service-learning research/texts in a particular discipline). Student affairs staff can also assist faculty in making connections with agencies and developing communication procedures for staying in contact with agency partners throughout the semester.

Student Affairs Roles

While student affairs professionals may play a much larger role in service-learning courses than in traditional courses, they must respect the boundaries of academic freedom and authorship. Faculty members, particularly those new to service-learning, cannot and should not be expected to hand over a course or syllabus to anyone. Additionally, while situations may differ, student affairs professionals "are primarily to provide academic support, not to be in the classroom. We are to advocate that principles of good practice are adhered to and serve as the liaison with the community so that the service-learning experience provides reciprocal benefits for all parties" (Engstrom & Tinto, 1997, p. 15). The best collaborations, though, are situations where faculty and student affairs staff work together to explore options and stay connected and involved before, during, and after the course. Student affairs staff should not hesitate to be in regular contact with faculty and look for ways to support faculty efforts. Partnerships will develop once relationships are formed and student affairs staff show they have assets to share.

Student affairs professionals, although they do not teach these courses, do have a great deal of responsibility. They should be the experts on community partnership opportunities, preparation activities, reflection models, locating resources, and service-learning best practices. Additionally, student affairs staff can bring skill and knowledge on important concerns related to liability issues, transportation, conflict resolution, national conferences, and listservs, for example. Perhaps the most important role for student affairs staff is to ask questions (Appendix D), understand faculty members' goals for their courses, and suggest options for further exploration in terms of agency partners, reflection and integration, and resources. In this way, student affairs professionals often play the role of an information clearinghouse. To be trusted as information sources, student affairs staff must understand their campus academic culture, general education curriculum, promotion and tenure process, and typical faculty development methods (used by groups like general studies, technology departments, and the teaching and learning center). In some situations, faculty will merely consult student affairs staff and will then make decisions on their own without any further collaboration. This is not a problem and should not stop student affairs staff from continuing to bring resources, ideas, reflection opportunities, connections with agency partners, and more to faculty members' attention. It is imperative that student affairs professionals demonstrate the skills, processes, and logistical support they can bring to the table.

Unfortunately, the inherent difficulty and frustration of the academic affairs–student affairs partnership will often rest on the shoulders of student affairs professionals. Stereotypical stylistic differences between collaborative student affairs staff and more individualistic faculty members can be both confusing and frustrating for student affairs staff. While service-learning requires mutual partnerships, there is no need to expect that student affairs staff will receive the same billing as faculty in the academic arena or will have equal access to course construction or course management. Student affairs professionals must realize that faculty members do not view courses as "joint projects." Rather, faculty members are completely responsible for the outcomes and delivery of their courses. While student affairs professionals may be excellent partners, advisors, resources, and service-learning experts, courses (and accompanying syllabi, pedagogy, and assignments) remain faculty members' full responsibility and determine their professional livelihood.

In other words, faculty members approach courses and their role in developing and teaching courses in completely different ways from their student affairs colleagues. Therefore, time spent wondering why professors don't see student affairs staff as equal colleagues or disciplinary experts is wasted. Disciplinary knowledge and responsibility will never match service-learning pedagogical know how, because student affairs staff cannot teach faculty's courses or receive faculty tenure. Thus, respect for faculty members' classroom, disciplinary knowledge, and academic freedom should always remain paramount. Faculty members come to student affairs staff for their input and pedagogical know-how. What faculty members do with that input is up to them.

Typical hurdles for student affairs staff include lack of authority to determine course construction; the need to serve as middle managers between faculty, students, and agency partners; lack of regular contact or direct communication with all partners at the same time; and the imbalance of academic and service content. Strategies for surmounting these hurdles include creating trainings for faculty, students, and community partners; developing roles and advisory board positions for both faculty members and community partners; ensuring that some form of assessment occurs in all service-learning efforts; remaining current on service-learning resources, national listservs, Web sites (from the National Clearinghouse to Campus Compact), syllabi banks, texts, and other resources for faculty across campus; and communicating student and faculty accomplishments to campus and community.

Senior Administration Roles

Senior administrators must encourage and facilitate service-learning and service-learning partnerships on campus. Building coalitions, providing resources and recognition, and reviewing promotion and tenure in relation to service-learning are all key roles for administration. Service-learning "must be integrated into the foundation of the institution...holistically" and throughout the institution—from academic affairs to student affairs to development offices to general education curricula to mission statements. If service-learning remains on the margins of college or university and fails to be fully integrated into the institution, it will achieve much less than its full potential. Instead, service-learning should be viewed by administration as "an opportunity to have entire campus structures reexamined and questioned for their efficacy in contributing to their local communities" (Ward, 1996, p. 57).

This process requires "strong, active leadership or advisory teams comprised of both faculty and student affairs professionals" (Engstrom

& Tinto, 2000, pp. 51–52). Advisory teams should consider obstacles and motivators for participating in service-learning for all parties as well as rewards (e.g., release time, course development monies, professional development opportunities) on both sides of the university structure. Part of the planning must include a full review or vision-setting for a wide range of both curricular and co-curricular service-learning efforts. Agendas should include reviews of best practices, prominent regional and national programs, prominence of programs on one's own campus, policy and funding support, leadership, recognition and rewards for faculty and student affairs, and examples of strong partnerships (Jacoby, 1999). Additionally, such leadership or task force groups should ensure that clear learning objectives and roles are defined. Identified roles should model an understanding and appreciation of the unique "jurisdiction, knowledge, and skills of faculty and student affairs professionals" (Engstrom & Tinto, 1997, p. 12). Once clear objectives are set, it is the task of the coordinating body to ensure that an assessment plan is put in action. Too often, campuses rely on participation numbers and anecdotal evidence to prove the validity of important initiatives like service-learning.

Finally, senior administration and advisory groups must keep in mind the important issue of institutional fit. Each campus will find a unique model that works with its curriculum, students, faculty promotion and tenure system, local community, and institutional scale. Throughout her research, Ward, for example, found that connecting distinct sectors of the institution was necessary in the development of inclusive partnerships for service-learning. But no matter the institution, her research showed that coordinating groups "must be aware of how campuses are organized and promote the institutionalization of service accordingly" (Ward, 1996, p. 62). Each campus must recognize

139

its resources and strengths and weaknesses. Each institution must set appropriate goals for service-learning and then translate those goals across its institutional structures. Engaged civic learning will be just as ineffective as lecture-style teaching without the commensurate understanding of campus and community cultures and subcultures (Ward, 1996). In other words, you have to know the map and design the transportation systems in order to meet at the crossroads.

Typical hurdles for senior administrators include staying in contact with all sectors involved in service-learning, meeting the needs for training and recognition in both student affairs and academic affairs, finding collaborative leaders in academic affairs and student affairs, and staying aware of changes and challenges occurring across the university in service-learning. Senior administrators should plan to invite key players in both academic affairs and student affairs to collaborate on service-learning curriculum, programs, and campus integration. Additionally, it will help to charge key individuals from both student affairs and academic affairs to spearhead the development of a service-learning advisory board and a plan for campus-wide service-learning sustainability. Part of this process will require allocating resources for staff, pedagogical resources and texts, and a physical location to house service-learning. Senior administrators can also send fact-finding groups to conferences, campus compact, and site visits at strong service-learning institutions to connect with best practices and practitioners. Finally, it is the role of senior administrators to remove obstacles to service-learning for both faculty and student affairs professionals, paying close attention to rewards for staff and faculty through the promotion and tenure process.

SERVICE-LEARNING BEST PRACTICES

COLLABORATION AT INDIANA UNIVERSITY–PURDUE UNIVERSITY INDIANAPOLIS

The less than four-decade-old partnership that created Indiana University–Purdue University Indianapolis (IUPUI) is currently ranked 15th in the country based on the number of first professional degrees it has offered. It is no surprise that IUPUI has a stellar service-learning program. Two of service-learning's most well-respected researchers, Robert Bringle and Julie Hatcher, authors of countless research studies on service-learning, lead a wide range of curricular and co-curricular offerings at IUPUI. Bringle serves as director of the Center for Service and Learning, whose mission is "to involve students, faculty, and staff in service activities that mutually benefit the campus and community." Bringle reports directly to the executive vice chancellor and dean of faculties, William Plater. In 1993, the center started focusing on development of service-learning courses but later combined with other service-related offices under the auspices of the center. The Office of Service and Learning still coordinates all service-learning courses across the 29,000-student campus through four different offices supervised by Bringle: the Office of Service and Learning (focused on faculty teaching service-learning classes), the Office of Community Service (coordinating service programs, organizations, and events), the Office of Neighborhood Partnerships (collaborating with community organizations and other campus units to build long-term partnerships), and the Office of Community Work Study (involving students in the community through federal work-study). By 2002 the center was named eighth best in the country by *U.S. News and World Report*; in 2005 IUPUI became one of 13 campuses selected by The Carnegie Foundation for the Advancement of Teaching to participate in a pilot project to help develop the new Carnegie Classifications related to community engagement.

Unique Structure

Julie Hatcher, associate director of the Center for Service and Learning at IUPUI, describes student affairs–academic affairs collaborations as "a very common tension within service-learning." She realizes that service-learning often "emerges out of the volunteer side and student affairs" and must be creatively addressed when combined with academics. At IUPUI, though service-learning began in academic affairs, academics later subsumed the student affairs service efforts. Hatcher sees that the unique origination point for service-learning at IUPUI "has impacted our success because service-learning has always been seen as an academic enterprise." In other words, the institution has managed to deal early on with typical challenges of faculty development and rewards through participation in service-learning because both the "lens and foundation" for service-learning is one of faculty work (personal communication, July 5, 2005).

Yet the IUPUI model still involves unique collaboration with student affairs in terms of structure and staffing. When Executive Vice Chancellor Plater asked Bringle to take on the coordination of volunteer service through the Office of Community Service, he provided a staff person with a dual appointment in both academic and student affairs. Hatcher says that this staff person has unique access to funding, student traffic, student interests, student government, and other student affairs programs. Hatcher points out that although she expected student affairs professionals and programs to be less focused on connecting to the curriculum or documenting learning, she has found their program design has actually been much stronger than she expected. The center is also in the process of aligning its programs more clearly with its educational philosophies. But Hatcher notes that part of its success is dependent on collaboration; student affairs does a better job gaining and "leveraging students' attention and interests" both into programs and the center itself (personal communication, July 5, 2005). So both sides need that clear focus on student learning outcomes, but their partnerships are helping to disperse and deliver strong programs to much wider audiences.

Benefits, Challenges, and Outcomes

Overall, these collaborations seem to work because both academic affairs and student affairs philosophically commit and also see advantages. Flexibility seems to be a key component to their success, partly owing to the shared staff member and also to the notion of shared involvement with all students. Fiscally, as Hatcher points out, both sides realize that by sharing this staff member, they each get the full benefits of her work while paying only half her salary. Certainly, this shared professional faces time constraints. Hatcher states that the arrangement "requires a certain level of adaptability and trust" from both sides (personal communication, July 5, 2005). By working together, these divisions and the four offices within the center actually represent a sort of coalition of shared staff and funding developing all forms of service-learning across campus. Their efforts may not have started out collaboratively. But they seem to have found they are stronger together and get that much closer to the university's mission of excellence in civic engagement, including collaboration across the campus and community.

CALIFORNIA STATE UNIVERSITY, FRESNO

The 388-acre California State University, Fresno (Fresno State) main campus is at the foot of the Sierra Nevada mountains on the northeast edge of Fresno, California. It is not surprising that agricultural sciences and technology is a prominent undergraduate focus (along with arts and humanities, business, education and human development, engineering, health and human services, science and math, and social sciences), since the surrounding San Joaquin Valley is described as one of the most fertile agricultural areas in the world. The area also boasts a large Southeast Asian community, including a large population of Hmong refugees. A recent Hmong refugee group immigrating to the area numbered more than 3,000.

Responses to these refugees show the multifaceted approach to social issues and service-learning at Fresno State. According to Chris Fiorentino, director of the Students for Community Service Office, student affairs professionals tend to recognize the unique needs of the Hmong student population by focusing on outreach and student support services like advising, and they engage students to meet those needs. Faculty members, on the other hand, tend to look at the Hmong community needs through disciplinary lenses related to specific academic topics. But at Fresno State, these divergent analyses have not caused dissension. Instead, upper-level administration supports and values collaboration and melding the best of both areas. Fiorentino explains that the more than 20,000 students have a wide range of service and civic involvement opportunities, ranging from one-time experiences to service-learning to internships and more. These opportunities are provided by both student affairs and academic affairs, in a cooperative environment.

Unique Structure

Fiorentino describes Fresno State's approach as organizational flexibility, stating, "There is no clear rationale division on what belongs in student affairs or academic affairs (turf)." At most institutions, the first question asked about a new program is where it makes the most sense to locate the program. Fiorentino believes there are no hard-and-fast rules. He describes how academic affairs coordinates campus-wide blood drives. It made sense to locate them in academic affairs when the blood drives started, based on the prevailing logic of spreading the work around—a sort of nonhierarchical "all hands on deck" mentality that distributes work across the board (personal communication, July 14, 2005). Certainly, student affairs and academic affairs bring different perspectives, but these different views seem to cause campus officials little difficulty. Turf wars are naturally avoided because a mix of academic affairs and student affairs staff work on service-learning. They seem to understand each other's work. In fact, while the Students for Community Service Office currently resides on the academic side, its philosophy focuses on the kinds of personal, leadership, and career development often linked to student affairs programs. A primary focus of the office remains connected to the academic affairs and student affairs efforts; Fiorentino supports both areas including teaching the academic components for American Humanities Certification and CSSP (Community Service Scholarship Program) in career services and the Community Service 101 internship course.

Clearly, this bipartisan spirit comes from the top through an administration that supports and values collaboration. Fiorentino feels that John D. Welty, president of Fresno State since 1991, has created a culture focused on accomplishment rather than strict distribution of tasks by rank or area. Jeronima Echeverria, provost and vice president for academic affairs, and Paul Oliaro, vice president for student affairs and dean of students, have co-chaired a joint task force on student success for the past four years, and Echeverria attributes much of its success to the fact that both academic affairs and student affairs mutually own this effort (personal communication January, 23, 2006).

Benefits, Challenges, and Outcomes

Echeverria states forthrightly "the benefits [of collaboration] outweigh the drawbacks" and believes "this sense of partnership and alignment on mutual goals on behalf of our students is the key to the success of all of our initiatives." She describes the "minimal" drawbacks to collaboration as the simple confusion about who is taking the lead on initiatives when responsibilities are shared. Echeverria includes mandatory incoming student orientation (for both first-year students and transfers), an electronic road map to graduation, first-year student learning communities, the student mentoring institute, and civic engagement and service-learning as examples of accomplishments built on collaborative efforts (personal communication, January, 23, 2006). Fiorentino, on the other hand, as someone more entrenched in the day-to-day operations of these collaborations, admits that stereotypes of each area still exist. When his office was housed in student affairs in the past, staff and faculty often assumed all service-learning programs were student affairs programs with little to no learning. Because he is housed in academic affairs now, he carries a sort of mythical pass in the form of academic credentials, focuses on faculty needs and concerns, and uses academic/faculty "lingo." When working with student affairs staff, he is more focused on leadership skills and personal and career development aspects of service-learning. Both Fiorentino and Echeverria, though, see that everyone, including students, benefits from the two areas crossing boundaries into collaborative work and from the Students for Community Service Office bringing together academic affairs and student affairs efforts. Certainly faculty still teach and student affairs staff still develop co-curricular programs, but each seems to be transformed in this process of placing students' transformation first.

ELON UNIVERSITY

While IUPUI's service-learning programs reside more prominently in academic affairs and Fresno State's rest between academic affairs and student affairs, Elon University's service-learning programs have always originated in student affairs. Service-learning is described as one of five core experiences at Elon, a comprehensive university in central North Carolina enrolling just under 5,000 undergraduates. The university's organized approach to service began in 1988 with a Habitat for Humanity chapter and a visit from former President Jimmy Carter. After the creation of Elon Volunteers! (EV!), the student organization coordinating all service-learning on campus in 1994 through the Provost's Office, service-learning officially moved to Student Life and later to the John Robert Kernodle Center for Service-Learning in 1997. EV! now serves as the 60-member student staff of coordinators, directors, and interns running the Kernodle Center. The center still coordinates both curricular and co-curricular service-learning opportunities, working closely with both student organizations and faculty members using service-learning in their courses. A wide range of programs, including the Service-Learning Community, domestic and international service trips, PreServe summer experience, and service clubs and events, have been created by student affairs staff with involvement of key faculty. In 2005–06, Elon students completed more than 88,000 hours of service, and 89% of graduating seniors had participated in service. Those hours are recorded, along with the other core Elon experiences, on the Elon Experience Transcript, an official university document recording students' out-of-class work in service, leadership, internships and co-ops, undergraduate research, and study abroad.

Unique Structures

The Kernodle Center, and therefore service-learning, remains student-run and connected to both academic affairs and student affairs through intentional efforts. For example, Provost Gerry Francis supervises Vice President of Student Life and Dean of Students Smith Jackson. The two work closely and have presented at conferences across the country on both engaged and seamless learning at Elon. They also authored a white paper on the topic, which led in 1997 to the formation of the Joint Deans' Council, a monthly gathering of academic and student life deans as well as directors of the library and general studies and the registrar.

Francis and Jackson also took on leadership within North Carolina Campus Compact to host a joint meeting of more than 40 chief academic and chief student affairs officers throughout the state in order to achieve a higher level of support from participating campuses to work closer together on fulfilling the civic mission of their own institutions. Elon has become a model for collaboration, specifically around areas such as service-learning. In 2002, the new assistant dean of students for service-learning, who also holds academic credentials, began teaching service-learning courses in the English Department and working to pull service-learning faculty into the partnership with the Kernodle Center staff. In fall 2003, academic affairs and student life designed a more structured role to collaborate in advancing the course-based service-learning program with faculty across campus. The chair of the Human Services Department, Pam Kiser, was invited to serve as the first Kernodle Center faculty fellow for academic service-learning. Kiser chairs the Academic Service-Learning Faculty Advisory Board, leads faculty development efforts with Kernodle Center staff, and has championed a number of service-learning programs across campus, including a new Academic Service-Learning Faculty Scholars development program and regular brown-bag lunches on service-learning topics. While faculty development related to service-learning had occurred for years on campus, faculty participation has changed since these efforts became a partnership between Kiser and the Kernodle Center staff. In other words, the message seemed to change when delivered by a respected faculty champion. Since Kiser's involvement, the collaboration has resulted in a service-learning course designation in the campus course book, the year-long Faculty Scholars program, and more recently, a $15,000 grant from the Charles A. Frueauff Foundation to fund collaborations among students, community agencies, and faculty.

Benefits, Challenges, and Outcomes

While Elon has a long history of academic affairs–student affairs collaboration, strong involvement and support of upper administration has combined with "crossover" staff and faculty to advance collaborative efforts. Structural shifts and connections such as the faculty fellow, faculty advisory board, faculty advising service trips, and teaching core courses for the service-learning community seem to have made quite a difference as well. Of course, there are challenges. At times, it is unclear who is leading the charge or an individual project. Even worse, student affairs and academic affairs have seen their similar requests handled differently by different audiences. Even on a campus focused on student and civic engagement, seamless learning, and experiential

149

education, distinct campus perceptions and languages exist on each side of the border. As John Barnhill, executive director of North Carolina Campus Compact, states:

> Often, budget decisions, staff decisions, policy decisions, etc. can be perceived to benefit one division of a campus more than another. It takes a high level of commitment and communication between the two areas to sustain a partnership. But students and community members often don't understand the difference between academic affairs and student affairs; they just want to know "what office do I go to find out about service or service-learning opportunities?" (personal communication, January 14, 2006)

Continued communication, strong leadership, and a student learning focus seem to have kept the collaborations strong. "Without the leadership of the provost and the vice president for student affairs," says Barnhill, "there would not be the high level of support for service, service-learning, and civic engagement. One only needs to look at other institutions that have only one division or one leader's support to see why a campus succeeds or doesn't meet its stated goals" (personal communication, January 14, 2006). The consistent by-product and consistent goal of this shared focus on curricular and co-curricular service-learning remains student learning. And the leveraging of the best of both student and academic affairs is also manifested in the sheer numbers of students participating in service-learning. The annual number of hours of service completed by Elon students has increased by more than 50,000 hours in the last 10 years. Elon's program has been ranked in the top 20 service-learning programs by *U.S. News and World Report* for the last three years, and Elon just became one of 13 campuses selected to assist the Carnegie Foundation in developing a classification based on civic engagement.

CONCLUSION

It is unnecessary to review the history of higher education, the emergence of separation and specialization in both faculty and student affairs professions, and even the separate theoretical groundings of each camp. Merely identifying stereotypes and perceptions about "introverted" faculty and "bubbly" student affairs professionals illustrates the gap that can separate these two central, professional forces.

The groups do not have to completely agree on the value of in- and out-of-class experiences, to completely blur roles, or to see professional distinctions as ambiguous or permeable in order to bridge this gap. Rather, faculty and student affairs professionals must communicate regularly about how to work together toward shared goals, to connect in- and out- of-class experiences, to find common goals/outcomes, and to see what each can bring to new projects. In other words, the professions are not the same. Shared goals can coexist with disparate forms of expertise. Service-learning's emphasis on mutuality illustrates that distinct student affairs and academic affairs professionals can create one holistic educational program that *Learning Reconsidered* (Keeling, 2004) works so aptly to describe.

References

Anzaldua, Gloria. (1987). *Borderlands/la frontera: The new mestiza.* San Francisco: Aunt Lute Books.

Astin, A. W., & Sax, L. J. (1999). Long term effects of volunteerism during the undergraduate years. *The Review of Higher Education, 22,* 187–202.

Astin, A. W., Vogelgesang, L. J., Ikeda, E. K., & Yee, J. A. (2000). *How service learning affects students.* Los Angeles: Higher Education Research Institute, University of California-Los Angeles.

Battistoni, R. M. (2002). *Civic engagement across the curriculum: A resource book for service-learning in all disciplines.* Providence, RI: Campus Compact.

Blake, E. S. (1979). Classroom and context: An educational dialectic. *Academe, 65,* 280–292.

Boyer commission on educating undergraduates in the research university. (1998). *Reinventing undergraduate education: A blueprint for America's research universities.* Stony Brook: NY: State University of New York.

Delve, C. I., Mintz, S. D., & Stewart, G. M. (1990). Promoting values development through community service: A design. In C. Delve, S. Mintz, & G. Stewart (Eds.), *Community service as values education* (pp. 7–29). San Francisco: Jossey-Bass.

Dewey, J. (1916). *Democracy and education: An introduction to the philosophy of education.* New York: Macmillan.

Engstrom, C. M. (2003). Developing collaborative student affairs-academic affairs partnerships for service-learning. In Jacoby, B. (Ed.), *Building partnerships in service-learning* (pp. 65–84). San Francisco: Jossey-Bass.

Engstrom, C. M., & Tinto, V. (1997, July/August). Working together for service learning. *About Campus,* 10–15.

Engstrom, C. M., & Tinto, V. (2000). Developing partnerships with academic affairs to enhance student learning. In M. Barr, M. Desler (Eds.), *The handbook of student affairs administration* (pp. 425–452). San Francisco: Jossey-Bass.

Enos, S., & Morton, K. (2003). Developing a theory and practice of campus-community partnerships. In B. Jacoby (Ed.), *Building partnerships in service-learning* (pp. 20–41). San Francisco: Jossey-Bass.

Eyler, J., & Giles, D. E., Jr. (1999). *Where's the learning in service-learning?* San Francisco: Jossey-Bass.

Harkavy, I. (2003). Foreword. In B. Jacoby (Ed.) *Building partnerships in service-learning* (pp. xi–xvi). San Francisco: Jossey-Bass.

Jacoby, B. (1999). Partnerships for service learning. In J. H. Schuh, J. H. Whitt, & E. J. Whitt (Eds.), *Creating successful partnerships between academic and student affairs* (pp. 19–35). San Francisco: Jossey-Bass.

Jacoby, B. (2003). *Building partnerships in service-learning.* San Francisco: Jossey-Bass.

Keeling, R. P. (Ed.). (2004). *Learning reconsidered: A campus-wide focus on the student experience.* Washington, DC: National Association of Student Personnel Administrators and American College Personnel Association.

Kezar, A., & Rhoads, R. A. (2001). The dynamic tensions of service learning in higher education: A philosophical perspective. *Journal of Higher Education, 72,* 148–171.

Kolb, D. A. (1984). *Experiential learning: Experience as the source of learning and development*. Englewood Cliffs, NJ: Prentice-Hall.

National Commission on Civic Renewal. (1998). *A nation of spectators: How civic disengagement weakens America and what we can do about it*. College Park, MD: University of Maryland.

Sigmon, R. L. (1994). *Linking service with learning in liberal arts education*. Washington, DC: Council of Independent Colleges.

Terenzini, P. T., & Pascarelli, E. T. (1994). Living with myths: Undergraduate education in America. *Change, 26,* 28–32.

Ward, K. (1996). Service-learning and student volunteerism: Reflections on institutional commitment. *Michigan Journal of Community Service, 3,* 55–65.

Wingspread group on higher education. (1993). *An American imperative: Higher expectations for higher education.* Racine, WI: Johnson Foundation.

CHAPTER NINE

Circle Seven: Classroom– Residence Hall Continuity

John W. Schmidt

College faculties across the country are beginning to adopt new practices that raise the level of student effort and achievement. [The intent] is to help college students become intentional, empowered, informed and responsible learners. (AAC&U, 2002)

T o achieve new levels of student learning will require successful collaborators. Two areas of university life that must be more collaborative are those of student affairs and academic affairs.

Both elements share common goals in preparing students to become life-long learners in a more complex world. Yet, often, pursuit of these goals in academe travels parallel paths where intersecting and overlapping junctures are avoided based on culture, climate, and competing interests.

Fostering shared learning practices where student service and academic leaders travel jointly toward a common goal of student success requires a change agent. This facilitative leader helps others achieve common goals of learning, creates a process for change, and then guides as well as sustains the learning process.

This chapter illustrates the importance of creating shared visions that build bonds of enhanced learning and student success through collaboration by student affairs and academic affairs leaders. It focuses on collaboration and innovation involving residence hall learning communities that facilitate student learning, development, and campus involvement. Next, it offers examples of learning communities as living extensions of classroom learning. Finally, it provides a synthesis of key ingredients that enable collaboration and sustains momentum for classroom–residence hall learning continuity. Examples provided in this chapter have been synthesized within Appendix E.

A CAMPUS X-RAY

Creating and sustaining academic and student affairs collaboration requires two essential elements. The first is a commitment to change focused on a common purpose or objective. Closely related to commitment is the second element: a champion who will fuel this change effort into collaboration leading to shared ownership. Kouzes and Posner (1995) referred to this process as helping others see a vision that results in shared destiny.

Friedman (2005) suggests that enabling others to see the way ahead requires an "organizational x-ray" that identifies core components for improvement (p. 357). Such an x-ray often begins with an examination of the institution's stated goals, trends, and retention rates.

Troy University in Alabama and Mansfield University in Pennsylvania used strategic planning to assess student learning and leadership beyond the classroom. Similarly, Elon University, recognized as a leader in student engagement, reviewed its overall campus setting as a means of building an environment supportive of student growth and leadership. Some universities use first-year retention as a gauge of both academic delivery and student satisfaction. For example, Northern Kentucky University employed institutional data that showed many students were leaving the university due to lack of vital student support services and a stated need for a more vibrant campus life. University of North Carolina–Charlotte planners also focused on retention improvement. Leadership responsibilities for these initiatives often fade away due to lack of attention. Thus, the role of the senior student affairs officer or practitioner becomes important in creating a structure for collaborative learning.

Indeed, observers of collaborative learning processes advocate the role of student affairs leaders in such processes. Astin (1999) stated, "Our findings...suggest that student affairs professionals and student affairs work in general should play a much more central role in academic planning and policy making" (p. 590). Gardner (2002) and Barefoot, King, and Kuh (2003) also encourage greater faculty and student affairs collaboration to improve student learning as a central goal for all higher education institutions. Truly, as Moneta (2003) pointed out, "The lines between traditional student affairs and academic support services...are blurring beyond distinction" (p. 6).

A Shared Learning Challenge

The blurring of the distinction between academic and student affairs has been prompted by greater accountability in higher education, especially for first-year students. Academic and student affairs leaders have used this impetus to develop various forms of campus learning models. Terenzini and Reason (2005) encouraged academic and student affairs leaders to integrate learning programs horizontally and vertically throughout campus life. These shared learning partnerships are a return to the earlier work of Tinto (1987), who advocated academic and social integration of first-year students into the institutional fabric of the university. These learning partnerships take various form and functions based on the campus culture. One size does not fit all. However, some commonalities exist.

Eison (2002) and Barefoot et al. (2003) provided an assessment of these learning partnerships from which four broad categories emerged, three of which center on residence hall living and learning. The initiatives include first-year seminars centered on specific topics, linked first-year courses further connected to on-campus residence living, holistic learning blending in-class objectives with out-of-class service projects, and residence halls organized to support specific academic programs. An overarching goal in these programs is to facilitate out-of-class interaction with peers and faculty members through shared learning assignments together with shared living arrangements. Pike (2000) offers a cautionary viewpoint regarding learning community expectations: "Learning communities, in and of themselves, do not cause a student to learn, make good grades or be retained" (p. 14). More often, the outcomes are more subtle where a climate for overall learning becomes the norm at all campus levels. Perhaps the reason for forming learning communities was best summarized by the former University of Michigan president who observed, "Memories of learning communities…may be far closer to the real world of college education…college should be as much a place to live as it is to live to learn" (Duderstadt, 2000, p. 76).

The theory and research behind learning communities are not new. Yet the concept has only recently been renewed on college campuses. A review of various collaborative efforts shows that many have emerged from the necessity for greater accountability and retention mentioned earlier. Other factors include strategic planning focused on being more student centered, reduced resources (funds, people, buildings) requiring new approaches, and a deliberate intent to improve campus learning processes in a shared fashion.

THE LEARNING COMMUNITY EXPERIENCE

Hit the Google search button for "campus residence hall learning" and more than 17 million sites appear. Indeed, many college campuses have either full-blown, robust learning communities or emerging initiatives. A more deliberate review of best practices submitted by student affairs practitioners reveals a trend similar to the Google search. Each campus has variations of classroom–residence hall learning.

Of all the universities surveyed in the promising practices submissions for this chapter, Elon University has the most robust program with a totally integrated campus learning environment. Well-defined academic and student services partnerships exist, coupled with annual report structures that offer feedback on the learning linkages and are used to improve the learning process.

Elon has established a series of residentially based learning communities. Students co-enroll in at least one class and reside in the same residence hall. Several communities have overarching themes, such as religious and spiritual life, service-learning, and science. A joint deans' group comprising both academic and student affairs leaders meets regularly to review the goal of seamless and connected learning.

Closely aligned to the Elon model is the "Village" concept at North Carolina State University (NCSU). NCSU created a living–learning village that blends residence hall living with a well-defined first-year college program. Resident assistants are trained to teach study skills, time management, and career choices. Programs to broaden classroom experiences include museum trips, attendance at theater productions, and leadership development. Students are required to attend these functions as part of an integrated first-year curriculum. These inquiry classes are usually taught with a ratio of 20 students to one faculty member. So the environment provides an open arena for inquiry and getting to know fellow students. The outcomes are focused on student development and learning.

Mansfield University of Pennsylvania is a newcomer to the learning community process, which emerged from its strategic plan to build collaborative practices and engage students in learning. Mansfield's learning community developed from a relationship between the provost/vice president of academic affairs and the vice president for student affairs. A co-curricula model emerged with the establishment of a faculty-in-residence program established in the residence halls. The intent is to have faculty engage students on their turf. Faculty augment academic and scholarly programs with learning for fun. The latter programs have included country line dancing, Native American jewelry making, and sharing reflections on a nonacademic book.

Bringing academic programs and faculty into the residence halls was the focus of learning for the University of South Carolina (USC) and the University of Florida (UF). USC uses non-revenue space inside the residence halls for classes. More than 50 courses are taught from these locations, including the university's first-year orientation course. USC's intent is to create an academic atmosphere, share space and resources, and enhance the undergraduate experience within the residence hall setting. USC believes that residence hall learning arrangements provide the "canvas upon which their academic partners are able to paint a picture of student success and engaged learning."

Similar to the USC model, UF houses three faculty members in residence halls. The faculty-in-residence members serve as liaisons for their academic colleagues, mentor students, and offer special programs for students in the residence hall. UF is also deliberate in linking specific colleges with residence halls, such as its College of Fine Arts that is linked with students living in an assigned campus house.

Another UF commitment to learning outside the classroom is its Honors Residential College, oriented toward high academic achievers. This collaborative effort emerged from a partnership between the residence hall staff and the associate provost. Faculty assist with residence hall programming, advising students where they reside, and facilitating student engagement (Keeling, 2006). In similar fashion, Western Carolina University employs its honors students as "academic achievement advocates" who teach academic survival skills to their classmates in the residence halls. This program resulted from cooperative efforts between the honors dean and vice chancellor for student affairs.

Necessity and merging mutual goals were the catalyst for the learning community program at Furman University in Greenville, South Carolina. The faculty associated with the Department of Health and Exercise Department wanted more first-year students enrolled in the wellness course. Concurrently, the residence hall director was interested in beginning a linked learning community. From these mutual interests emerged Furman's learning community. Students enrolled in the wellness course are housed in the same residence hall. On weekends, special evening dinners are scheduled where the faculty members meet with students to discuss wellness issues and map out healthy lifestyle habits.

Another use of the dining approach for residence hall learning is found at the University of Wyoming. Here, the emphasis is on cross-cultural awareness with the inclusion of international students. Residence life personnel working with dining services built learning themes into menu planning centered on specific ethnic cultures. Such an idea can be tied to world studies, political science endeavors, or geography to engage the entire campus in a central learning theme (Keeling, 2006).

Institutional reorganization prompting collaborative learning formed the basis for residence hall learning and beyond at Slippery Rock University in Slippery Rock, Pennsylvania, and Troy University in Troy, Alabama.

At Slippery Rock, a series of joint retreats with student affairs and academic affairs leaders yielded residence hall "commons" floors. Program funding comes from student affairs, with program and tutoring services provided by the faculty. It was noted that in these relationships humility is a factor. That is, students win in these environments and no one dwells on who gets the credit.

Student affairs leaders at Troy University created a first-year task force supported by the provost. The task force of student affairs and academic leaders began by creating a learning community that included weekly meetings with peer mentors, faculty advisors, and a signed learning contract used for semester evaluation. This initial partnership is yielding new programs such as a first-year reading initiative. Next fall, all incoming first-year students will be required to read a designated book that will be discussed in classes as well as in the residence halls.

CONTINUING THE MOMENTUM FOR LEARNING COLLABORATION

Based on a review of campus collaborative efforts that expand learning, some reflections are worth noting to enable the establishment and maintenance of the learning community momentum.

The Problem of Ownership

The question of who has responsibility for learning outside the classroom often remains a grey area. Student services leaders are the ones who most often detect student dissatisfaction expressed by missing classes, voiced in confidence to counselors, or seen in first-year grade point averages and poor retention rates. Campus experience shows that student services leaders should make a difference by taking the leadership role with their academic colleagues to improve first-year learning. One of the common base points is the merger of living and learning in the residence hall. What gradually emerges with some determined leadership is shared ownership of the overall learning process. As a senior administrator at Western Carolina noted, actions such as taking learning beyond the classroom into the residence halls break down traditional silos and create the necessary learning connections.

A Foundation for Learning

Collaborative learning requires collaborative team-building with

163

the right players. Campus leaders must be chosen who will contribute to the goal. Senior leadership must be involved. Faculty mentors in the residence halls are usually volunteers with reputations for being engaged with students. Volunteers should be rewarded with free dining in the campus dining facility or provided tickets to selected campus events. Faculty should also be recognized for their participation in their residence hall learning engagement in promotion and tenure processes. These actions will build visibility and campus support across all sectors.

Engaged Students

Students come to campus with differing learning styles and expectations. Strong residential life programs connected to course curricula, supported by dedicated faculty, augmented by motivated peers, and delivered to meet student needs result in enhanced learning and build social skills outside class. The end result is persistent students who will ultimately become loyal alumni.

Assessment Awareness and Refinement

No project or plan ever unfolds exactly as envisioned. Continual assessment is required to sustain momentum of these learning arrangements within residence halls. Each university reviewed for this project had a definitive assessment model attached to its learning community program. Each learning community concept recognized the connectedness of academic progress or professional development and personal growth that leads to retention and persistence to graduation. Figure 9.1 captures the unique aspects of learning communities with the student at the center supported mutually by academic and student services.

Figure 9.1. Living and learning pathways.

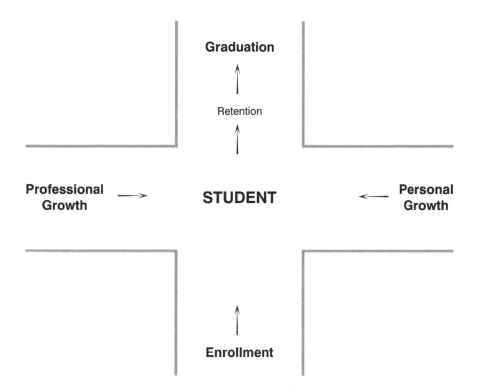

Academic and student services leaders must ensure that the horizontal pathway is mutually supportive. Simple, measurable, defined goals keep the learning engagement alive and keep students on course for retention resulting in graduation on the vertical path. For example, in the academic area of professional growth, meeting with mentors, midterm grade assessments, and learning style evaluations are key interventions. Concurrently, in the area of personal growth, usually the purview of student services, participation in community projects, involvement in campus organizations, and maintaining a healthy lifestyle serve as essential assessments. Remember, however, that the horizontal

165

pathway is mutually supported, not mutually exclusive. With this in mind, collaboration among colleagues in these ventures offers its own learning loop and provides an open forum for constructive dialogue to improve the learning community process. The final assessment and outcome should be students who are motivated to learn and who see their own potential being developed for leadership roles after graduation.

DEFINING A SUITABLE LEARNING COMMUNITY

Each of the many classroom–learning communities cited arose in response to a need unique to that campus. Common to all is the shared academic and student services quest for learning involvement. Campus leadership must determine how to achieve that goal and define the outcome.

Common Classroom–Residence Hall Learning Practices

These practices include:

* Sustaining a vision to build a total campus learning environment

* Integrating and expanding classroom learning with outside class experiences

* Building first-year student persistence and campus involvement

* Recognizing that residence halls are a ready avenue connecting academic and student affairs in a shared commitment to intentional learning

* Providing an excellent evaluation tool to measure learning outcomes based on engagement, grade point achievement, participation in campus events, and faculty interaction with students

Conclusion

Student affairs leaders tend to be collaborators and risk takers by nature. When one assembles assorted service functions into a cohesive whole for others, collaboration comes easy. Expanding learning outside the classroom requires leaders who are creative, flexible, initiative-oriented, and team builders. Sharing the credit is more important than deciding who gets the credit in these environments. Leaders who can apply these skills will be valuable assets to any college or university. Most of all, students will be the beneficiaries of an atmosphere that cares about their overall success and well-being.

REFERENCES

Association of American Colleges and Universities. (2002). *Greater expectations: A new vision for learning as a nation goes to college* [National panel]. Washington, DC: Author.

Astin, A. W. (1999). Involvement in learning revisited: Lessons we have learned. *Journal of College Student Development, 40*(5), 587–597.

Astin, A. W., Korn, W. S., Lindholm, J. A., & Mahoney, K. M. (2002). *The American freshmen norms for 2002.* Los Angeles: University of California, Los Angeles, Higher Education Research Institute.

Barefoot, B., King, P., & Kuh, G. (2003, March). *Engaging students in learning.* Teleconference presented by the National Resource Center for The First-Year Experience and Students in Transition, University of South Carolina, Columbia, SC.

Duderstadt, J. J. (2000). *A university for the 21st century.* Ann Arbor, MI: The University of Michigan Press.

Eaton, M. (2005). *Searching for the new university: Changing faculty roles.* Retrieved August 1, 2005, from http:// www.pfhe.org

Eison, J. (2002). Teaching strategies for the 21st century. In R. M. Diamond (Ed.) *Field guide to academic leadership* (pp. 157–173). San Francisco: Jossey-Bass.

Friedman, T. L. (2005). *The world is flat.* New York: Farrar, Straus and Giroux.

Gardner, J. (2002, August). *Making the most of the undergraduate experience.* Paper presented to Troy University faculty and staff, Troy, AL.

Hawkins, J. (2001). *Over the horizon: Strong values–clear vision.* Troy, AL: Troy University Chancellor's Office.

Hayes, R. Q. (Ed.). (2002). *The retention and graduation rates of 1994–2000 entering freshmen cohorts in 360 colleges and universities.* Consortium for Student Retention Data Exchange Report. Norman, OK: The University of Oklahoma, College of Continuing Education.

Keeling, R. P. (Ed.). (2004). *Learning reconsidered: A campus-wide focus on the student experience.* Washington, DC: National Association of Student Personnel Administrators and the American College Personnel Association.

Keeling, R. P. (Ed.). (2006). *Learning reconsidered 2: A practical guide to implementing A campus-wide focus on the student experience.* Washington, DC: American College Personnel Association, Association of College and University Housing Officers–International, Association of College Unions International, National Academic Advising Association, National Association for Campus Activities, National Association of Student Personnel Administrators, and National Intramural-Recreational Sports Association.

Kotter, J. P. (1996). *Leading change.* Boston: Harvard Business School Press.

Kouzes, J., & Posner, B. (1995). *The leadership challenge.* San Francisco: Jossey-Bass.

Kuh, G. D., & Pace, C. R. (1998). *CSXQ and CSEQ surveys.* (Available from Indiana University, Ashton Aley Hall, Suite 102, 1913 East Seventh Street, Bloomington, IN 47405-7510).

Moneta, L. (2003, Spring). Future trends and challenges for

student affairs: A senior student affairs officer's perspective. *Leadership Exchange, 1,* 6–9.

National Center for Public Policy and Higher Education. (2004). *Measuring up 2004.* Special Report. San Jose, CA: Author.

Pascarella, E. T., & Terenzini, P. T. (1991). *How college affects students.* San Francisco: Jossey-Bass.

Pierce, S. (2002). *Undergraduate attrition report for 2001–2002.* Troy, AL: Troy University Office of Student Development/Counseling.

Pike, G. (2000, March-April). Methodological issues in the assessment of learning communities. *Assessment Update, 12,* 14–15.

Roling, A. (Ed.). (2005). *Annual fact book 2005.* Troy, AL: Troy University, Office of Institutional Research and Planning Effectiveness.

Rowden, R. W. (2001). The learning organization and strategic change. *Advanced Management Journal, 66*(3), 11–16.

Shapiro, N., & Levine, J. (1999). *Creating learning communities.* San Francisco: Jossey-Bass.

Terenzini, P. T., & Reason, R. D. (2005). *Parsing the first year of college: Rethinking the effects of college on students.* Paper presented at the meeting of the Association for the Study of Higher Education, Philadelphia, PA.

Tinto, V. (1987). *Leaving college.* Chicago: The University of Chicago Press.

Tinto, V. (1997). Classrooms as communities: Exploring the educational character of student Persistence. *The Journal of Higher Education 68,* 599–623.

CHAPTER TEN
Circle Eight:
Well-Coordinated Assessment

Sandi N. Osters

Making a case for effective assessment collaboration between student affairs and academic affairs is not a new
call. In 1991, Peter Ewell observed that there was a general lack of integration among assessment functions between academic
and student affairs. He commented that institutions treated these assessments as separate activities, and findings rarely became integrated
or became recommendations for improvement. He acknowledged that
the then-new living–learning community initiative was an example of
bridges between the two areas; however, "In all too many institutions,

171

these functions remain worlds unto themselves, and in the absence of vigorous, top-level leadership to span organizational boundaries they are likely to remain so" (p. 730).

> Seven years later, Trudy Banta and George Kuh (1998) would echo the same call: Improving the quality of undergraduate experience at any institution is so complex and multifaceted that it demands cooperation by the two groups on campus that spend the most time with students: faculty members and student affairs professionals. To improve, all institutions need the best information they can get about the quality of their students' learning; they need to know where learning occurs and what changes will enhance it. (p. 42)

Banta and Kuh (1998) believed that "one of the most promising but underused opportunities for collaboration comes in the form of outcomes assessment" (p. 42). Although emphasizing different aspects of student learning, student and academic affairs can participate as equal partners in this effort. These collaborations allow first hand observations of what college impact research shows: "that cognitive and affective development are inextricable intertwined and that the curricular and out-of-class activities are not discrete, independent events; they affect one another (sometimes profoundly) in ways that often are not immediately obvious" (p. 42).

James Anderson repeated the call in 2001 when he stressed the need for student development professionals to "inform the academic side of the institution of their desire to establish, maintain, and assess functional collaborations" (p. 2). He challenged student affairs to develop "conceptual clarity" about the work it does and what it seeks to accomplish.

172

Banta and Kuh (1998) identified six themes common to effective academic-student affairs collaborations: (1) strong institutional administrative support; (2) joint planning of curriculum and assessment; (3) shared institutional understanding of student learning and development; (4) coordination of in- and out-of-class learning experiences in order to accurately document the impact of college on students; (5) developed, shared process indicators of desired outcomes; and (6) use of assessment findings to improve the entire student experience.

Banta and Kuh (1998) concluded:

> By working together on assessment, faculty and student affairs professionals can broaden acceptable definitions and develop a common language of learning; accumulate institution-specific evidence linking out-of-class experiences to valued outcomes of undergraduate education; help identify complementary activities, services, and practices; and experiment with ways to realize these conditions more of the time. (p. 46)

To garner evidence of academic and student affairs collaborations, the Educational Resources Information Center Clearinghouse on Education, the National Association of Student Personnel Administrators (NASPA), and the American College Personnel Association (ACPA) conducted a joint national study (Kezar, Hirsch, & Burack, 2002). The study found that 45% of the institutions surveyed were conducting outcomes assessments of academic and student affairs collaborations. More than 33% also conducted focus groups and interviews on the impact of these partnerships. In the same study, respondents were asked what they perceived the benefits of their collaboration to be and whether they were achieving their stated goals and outcomes. "Although there were too few responses to report reliable trends, an improved learning environment, retention, enhanced institutional communication, culture of trust, better campus relationships, and increased attention to the work of student affairs were most often mentioned" (p. 49).

Most recently, Bresciani, Zelna, and Anderson (2004) noted that one of the expectations in the 21st century is that various campus groups will learn to collaborate on common goals. "The most important—and yet most underdeveloped—collaboration on many campuses is between Academic Affairs (especially the faculty) and the Academic and Student Supports services areas, or the curricular and the cocurriuclar" (p. 1).

Bresciani et al. (2004) highlighted several institutions and programs that are successfully accomplishing assessment collaborations. What stands out at each of these institutions is the blending of a philosophical commitment to being learning-centered, and the real commitment to develop a best practice that can be assessed and evaluated. The collaborative nature of the contributions from student and academic affairs assures a best fit for each entity. Both divisions work through and agree upon a common language and process while maintaining their focus on the student (p. 5).

Learning Reconsidered (Keeling, 2004) set high standards for assessment of academic–student affairs collaborations. It suggested that student affairs assume leadership in collaborative efforts to define and assess student learning outcomes for the institution and for ensuring that student affairs goals, outcomes, and assessment plans are in alignment with institutional outcomes. It called for innovative multiple assessment methods of student learning rather than satisfaction and looked at direct and indirect assessment methods both within and outside the classroom and in follow-up work with graduates and employers. It challenged student affairs practitioners to work with faculty to complete "conceptual mapping of student learning" and to know what institutional opportunities "support and supplement learning objectives" (p. 24). Taking the collaboration even further, *Learning Reconsidered* suggested that student and academic affairs educators work in teams not only to understand the learning that is occurring but also to decide on how improvements should be structured.

Sharing the results should encourage inquiry and discussion, creating an interactive assessment cycle that places value on faculty and staff efforts as well as on student feedback. Such a cycle engages academic and student affair educators, empowers them to continue assessment, and closes the assessment loop (Keeling, 2004).

CHOOSING BEST PRACTICE EXAMPLES

To begin the search for best practice institutions, Cynthia Wells, a Boyer Fellow at Messiah College's Boyer Center, recommended DePaul University in Chicago and St. Mary's College in Moraga, California. Both institutions participated in the Boyer Partnership Project, a three-year assessment of partnerships between academic affairs and student affairs at 18 different institutions (Kraybill, 2001). The academic and student affairs partnerships in the Boyer Project had to be educational programs that directly impacted student learning and that showed some evidence of assessment of that learning.

Oregon State is featured based on the recommendation of Marilee Bresciani, associate professor, San Diego State University.

Paradise Valley Community College was chosen based on a literature review of institutions that had published research studies of successful academic and student affairs collaborations, as well as on the recommendation of Bresciani.

PRESENTING BEST PRACTICE EXAMPLES

Best practice institutions were asked to explain and provide evidence of their collaborative programs based on the Bresciani et al. (2004) iterative outcomes assessment model. Not every element is present in each best practice example, and there is no attempt here to say that they should be. However, this is a well-articulated and -supported outcomes assessment model that serves to convey the nature and scope of the best practice example.

The question posed to each best practice institutional representative was what collaboration occurred in the following areas:

* In the development of the program

* In the mission or purpose of the program

* In the goals and objectives of the program

* In the development of learning and program outcomes

* In the evaluation methods used and the criteria for success

* In the implementation of the assessment

* In the data analysis

* In the development of results, decisions, and recommendations

* In the assessment of any changes and improvements
made from that assessment

Best Practice Programs

Paradise Valley Community College, Phoenix

According to the Paradise Valley Community College (PVCC)
Web site, PVCC is one of 10 colleges, two skill centers, and multiple
satellite locations that comprise the Maricopa County Community
College District located throughout metropolitan Phoenix. PVCC was
founded in 1985 and has a per-semester enrollment of 7,800 students.
Its "unduplicated headcount per year is over 12,400 students, with an
additional 7,000 in non-credit and continuing education programs"
(Maricopa County Community College District, p. 1).

In March 2000 Paul Dale, then dean of students, and Cindy
Shoenhair, human development faculty at PVCC, coauthored a presentation on Learning-Centered Practices in Student Services. Dale and
Shoenhair indicated that "significant collaborations with faculty and
programmatic partnerships, sharing resources" was a characteristic of
learning-oriented student services programs (p. 8). On June 30, 2005,
Dale accepted an offer to be featured in *Divine Comity* and suggested
several of PVCC's programs that would meet the criteria for participation: an athletic academic success program, an under-prepared student
initiative (developmental math and a student success class), First Year
Experience (FYE), emerging leaders program, and an out-of-class assessment of general education outcomes program. In a personal conversation on July 21, 2005, Dale shared another collaboration between
media services (in student affairs) and faculty. FYE and the media ser-

vices program are discussed here because of the amount of assessment provided to support their inclusion as best practices.

First Year Experience is part of the university's learning community program. (A learning community is a one-semester program at PVCC. FYE is also considered a learning community but is a year-long program.) Dale (personal communication, July 21, 2005) had an interest in the first-year experience and "invited himself" to the Learning Community Steering Committee, whose membership at the time comprised only faculty and academic administrators. During the next year Dale worked with a faculty member to develop a first-year experience learning community. At the same time, another faculty member was developing a 12-credit-hour first-year experience block. The two programs were developed separately until they were brought under the learning community committee. "It was a confluence of my personal interest and a faculty member that was out on her own doing it and the faculty member who I was working with." Subsequently, student affairs provided funding for faculty to attend the National Conference on the First Year Experience as well as providing co-curricular support for the program. Faculty and student affairs staffs also have attended Evergreen State's summer workshops, which were the genesis of the notion of shared resources for PVCC's FYE. Faculty in English and health and exercise science were the first to develop the curriculum for a first-year experience. Currently, FYE has become a priority for the colleges and has resulted in additional budget requests.

According to the internal First Year Experience Program: Report on the 2003–2004 Year provided to the researcher, FYE blocks were piloted at PVCC in fall 2000 with a mission to "innovatively integrate academic and co-curricular learning activities to help new students transition successfully to college life" (p. 1). The blocks thematically link two or more courses. In fall 2003, "Exploring Your Options in a Changing World" thematically linked English Composition 101, Introduction to Sociology 101, Strategies for College Success, and Survey of Computer Information Systems. "Computers and College Success for the ESL Student" linked English as a Second Language, Orientation for Student Development, and Introduction to Microcomputers I.

FYE courses are team-taught and have student peer mentors and staff counselors assigned to the block of courses. Initially, peer mentors were simply graduates of FYE without formal training, but now they enroll in a counseling-based course on mentoring. Student affairs pays the mentors a stipend. The block counselors report both to academic affairs and student affairs. The faculty division chair of counseling also reports to both academic and student affairs.

Developing and implementing an ongoing assessment plan for improving the Learning Community program is the responsibility of the Learning Community Steering Committee. Student affairs also has input into the FYE master plan. According to Dale (personal communication, July 21, 2005), most assessment to date has been program assessment, but there is now an active effort to develop both learning and program outcomes for FYE and learning communities across disciplines. The internal PVCC document, The First Year Experience Program: Report on the 2003–2004 Year, noted that student retention/persistence, academic preparedness and success, and personal development and transition to college life were the three FYE goals supported by six outcomes. Assessment for the fall semester in the "Exploring Your Options in a Changing World" block included quantitative enrollment/grade data and a qualitative survey completed by FYE students and a control group of English 101 students taught by a full-time professor. Evidence from this assessment strongly supported FYE. Even anecdotal evidence provided support when it was noted that "students who were failing one or more of the classes remained enrolled and in attendance through final exams because they were committed to other students in final group projects and because they had formed relationships with other students and faculty" (p. 4).

The "Computers and College Success for the ESL Student" block in fall 2003 enrolled only eight students. An interesting collaborative venture occurred when ESL students informed the instructors that one reason for low enrollment might be the expense of this five-credit block. The FYE coordinator and the Financial Aid Office worked together to make instructors and students aware of the Opportunity Grants and Scholarship Application that targets students who are ineligible for federal financial aid. Financial Aid representatives visited each class, distributed flyers, and explained this grant. Retention and persistence for these eight students was tracked, as was qualitative commentary from instructors.

In spring 2004, the "Exploring Connections in a Global Community" block linked three essays and a research paper. Co-curricular activities were also linked. Students chose two of five co-curricular activities, which included viewing films, visiting museums, and attending an activity on campus.

The internal PVCC document, The First Year Experience Program: Report on the 2003–2004 Year, identified program strengths and challenges for both faculty and students, program direction for the 2004–2005 academic year, and recommendations for continuing improvement. The report clearly showed the collaborative nature of most of the elements in Bresciani et al. (2004) iterative outcomes assessment model. In fact, Dale (personal communication, July 21, 2005) indicated that PVCC had used Bresciani's work to develop assessment strategies for these programs.

Paula Vaughn, director of service learning, who also does assessment for the Division of Student Affairs, and Dale are both on the Learning Community Committee. Vaughn is the co-chair of the Learning Community Steering Committee, which is essentially an academic committee. Dale (personal communication, July 21, 2005) says the fact that Vaughn co-chairs the Steering Committee speaks strongly to the collaboration in this effort. Dale admits that it is a continuing ownership and coordination challenge to make learning communities work well between two different divisions of the college. Who "owns" the program is always at issue.

Another interesting collaborative initiative at PVCC that speaks not only to collaboration but to student affairs promotion of students' academic success is between student affairs' Media Services and faculty. The coordinator of Media Services, Lily Fultz, intuitively understands learning outcomes and assessment, according to Dale (personal communication, July 21, 2005), and was responsible for initiating this innovate practice.

As indicated in an internal Media Services Assessment Plan provided to the researcher, PVCC students are often asked to give presentations in class and are expected to be able to "...use technological resources appropriately and efficiently" (p. 1). When Ms. Fultz recognized that students had little or no idea of the support services available to them, she developed an assessment rubric to measure student learning. The actual student learning outcome for Media Services is "Employ media production materials and technical resource tools to enhance academic review, classroom presentations and learning, through media technology training and support" (p. 1). Media Services

presentations were made in classes and included a pre-survey before
the classroom training and a post-survey after students had completed
their actual media presentations in the classroom. Walk-in surveys were
also conducted with walk-in student patrons. In addition, analysis was
conducted of the assessment rubric itself to determine student competency in its six criteria.

The PVCC internal document, 2004–05 PVCC Media Services
Student Learning Assessment and Findings Final Report was provided to this author. Improvements on this assessment included the
development of a Solutions Computer Mini Lab course offered by
the Computer Commons to supplement Media Services training with
computer/software literacy. The Mini Lab course was developed in collaboration with other divisions and with a desire for "...deeper learning
for students," (p. 3). Media Services advertises this Mini Lab course
to students during its own workshops to "...encourage more profound
presentation effectiveness for the students " (p. 3).

The post-findings survey suggested some question about the
redundancy of a pre/post survey given each semester in the classroom
and instructor support of the survey as measurement. This assessment
tool will be reevaluated in the 2005–06 academic year.

CHICAGO QUARTER, DEPAUL UNIVERSITY, CHICAGO

DePaul University, founded in 1898, has grown to become the
country's largest Catholic university and its eighth-largest private
university. Total enrollment in fall 2004 was 23,570 undergraduate,
graduate, and law students, both full and part time (DePaul University,
2005a). The freshman class size was 2,317, all of whom participate in
the Chicago Quarter in their first quarter at DePaul. Because DePaul is
in the heart of Chicago with its "...rich cultural heritage, lively business

communities, vibrant arts centers, diverse neighborhoods and active community and religious organizations," all first-year students register for a Chicago-themed course during their first autumn quarter (DePaul University, 2005b).

Students select Explore Chicago, a 10-week course; or Discover Chicago, a one-week immersion study the week before classes begin followed by 7 weeks of traditional course work in the fall quarter. In fall 2005, students could choose from 33 courses from a wide variety of academic disciplines for participation in Discover Chicago and 39 for Explore Chicago. Courses allow students to investigate the particular topic of that course using the city as its learning center. All courses familiarize students with "the metropolitan community, its neighborhoods, cultures, people, institutions, organizations and issues" (DePaul University, 2005b). According to Midge Wilson, director of First Year Program and professor of psychology (personal communication, August 15, 2005), 30 hours are in a course and 10 hours in the Common Hour. The Common Hour is the freshman seminar/co-curricular part of the Chicago Quarter that addresses transition to university life.

All courses are team-led by a faculty member, a staff professional, and a student mentor. The academic instructor proposes the class and is responsible for its core content. The staff professional is trained to help students learn about campus life and the administrative services available to them. The student leader receives a stipend, course credit, and training in how to teach students about issues of transition.

This early exposure to this unique relationship likely conveys to students in more ways than one—and perhaps especially to those who are first-generation Americans and belong to a group that DePaul seeks to admit and serve—that professors are approachable people, willing to work collaboratively with students and staff professionals alike (M. Wilson, personal communication, November 7, 2005).

According to Wilson, the Chicago Quarter Committee is comprised of six to seven faculty members and one student affairs member, currently the associate director of academic enhancement. The committee, which reports to the associate dean of liberal arts, reviews proposals for new classes and determines the annual assessment project. Although the program is housed in the Liberal Arts Department, courses are taught by faculty from a wide variety of disciplines and colleges.

Learning outcomes are developed for Discover and Explore Chicago as well as separate learning outcomes for the Common Hour. Assessment projects target one of these learning outcomes annually. This author was provided examples of two years of assessment results for the Chicago Quarter Program, one of which was more than six years old and one for 2004. In addition, the Proposed Learning Goal/Assessment Project for 2005 was provided.

The first assessment of the program took a broad look at its six major learning goals. The assessment concentrated on the pedagogical means of attaining program goals by the approximately 200 teaching participants. Only 10% of the teaching faculty participated in the assessment; however, they provided detailed descriptions of their best practices as well as methods that had not worked. As a result of this assessment, the program intended to do an assessment of student work in the next and subsequent years based on some of these best practices. Assessment of the Common Hour was also planned in coordination with the academic enhancement group of student affairs. The assessment was conducted and reported by the chair of the Chicago Quarter Committee.

The chair of the Chicago Quarter Committee and three of its members conducted the annual 2004 assessment project, "Reading into Writing":

> We have examined students' work: in this case, their final projects. Nearly all of these, we find, have required some writing based on course readings. Our interest in how students read, and what they do with the knowledge that comes from reading, dovetails nicely, we think, with the university's interest in student writing. (p. 1)

The report describes the sample, the assessment rubric used to examine final class project assignments, and results and conclusions.

In 2004 the annual assessment project examined student learning outcomes in relation to the fourth learning goal of Chicago Quarter classes—acquainting students with "...the Chicago metropolitan area, its neighborhoods, cultures, people, institutions, organizations, or issues" (p. 1). This assessment project was chosen as a result of suggestions made in an academic program review response to a self-study of the program. The response encouraged the Chicago Quarter Program "...to examine and enhance those aspects of the program that make the Chicago Quarter unique" (p. 1). Students' final project work would be examined and assessed based on a rubric developed by the Chicago Quarter Committee.

The Office of Academic Enhancement in Student Affairs also planned the assessment of the Common Hour as a result of the Academic Program Review. To date, there have been two assessment projects for the Common Hour. The chair of the Common Hour Steering Committee along with four committee members conducted the 2003–04 assessment project of "Student Mentor Lesson Plans and Academic

Success" and the 2004–05 assessment project of "Explore Chicago Letter to Students." The author was provided copies of both internal assessment documents.

The 2003–04 assessment project examined the effectiveness of the Common Hour lesson plans created by the student mentors to address the Academic Success Skills learning goal. Work from first-year students participating in the Common Hour was unavailable, so the Common Hour Steering Committee decided to collect lesson plans from Student Leaders teaching in fall 2003 and compare them to the results of the Academic Success Skills questions listed on the final course evaluations.

> From this assessment, it was important to note that well over 79% of the students felt they knew how to locate and use various university resources. Knowing where to go and who to call is key to a successful transition. This indicator clearly meets one main objective of the Common Hour. In addition, it became clear that the evaluation tool for measuring the Common Hour needed to be revised and the Common Hour Steering Committee would work to make sure that it accurately represents the Common Hour learning goals and objectives. (p. 3)

In 2004–05 Explore Chicago, students "were asked to generate a letter to new first year students sharing with them how the Chicago Quarter has assisted in their transition. Specifically, students were asked to provide insight and detail to the common hour learning goals" (p. 1).

> From this assessment, it was found that students were able to articulate the purpose of the common hour and

how it supported them in their transition. In addition, through the qualitative data assessment, three themes were revealed. These include personal growth; navigation and management of campus resources; and community and cultural experiences. (p. 2)

The Chicago Quarter has a comprehensive Web site that supports both faculty and students. The Faculty Information Center (http://condor.depaul.edu/~firstyr/faculty/index.html) includes a "Best Practices of First-Year Learning Goals" page with commentaries by individual faculty members and a "Best Practices of General Assignments and Activities" for seven different aspects of the program. Full descriptions of all courses in Explore and Discover Chicago as well as end-of-course evaluations are available for students.

The Common Hour also posts a description and specific student learning outcomes for its six goals (http://condor.depaul.edu/~firstyr/faculty/Common%20Hour%20Learning%20 Goals.doc). In addition, the Office of Academic Enhancement maintains a Blackboard site for all teaching team members that contains sample lesson plans and activities to fulfill the six Common Hour learning goals.

Wilson (personal communication, August 15, 2005) says that the challenge for the Chicago Quarter surrounds what changes are made and knowing if the changes are working. It is sometimes difficult to get faculty to change their ways and to attend best practice meetings to talk about standards and expectations. Making the proposal process for new courses in the Chicago Quarter curriculum more specific as to criteria and expectations of faculty members has helped improve the program.

WEATHERFORD RESIDENTIAL COLLEGE: AUSTIN ENTREPRENEURIAL PROGRAM, OREGON STATE UNIVERSITY

A land grant university, Oregon State University (OSU) was designated Oregon's state-assisted agricultural college in 1868 and would later add space, sea, and sun grant designations. More than 19,000 students attend OSU's Corvallis campus (Oregon State University, 2005a).

According to Rebecca Sanderson, director of student affairs research and evaluation (personal communication, October 27, 2005), in the center of campus is an architecturally pleasing 1928 building that had badly deteriorated over the years and had been unused since it closed in 1994, waiting for the funds to rehabilitate it as a residential college. The director of housing and dining approached the dean of the College of Engineering about the possibilities for a residential college during the College of Engineering's financial campaign to become a top 25 engineering school. The College of Engineering and the College of Business then discussed entrepreneurship as a focus for this venture, with the desired outcome that engineering students would benefit from learning business skills and business students would benefit from applied learning experiences. Visits to the University of Maryland, College Park, and the University of Virginia's residential colleges helped form the basis of Oregon State's program.

The Austin Entrepreneurship Program (AEP), named after its major benefactor, in the Weatherford Residential College opened its doors to students in fall 2004. Any students in any majors who see themselves in the entrepreneurial process are welcome. "The umbrella is the entrepreneurial concept, not a particular discipline or department," according to Dan Larson, assistant director of university housing and dining (personal communication, November 4, 2005).

188

AEP has the vision of developing entrepreneurs to fulfill the university's historical land grant and economic development mission. As the AEP Web site states, "Focused exclusively on entrepreneurship, Weatherford Hall has been renovated to meet the needs of entrepreneurs. Business, engineering and other OSU students with entrepreneurial interests live, dine, work and dream together 24–7" (Oregon State University, 2005b).

According to Sanderson and Larson (personal communications, October 27 and November 4, 2005, respectively), a good portion of the first year involved acclimating to the new space, the new program, and the new students. A faculty-in-residence program, faculty offices and classrooms, students, resident assistants, and programs were all in pilot mode. Basically, AEP had taken a curriculum and put it into a residence hall. There were lots of good concepts, but fitting it all together was a work in progress.

By the end of the first quarter, a positive vision and hard work gave way to the realization that some things needed to be changed (R. Sanderson, personal communication, October 27, 2005). Students were unclear about expectations or how to begin, primarily because the program and its leadership had not fully clarified those matters for themselves or the students. Faculty were unfamiliar with the concept of incorporating the student voice into the program. Residence hall staff were not clear about their roles beyond the traditional and did not feel they were a part of the initiative. Residents had a mixed investment in the program, and attendance at planned events was inconsistent. There was a lack of clarity about what students were to learn and invest in the experience. Leadership was not entirely clear on the curriculum in terms of what it was the students were to learn and how they would demonstrate that learning within a residential community. There was

189

some frustration among all involved, "yet, the desire to learn from that first year experience persisted and continued to be guided by the vision" (R. Sanderson, personal communication, October 27, 2005).

In the later part of the fall quarter, Sanderson was brought into the project to assist with discussions about formal assessment for the program. Questions persisted about how to develop a curriculum that leveraged the best from an entrepreneurship curriculum and a residential curriculum and that was transparent to students. The live-in faculty member, Justin Craig, assistant professor of entrepreneurship, knew the entrepreneurship curriculum and how to motivate and teach, but the educational process was not making the transition to a residential setting. Residential Life knew how to train resident assistants (RAs) and how to program for students, but not how to connect it all to the entrepreneurship curriculum. Larson joined Sanderson and Craig in order to have all parties present in the conversation and to attain greater understanding of all the roles in the curriculum development and delivery. The following questions needed to be answered: How do both curricular and co-curricular programs join with greater structure and greater transparency to students and others? What are the expectations for membership in the AEP and Weatherford Residential College? What do we want students to learn from this type of program? What methods are we using to deliver these outcomes? Are we maximizing the resources—staffing, hall environment, and the like? What is the role of hall staff—are they part of the delivery of the curriculum through the co-curriculum? How do we speak with one language? How does student development language fit with or translate into entrepreneurial language and vice versa? With these questions to form their discussion, Larson began consulting with student affairs and Craig with business and engineering faculty.

190

At the point that answers to these questions were developed and documented, the energy and creativity between residence life and the business and engineering faculty was incredible, according to Sanderson (personal communication, October 27, 2005). Larson, Craig, and Sanderson engaged in active and continuing conversations with department heads and the AEP steering committee. They reviewed the literature on entrepreneurship and student development and wrote a formal AEP curriculum. Four pillars of excellence and outcomes for each were developed (Oregon State University, 2005c). (Larson provided the author with the curriculum map for each term and each week in each term that covers delivery methods and the 19 core competencies from the four pillars of excellence (see Appendix F). RA selection and spring training were revamped into a combined RA/entrepreneurial training involving both residence life staff and entrepreneurial faculty that helped RAs understand how their roles fit with the entrepreneurial curriculum of the Residential College. Larson, Craig, and Sanderson worked with outcomes in mind and then set methods for measuring or tracking those outcomes over time—using a Web page for tracking and for assessment—so that students always know where they are in the process and what they are to get from the activities and programs in the hall. A two-year designation program in entrepreneurship was developed so students would have a tangible academic achievement from their involvement in the program. And, they kept the conversations going.

Reflection on the quality of the collaboration between Larson and Craig provides insight into why the end results were so generative. According to Larson (personal communication, November 4, 2005) both he and Craig recognized that they had to be deliberate about learning and learning support activities—that it was not an informal curriculum but a real curriculum with ties to research in student development and entrepreneurship. Their collaborative efforts began with the end in mind—what they wanted students to achieve by living in Weatherford Hall. Both men believed not only in the end product but in the process of delivering it. Craig had come to higher education from the business sector and understood the deliverables, while Larson had come into higher education as a student development specialist in residence life. These diverse backgrounds and their work to find a common language was another aid to the mutuality of their efforts. Actually, their collaboration was like an entrepreneurial venture itself—they became the start-up company for this project with the right team assembled—the scholarly knowledge and idea person, and the process and deliverables person. Larson says, "I never thought of myself as an entrepreneur," but "Justin says that I am, and it's just a different way that you look at what you do" (personal communication, November 4, 2005).

The focus in the 2005–06 academic year is still on first-year students, although the desire is to retain residents into their second year and beyond. A prerequisite for participation in the certificate program is that the student live in Weatherford. RAs are eligible to participate in the program as well.

Looking back, Sanderson and Larson agree that at inception, no one knew where the bumps were going to be. Everyone in the project had the same concept and thought that was enough to carry them through, but they didn't know what the end results would be and how all the pieces would fit. Once they sat down and started talking about assessment, the adage of "first things first" shaped and led them into enormous generativity.

According to Larson (personal communication, November 4, 2005), there has been unexpected learning for residence life as well. In the attempts to have Weatherford RAs understand the seamlessness of the curriculum and co-curriculum in a residential college model, he had to work with them to extend learning beyond the traditional RA experience. A pizza party can include a speaker who shares information or experiences on an entrepreneurial competency. A roommate conflict is not only about resolution of the conflict but also about what the residents learn from the experience that applies to entrepreneurship. RAs began to realize that they were actually participating in building residents' competencies and could see some end products, such as building teams, finding resources, and using daily action to build competency. This new way of looking at the role of an RA could lead to changing all residence hall staff training to a more curricular and competency-based program. What does residence life want students to learn from participation in hall programs? What should students learn from a conflict situation? What should they learn from a speaker? In other words, student learning outcomes include evidence of the transferability from the out-of-class experience to the in-class experience and vice versa, whether the setting is a residential college or a traditional residence hall. In essence, this venture operationalized the development and implementation of one curriculum designed for student learning versus the traditional two-curriculum model of the academic curriculum and co-curriculum.

CATHOLIC INSTITUTE FOR LASALLIAN SOCIAL ACTION (CILSA), SAINT MARY'S COLLEGE, MORAGA, CALIFORNIA

Founded in 1863 by the Roman Catholic Archdiocese of San Francisco, Saint Mary's College of California is one of the oldest colleges in the West. The campus originally was located in San Francisco but moved to Moraga in 1927. It was a men's college until 1970, when it became coeducational. Undergraduate students and graduate students each number about 2,500. According to its home page:

> Saint Mary's College celebrates three traditions: the classical tradition of liberal arts education, the intellectual and spiritual legacy of the Catholic Church, and the vision of education enunciated by Saint John Baptist De La Salle and developed by the Brothers of the Christian Schools and their colleagues in a tradition now more than 300 years old.
>
> The Catholic tradition fosters a Christian understanding of the whole person. The Lasallian tradition, rooted in the Christian Brothers' commitment to teaching, supports education that is truly transformative. The Liberal Arts tradition ensures that students develop habits of critical thinking and a desire for lifelong learning. (Saint Mary's College of California, 2005)

In September 1999, the Catholic Institute for Lasallian Social Action (CILSA) was created. According to its director, Janet Luce (personal communication, November 7, 2005) CILSA's inspiration came from the timing of several events. National Survey of Student Engagement data indicated that Saint Mary's students fell behind their peers in the area of community service. A new president and new vice provost for student life began their tenures. Students were indicating that service was occurring on campus but that the college was not providing any support for it. (There was no volunteer or community service office in student life at the time.) The district office in Napa, California, also was interested in Lasallian schools having a greater focus on student learning, and ultimately the district office and the president seeded two years of soft money to make CILSA a reality.

Luce began her tenure as director as sole employee of the center until another full-time staff member was added in January, followed by a half-time administrative assistant. Today CILSA has the director, an associate director for faith and justice formation, an assistant director for residential service learning, an associate director for community partnerships, and a part-time community service coordinator. Initially CILSA reported to the vice provost for student life. A faculty steering committee was formed and a good relationship developed with the dean of liberal arts. In 2002, CILSA's formal reporting relationship changed to the dean of liberal arts, who subsequently was promoted to vice provost of academics— a new position for Saint Mary's. The new vice provost brought CILSA along with her, symbolically focusing its importance and mission for the entire campus.

CILSA's mission parallels the institutional mission:

> Guided by the vision of Catholic social thought, animated by the Lasallian concern for the poor, and informed by the wisdom of the liberal arts, CILSA seeks to promote a culture of service as a means of embodying the values of faith, charity, and justice. (Catholic Institute for Lasallian Social Action, 2005)

Although CILSA has engaged in continuous assessment of the quality and impact of its service-learning efforts, the most extensive assessment came through the Western Association of Schools and Colleges (WACS) reaffirmation process and participation in the three-year research project led by the Boyer Center and funded by the Fund for the Improvement of Post-Secondary Education (FIPSE) to identify and assess best practices in academic and student affairs partnership programs. CILSA's director co-chaired the WACS social justice educational effectiveness committee with a faculty member. The extensive results of

195

that assessment can be found in Saint Mary's Self-Study for the Educational Effectiveness Review (Saint Mary's College of California, 2004, pp. 41–54). Benefits from participation in the Boyer FIPSE project have included developing and refining CILSA assessment procedures for program improvement. In addition, CILSA continues a relationship with its Boyer partner, who continues to provide assessment services that focus study on particular program offerings. CILSA's mission is an integral a part of the institution's mission and its focus on social justice. CILSA's programs include a social action clearinghouse that directs students to off-campus service opportunities; service immersion and leadership development opportunities that include the Bonner Leadership Americorps Program, which has quadrupled student participation since its inception; social justice forums (speaker series); and course-based social action programs. CILSA is both curricular and co-curricular, but its vision and the passion of its staff blur those distinctions. It provides the opportunity for all campus members to articulate and practice their faith and commitment in action.

CONCLUSION

Banta and Kuh (1998) identified six themes common to effective academic–student affairs collaborations that are evidenced in these four best practice institutions. All of these institutions have leadership support. Sometimes that is the president, but it is always the vice president of student or academic affairs who provides continuing vision and motivation for the collaboration. Additionally, leadership support flows from a strong institutional mission that supports "the blending of a philosophical commitment to being learning-centered, and the real commitment to develop a 'best practice' that can be assessed and evaluated" (Bresciani et al., 2004, p. 5).

In all four institutions, planning of curriculum (or program goals and outcomes) and assessment are shared responsibilities of faculty and student affairs staff committees. Coordination of in- and out-of-class learning experiences in these programs is supported by the collaborative assessment of their impact on students, and assessment findings are used to improve the student experience—be it with a learning community, a first-year program, a residential college, or a social justice mission.

Each institution has a different level of maturity in the expression of student learning and development outcomes and process indicators. Most admit that it is or has been an evolutionary process. They still see assessment as an iterative process from which they will continually learn and improve.

Each case institution reports, to different degrees, a continuing struggle over who "owns" the program and challenges in the development of trust based on mutual respect and understanding. Collaboration between student affairs and academic affairs may be a journey rather than a destination and a goal that will always need nurture and care. However, as these institutions show, the vision of what can be accomplished for students is stronger than any obstacle.

REFERENCES

Anderson, J. (2001, August 7). Why assessment is important to student affairs. *NetResults.* Retrieved September 1, 2003, from http://www.naspa.org/NetREsults/ PrinterFriendly.cfm?id=393

Banta, T. W., & Kuh, G. D. (1998). A missing link in assessment: Collaboration between academic and student affairs professionals. *Change,* 40–46.

Bresciani, M. J., Zelna, C. L., & Anderson, J. A. (2004). *Assessing student learning and development.* Washington, DC: National Association of Student Personnel Administrators.

Catholic Institute for Lasallian Social Action (CILSA). Retrieved August 11, 2005, from http://www.stmarys-ca.edu/prospective/ undergraduate_admissions/student_life_ and_services/life_on_ campus/cilsa/

Dale, P., & Shoenhair, C. (2002, March). *Learning-centered practice in student services.* Retrieved May 21, 2005, from http://www. eric.ed.gov. (ERIC Document Reproduction Service No. ED445732).

DePaul University. (2005a). About our students. Retrieved October 31, 2005, from http://www.depalu.edu/about-DP/about-students.asp

DePaul University. (2005b). The DePaul First-Year Program. Retrieved June 29, 2005, from http://www.condor.depaul. edu/~firstyr/chicago_qtr/index/html

Ewell, P. T. (1991). Assessment and TQM: In search of convergence. In J. S. Stark & A. Thomas (Eds.), *Assessment and program evaluation.* ASHE Reader Series, 1994. Needham Heights, MA: Simon & Schuster Custom Publishing.

Keeling, R. P. (Ed.). (2004). *Learning reconsidered: A campus-wide focus on the student experience.* Washington, DC: National Association of Student Personnel Administrators and American College Personnel Association.

Kezar, A., Hirsch, D. J., & Burack, C. (Eds.). (2002). *Understanding the role of academic and student affairs collaboration in creating a successful learning environment.* New Directions for Higher Education, no. 116. San Francisco: Jossey-Bass.

Kraybill, D. B. (2001, November 13). Can partnerships be assessed? The Boyer partnership project. *NetResults.* Retrieved August 18, 2005, from http://www.naspa.org/membershipmem/nr/PrinterFriendly.cfm?id=508

Maricopa County Community College District. (2004). *About PVCC.* Retrieved October 3,2005, from www.pvc.maricopa.edu/about.html

Oregon State University. (2005a). *About OSU.* Retrieved November 6, 2005, from http://oregonstate.edu/about

Oregon State University. (2005b). *Austin Entrepreneurial Program.* Retrieved November 6, 2005, from http://www.bus.OregonState.edu%5Cprograms%5CAustin_entrep.htm

Oregon State University. (2005c). *A.E.P. Tick.* Retrieved November 1, 2005, from http://www.bus.oregonstate.edu/programs/aeptick/aeptick.htm

Saint Mary's College of California. (2004, Fall). *Self-study for the educational effectiveness review: Western Association of Schools and Colleges.* Moraga, CA: Saint Mary's College.

Saint Mary's College of California. (2005). *About SMC.* Retrieved November 7, 2005, from http://www.stmarys-ca.edu

CHAPTER ELEVEN

Collaboration in the Community College

Edward J. Shenk
and Magdalena H. de la Teja

The community college is an egalitarian institution within the post-secondary system that provides higher education opportunities for about 40% of all college students. To ensure the success of these students as they matriculate through a community college, it is imperative that academic affairs and student affairs collaborate. This collaboration allows for the total immersion of the student in an environment where learning occurs both within and outside the classroom. Whether the partnership is initiated in academic affairs or student affairs, the executive leadership at the college must endorse and support these efforts. As noted in *Learning Reconsidered* (Keeling, 2004), "Learning is a complex, holistic, multi-centric activity that occurs throughout and across the college experience" (p. 6). This holistic view of learning will be referred to in this chapter as it relates to collaboration in the community college.

With the emergence of accreditation standards requiring student learning outcomes to be tied to the institution's mission, a successful effort requires close alignment of the learning outcomes in academic and student affairs with the mission of the college. The public demands that students acquire the skill sets that will enable them to succeed in the next stage of their lives, whether at work, at a transfer college or university, or for personal goal achievement. These transformative efforts in learning delivery and assessment create a more learning-centered institution and enable the college to allocate resources precisely. Another significant result will be "vibrant educational partnerships among members of the academic faculty and student affairs personnel in which all campus educators share broad responsibility for achieving defined student outcomes" (Keeling, 2004, p. 30).

This chapter suggests ways academic and student affairs personnel in community colleges can collaborate more effectively and addresses challenges associated with forming and sustaining effective collaborations. Selected community colleges nationwide are identified and their experiences with collaboration are featured. Below are a brief history of the community college and a description of its diverse student learners to set the context.

MISSION OF THE COMMUNITY COLLEGE

Somewhat paralleling the evolution of student services, the

community college, first referred to as a "junior college," emerged in 1897. Blocker, Plummer, and Richardson (1965) referred to the community college as an innovation of the 20th century. William Rainy Harper, president of The University of Chicago, was instrumental in implementing the concept of a two-year college as an extension of the university in 1897. Harper envisioned this new post-secondary institution as providing a college orientation and two years of academic preparation, thus freeing the university to focus on upper-division and graduate study. The concept also emerged on the West Coast in 1907. The California legislature established the junior college as part of the state system of education. Concurrently, public high school leaders envisioned the two-year college as an outgrowth of high school that would provide for the last two years of technical and vocational education. While the origin of the community college varies from state to state, the dual purpose of technical and vocational education and academic preparation for university transfer were the key components of the earliest models of these institutions (Monroe, 1972).

These purposes provided the basis for a comprehensive institution with a local contract. After World War II, the junior college became the community college and added continuing education community service classes as a means to educate a wider variety of people. A detailed account of the evolution of the community college can be found in Monroe (1972, pp. 1–20).

The community college was evolving into a democratized school that helped to meet the goals of a 1947 Truman report that aimed to increase access to post-secondary education for all U.S. citizens (Parker & Vecchitto, 1973). This effort resulted in the "open door college" with little or no tuition, mirroring the cost structure applied to public secondary education.

During this early period, community colleges also expanded services to students outside the classroom. Lillard (1930) examined the growth of Sacramento Junior College in California from 1922 to 1930. He wrote about the roles of the president, the faculty, the dean of men, and dean of women, who often had dual roles as faculty. At Sacramento Junior College, the student personnel committee (comprising the student services division) was composed of the dean of men (chairman), the dean of women, and the president, ex officio. Lillard stated, "This committee is responsible for admission and placement of students, physical, mental, and aptitude examinations, counseling, student personnel records and reports, keeping in touch with parents, work of student counselors, and checking students' scholastic standing" (pp. 82–83). Student enrollment at the college was 198.

Over time, the dual purposes of these two-year institutions were confounded with the expansion of the comprehensive community college, leading to confusion as to its mission. Shenk (1981) explained that these two divergent points of view resulted in an identity crisis in the 1960s and 1970s that remains to some extent today. The crisis revolved around the debate over the egalitarian (public schools) or equal opportunity model of the community college as opposed to the elitist (university) or meritocratic model. This conflict created much of the debate over the place of the community college in the higher education hierarchy. Most of the debate was resolved indirectly by the overall decline in resources from the late 1970s through the 1990s.

In the end, the community college accepted an educational mission based on universal access to enable students to transfer to four-year schools by completing lower-division course work, to provide students with high-quality technical and vocational education, to allow students to pursue lifelong education through noncredit community education and community service classes, and to provide student services as a retention support system. These components of the mission required collaborative effort between academic affairs and student affairs personnel to provide students the services that minimized barriers to access and allowed for the students' full attention in the classroom.

As one examines the evolution of student services (i.e., student affairs) from an arm of the president to address discipline issues in the late 1800s to a full-blown, separate organizational structure containing an array of services today, it is logical to conclude that the community college embraced these offerings in order to ensure student access and retention to graduation. The changes in student services also paralleled the more focused role of instruction as it gave up addressing discipline and became more intent on instructional delivery. As student service personnel increased their attention to student development, the instructional unit became more comprehensive. Both the vocational and transfer degrees in the community college were expanded by type, level of education, and relation with four-year colleges and businesses. As student services were added, including but not limited to counseling, expanded admission and records, financial aid offices, testing and course placement, orientation, student activities, disability services, and child care, the instructional units were addressing falling transfer rates, writing skills across the curriculum, basic skills, and ESL programs. These parallel efforts seldom intersected and were perceived as organizationally distinct.

With the changing student demographics of the 1980s and 1990s, it became imperative for the colleges to re-examine the way in which services were delivered as related to retention, persistence, and the ability to benefit. In California, a matriculation program was created to help students achieve their educational goals by following a process of seven components: admission, orientation, assessment of basic skills, academic advising, follow-up, research, and coordination. This program was codified in the California Title V regulations and mandated for implementation at all California community colleges. While never fully funded, the program was aimed at ensuring that students were appropriately assessed and placed in the correct level of English and math classes. It was also assumed that adequate follow-up would ensure that the students adhered to the educational plan created early in their tenure at the college. This program brought the academic affairs and student services units together to plan and implement these requirements. While all of the student affairs' activity was outside the classroom, the requirements did force dialogue over basic skills assessment testing and course placement and other related student success issues in the classroom. This program was advanced in different ways throughout the nation. While community colleges struggled with budget declines and student fee increases during the 1990s, the need for greater collaboration began to emerge to better serve an increasingly diverse student population.

STUDENTS ENROLLED IN COMMUNITY COLLEGES

Because community colleges offer open-access admission, they attract a diverse group of nontraditional learners. In fact, most community college students are nontraditional. A nontraditional student is defined as one who is "financially independent, attends part time, works full time, delays enrollment after high school, has dependents, is a single parent, or does not have a high school diploma" (Boswell & Wilson, 2004, p. 29). Community college students account for about 38% of total post-secondary enrollments (Martinez, 2004). This share will continue to increase, as has been the trend for the last 30 years. A growing number of traditional-age 18- to-24-year-olds are enrolling in community colleges, approximately half of the total public community college enrollment, whereas students age 30 or older comprise one third (Wilson, 2004). A greater percentage of females (57.3%) than males (42.7%) are enrolled, while ethnic minority students make up about one third of the total enrollment (see Table 11.1). Most of these minority students are either Black or Hispanic, and their numbers are projected to increase. Almost one half of community college students are first-generation college attendees. A higher percentage of students with disabilities enroll in community colleges than any other post-secondary institution (Phillippe, 2000) comprising 11% of the student population, and of those students about 5% indicate having a learning disability. (Wilson, 2004). Most (84%) community college students are employed either part time (30.4%) or full time (53.8%). Two thirds of community college students are enrolled part time (Wilson, 2004) compared to 22% at four-year institutions (Phillippe, 2000).

Table 11.1. **Percentage distribution by race/ethnicity, public 2-year institutions.**

American Indian	1.3%
Asian/Pacific Islander	6.1%
Hispanic	12.9%
Black	13.2%
White	66.4%

Source: Wilson, 2004, p. 25.

Given this diversity, it is important to recognize the challenges facing community colleges in meeting the needs of their learners. Price

(2004, p. 36) writes about the gaps in access and success identified in community colleges and describes the characteristics known to adversely affect persistence and success in college (see Table 11.2).

Table 11.2. **Percentage distribution of students by risk factor and type of institution.**

At-Risk Factors for Beginning Students	Public 2-year	Public 4-year	Private 4-year
Delayed Enrollment	45.6	18.0	13.0
GED/HS dropout	12.1	1.8	2.5
Part-Time Attendance	47.4	11.2	5.7
Financial Independence	34.5	8.1	6.7
One or More Children	20.6	4.2	2.9
Single Parent	10.0	2.4	1.5
Worked Full-Time	35.1	10.5	8.4

Source: Price, 2004, p. 37.

Open admission has resulted in community colleges offering expanded developmental education (remedial) courses. Wilson (2004) stated, "42 percent of community college freshmen enroll in at least one developmental course is an indication that the open door policy is able to fill a very real educational access need" (p. 26). These underprepared learners are deficient in reading, writing, and/or math skills, underscoring the urgency for community college academic affairs and student affairs units to become learning centered and to systematically identify learning outcomes that support student success.

Hamm (2004) described community college students as patching together a college experience—referred to as "swirling"—by dropping in, stopping out, or attending more than one institution. McClenney (2004) noted that 33% of community college students start at another institution, 12% have already earned a degree, and 11% are taking courses concurrently at another institution. Milleron and de los Santos (2004) reported that "Learning Swirl" was one of the seven clusters identified as important in the League for Innovation in the Community College's 2003 survey of its board member institutions. Students increasingly use community colleges for short-cycle training, industry certification, reverse transfer, or a post-baccalaureate option, often for job-specific training to meet their goals. However, the gaps in educational goal attainment suggest that "swirling" is not an effective strategy for all students.

The nontraditional characteristics of community college students oftentimes translate into gaps in learning success. Hamm (2004) stated that 62% of students who have three or more nontraditional characteristics and seek an associate's degree (see Table 11.3) leave without a degree, compared to 19% of traditional students who leave without an associate's degree. Only 11% of students who seek a bachelor's degree obtain a degree within five years, compared to 51% of traditional students. However, it has been observed that students who transfer with an associate's degree succeed at the upper division level at the transfer university or college at a better rate than the native students.

Table 11.3. **Persistence to degree for traditional and nontraditional students.**

	Highly Non-Traditional Students	Traditional Students
Seek but do not earn associate's degree	62%	19%
Seek and obtain bachelor's degree	11%	51%

Source: Hamm, 2004, p. 30.

How community college students perceive their relationship to college makes a difference in their learning success. Hamm (2004) noted that about 20% of all college students perceive themselves as employees seeking an education rather than working to support themselves while in college. Most of these "employee students" begin their education in a community college and are less likely to persist in college and more likely to drop out due to their behaviors related to attendance.

Ethnic minorities are more likely to attend a community college for a variety of reasons, including open admissions, proximity to home, and affordability. According to the U.S. Census Bureau projections to 2010, the fastest growing groups in the 18- to-24-year-old population are ethnic minorities, who are projected to enroll in community colleges in large numbers. The fastest growing racial/ethnic group at community colleges is students of Hispanic origin, primarily self-identified as Mexican, Mexican American, or Chicano descent (Phillippe, 2000). According to the *New York Times* (Pear, 2005), the U.S. Census Bureau indicates that the nation as a whole will soon reflect what is happening in California and Texas, where racial and ethnic minorities account for more than half the population. Steve Murdock, the state demographer of Texas, has often said that the future of Texas, as well as the nation, depends on how effective we are in educating our ethnic minority populations who are presently the "new majority" in several states.

Furthermore, Price (2004) indicated that persons of color are proportionately overrepresented in lower income groups. This is an important characteristic because of demographic trends cited by Price (2004):

> In 2000, almost 50 percent of high school completers from low-income families enrolled in college immediately after finishing high school compared with 77 percent of high school completers from high-income families. A similar gap is present among students from different racial and ethnic backgrounds. (pp. 35–36)

As previously noted, one of the seven main risk factors for college failure is delayed college enrollment.

Other factors contribute to making learning a challenge for community college students. Almost 15% of students speak a language other than English in the home (most frequently Spanish) (Phillippe, 2000), resulting in the need for ESL programs (Wilson, 2004). The demand for ESL programs is projected to increase to accommodate these students' needs. More than one third of community college students have at least one dependent (Wilson, 2004). In addition, 93% of community college students commute to college, which limits their opportunities to engage in learning activities on the college campus (Hamm, 2004).

There are notable gaps in community college student persistence and degree or transfer goal attainment. Price (2004) explained that

211

35% of community college students who initially enrolled in 1995–96 attained a certificate or degree within six years, compared to 60% of students who initially enrolled in public four-year institutions. The gaps are greater for Blacks and Hispanics (see Table 11.4).

Table 11.4. **Persistence to certificate or degree over 6-year period, by race/ethnicity.**

Black	26%
Hispanic	29%
White	38%
Asian	39%

Source: Price, 2004, p. 36.

The diversity of students enrolled at community colleges and the gaps in success among varying student groups suggest that it is imperative for academic and student affairs professionals to collaborate in designing programs, services, and systems that place the student at the center of the transformative learning experience. The varying learning styles and needs of these diverse students must also be *reconsidered* since we know as educators that one size does not fit all.

Promoting Effective Collaboration: Opportunities and Challenges

The learning college movement began in community colleges under the leadership of Terry O'Banion in the late 1990s. Community college academic and student affairs professionals are in an ideal position to work collaboratively to build on their student-centered and teaching-centered values and mission to begin the transformation into a learning-centered organizational culture. Student affairs professionals at these two-year institutions have contributed to supporting a paradigm shift from teaching to learning and to promoting the notion that student learning takes place outside as well as inside the classroom. Although some very promising collaborative efforts have been initiated at a number of community colleges based on O'Banion's (1997) learning college principles, much more work remains to be done to realize the movement's potential.

O'Banion (1997) identified six learning college principles: (1) creating substantive change in learners; (2) engaging learners as full partners; (3) creating and offering a variety of learning options; (4) assisting learners in forming and participating in collaborative learning activities; (5) defining roles in response to the needs of learners; and (6) documenting improved and expanded learning. In the League for Innovation in the Community College's Learning College Project, O'Banion and others led an effort that began in 2000 to support several community colleges in applying these principles. Although collaboration is not specifically mentioned, principles 3 and 5 come closest to the concept. McClenney (2004) indicated that one of the significant lessons learned from the Learning College Project is that the transformation in institutional culture must result in a "collective responsibility for student learning" (p. 12) that cuts across classrooms, disciplines, departments, and divisions. *Learning Reconsidered* (Keeling, 2004) stated:

> Mapping the learning environment for sites in which learning can occur provides one approach to supporting transformative learning that identifies strength in col-

213

laboration—linking the best efforts of educators across
the institution to support student learning. (p. 13)

Learning Reconsidered 2 (Keeling, 2006), building on that principle,
provides a practical roadmap:

> Mapping a learning environment is the process of rec-
> ognizing, identifying, and documenting the sites for
> learning activities on campus; it provides the framework
> within which student affairs educators can link their
> programs and activities to learning opportunities. It is
> leveraging our programs and resources in ways that pro-
> mote opportunities to deepen student learning. Fresh
> collaborations for learning are realized by focusing on
> creating learning outcomes that support student suc-
> cess. A campus committed to engaging members in new
> paradigms of learning, practicing new pedagogies, and
> creating experiences to support learning must be truly
> 'learner-centered.' This means that all campus educators
> (both faculty and student affairs professionals) must re-
> view and consider changing their practice. Mapping an
> environment informs practitioners about the kinds of
> activities that will enhance classroom experiences and
> help the campus develop a broader understanding of
> transformative learning. (p. 12)

As practitioners, we all know, however, that collaboration between
academic and student affairs professionals in mapping the learning
environment, designing processes and programs that support student
learning, and identifying, measuring, and documenting student learning are oftentimes easier said than done. That said, it is worthwhile
to review what we have learned about the essential dimensions and

interconnections of effective collaborations between student affairs and academic affairs professionals within the community college.

Medsker (1960) describes the results of a survey in 1956–57 about student personnel services (i.e., student affairs) in 75 two-year colleges and recommended:

> There should be a plan for close coordination between those who perform personnel services and those who teach, so that the curriculum and the instructional program are strengthened by information and ideas from those who work closely with students outside the classroom. (p. 167)

As early as the mid-20th century, researchers recognized the need for student services personnel and teachers to work closely; however, the historical paradigm resulted in an emphasis on teaching and the curriculum and not on student learning. Also, at that time many of the personnel responsible for providing student services were teaching faculty who were assigned that role. It is almost half a century later, and researchers are challenging community colleges to make a paradigm shift from teaching to learning and to liberating the organization from historical processes, approaches, and systems so that organizational transformation can result (McPhail, 2005). *Learning Reconsidered* (Keeling, 2004) said, "Our vision of learning assumes that distinctions among terms such as personal development, student development, and learning are meaningless, if not destructive," and therefore proposes the "…integration of all domains of learning and involvement of all educators, regardless of their campus role" (p. 3). McPhail (2005) advocated for student affairs professionals to be "…change agents in the transformation of institutional cultures into environments more open and responsive to student learning" (p. 99).

215

Learning Reconsidered (Keeling, 2004) defined learning "as a comprehensive, holistic, transformative activity that integrates academic learning and student development, processes that have often been considered separate, and even independent of each other" (p. 2). Furthermore, to help today's learners adapt to a constantly evolving, information-based, global economy, *Learning Reconsidered* emphasized the need for the focus of education to shift from mere information transfer to identity development (transformation). "Such an approach to teaching and learning must include the full scope of a student's life. It cannot be accomplished in the classroom alone. It cannot be accomplished out of the classroom alone, either" (p. 10). *Learning Reconsidered 2* (Keeling, 2006) indicates "Learning has physiological, social and emotional, cognitive, and developmental dimensions...most people need to find patterns and meaning in what they are learning. Active, experiential learning followed by cognitive processing in emotionally safe environments produces extremely powerful, or transformative, learning" (p. 5). Knowing this about how students learn is a motivator for student affairs professionals to work collaboratively within the college setting to design programs, services, and activities for students that provide those safe learning environments outside the classroom that deliberatively contribute to student learning outcomes.

Two student affairs practitioners, Mitchel Livingston and Lucy Croft, in a June 2005 audio conference titled *Building Bridges Between Academic Affairs and Student Affairs*, described elements essential to effective collaborations and desirable interconnections. It is important to work laterally, relate across organizational boundaries, and transcend institutional silo culture. Academic and student affairs professionals should be encouraged to read the same literature about student learning and learning colleges and dialogue about these issues. *Learning*

216

Reconsidered 2 (Keeling, 2006) reinforces this concept by indicating that student affairs professionals need to become "dialogue experts," bringing diverse people together "to help them articulate common goals for learning and to design programs that support that goal in a variety of contexts, across numerous learning styles and kinds of intelligences" (p. 62). Livingston and Croft (2005) recommend that faculty and student affairs staff members participate in the same professional development activities to identify common goals about student learning and develop a shared knowledge base. To this end, community colleges should plan a joint retreat for academic and student affairs personnel to inventory the collaborations that already occur between them as a way to encourage further combined efforts. Working together to identify and assess student learning outcomes is essential. Infusing these collaborative practices into the institutional culture in an intentional and strategic manner can have a transforming effect.

De la Teja and Kramer (1999) offered this summary statement in their research about student learning in the community college:

> The challenge for student affairs professionals is to work collaboratively with faculty to understand the character of community college student involvement, to reward involvement in learning activities that naturally occur outside of class, and to provide co-curricular experiences that utilize learners' out of class experiences to enrich their in-class learning, and vice versa. (p. 95)

The resulting benefits for meeting this challenge and promoting effective collaboration between academic and student affairs personnel are (1) shared values, including mutual trust and respect for each other's roles in enhancing student learning; (2) a better understanding and holistic approach to addressing the needs of diverse community college learners; (3) shared responsibility and accountability for student learning by focusing on learning outcomes; and (4) a transformation in culture from silo to systemic change that places student learning at the center of the community college mission.

As we examine the collaborative efforts at select community colleges, an important consideration is how they overcome differences in learning models. The challenge exists between the academic learning model and the student affairs learning model. The academic affairs view of the centrality of the curriculum suggests that faculty consider learning as an intellectual development within the cognitive framework. Student affairs professionals view learning more broadly as a developmental process, not a product such as mastery of discipline, graduation, or post-degree employment (Arnold & Kuh, 1999). This factor, when coupled with the historical community college mission of teaching and a budget based on full-time equivalencies (FTEs) generated in the classroom, puts a lot of stress on the equal partnership in the student learning perspective.

Grund (2004) stated, "Part of the problem in entering the academic affairs/student affairs partnership is that faculty hold all of the cards" (p. 11). In-class and out-of-class learning fail to converge on many campuses due to the existence of silos that focus on learning environments that are exclusive of each other. Ways to minimize these silos include joint committees, organizational structures—usually where the student service administrator reports to the instructional vice president, very rarely the other way around—and student involvement outside the classroom specifically related to classroom objectives, such as Symposium on the Gulf War or Constitution Day. The challenge is further exacerbated by the language of the two areas and the role of the instructor versus the service provider. In this chapter, we will discuss

218

the efforts of several colleges that are working to overcome these challenges to transforming institutional culture and becoming more learning-centered.

CULTURE OF EVIDENCE

An increased interest in accountability in education in the past decade or so has arisen from declining resources and rising costs, increasing enrollments of diverse learners who have not fared well, more government intervention resulting from public distrust, and global competition in an evolving information-based economy. Although all of that may sound ominous, during the same period community colleges have received positive feedback from government entities as well as the public about their contributions to student access and success. According to McClenney (2004/05), a public opinion survey funded by the Ford Foundation indicates that Americans believe community colleges, besides being conveniently located and easily accessible as well as affordable, provide high-quality education and good job training. To maintain and enhance this public support, it behooves these institutions to promote a culture of evidence of accountability by documenting what their students have learned. Dowd (2005) characterizes "culture of evidence" as one in which "institutional research functions play a more prominent role and faculty and administrators are more fully engaged with data and research about success of their students, using those data to make decisions" (p. 6).

McClenney (2004) noted that in the League for Innovation's Learning College Project, O'Banion continuously posed two questions of the participants: "How will this decision/action/program/policy improve and expand student learning?" and "How do we know?" (p. 14). McClenney (2004) stated:

> To be specific, we will decide what questions need to be answered about student progress, student attainment, and student success in our institutions. We will identify the critical performance indicators that will tell us how we're doing. We will collect clear and credible evidence of institutional performance on those indicators. And we will break down the data by race and ethnicity, income, gender, and age so that we will have a genuine understanding of how student groups may differentially fare in our colleges. Then we will use the data and our understandings of it to target improvements in the work we do with students. (p. 14)

Medsker (1960), in a study of two-year colleges in the mid-1950s, recognized that an important role of student personnel staff was to gather and disseminate information about students, although he lamented that because of limited staff, this task was often left undone. Does this sound all too familiar and applicable today? Community colleges are much more complex in the 21st century compared to half a century ago; however, *Learning Reconsidered* (Keeling, 2004) nonetheless recommended that student affairs be "developed" (p. 25) as a source of key information about students, their lives, and their learning. Student affairs professionals have an opportunity to step up to the plate and be leaders and advocates for identifying learning outcomes, collecting data, and working with institutional effectiveness colleagues to analyze the data, helping staff and students on the campus make sense of it all—a process of meaning making—and implementing improvements that enhance student learning and success.

Being able to assess student learning and certify what competencies and skills a student has gained is a growth industry of the future (McClenney, 2004) as people move about the world for employment in the global economy. The shift from an industrial economy to an information-based, global economy is necessitating different skills, such as problem-solving skills; interpersonal skills; a positive "cognitive style" that allows workers to cope with an accelerated pace of change in the workplace (Carnevale & Desrochers, 2004); literacy skills, including computer literacy skills; self-directed, lifelong learning skills; and global diversity skills needed to build an inclusive work environment among employees of different backgrounds and cultures (Ruiz, 2002/03). These skills and others are learned in the classroom as well as outside the classroom in service-learning, in student government, in sessions with academic advisors, in student leadership development experiences, in workshops led by counselors, and in student life co-curricular programming. Student affairs professionals provide students opportunities "to learn through action, contemplation, reflection, and emotional engagement as well as information acquisition" (Keeling, 2004, p. 11). *Learning Reconsidered 2* (Keeling, 2006) specifically defines as significant student learning outcomes: (1) cognitive complexity; (2) knowledge acquisition, integration, and application; (3) humanitarianism; (4) civic engagement; (5) interpersonal and intrapersonal competence; (6) practical competence; and (7) persistence and academic achievement.

Accrediting agencies, parents, business and industry, and government will continue to demand accountability. Community colleges must provide documented evidence that students are learning and are meeting their educational goals within a reasonable period of time, as well as being prepared to work in a diverse and technologically complex global economy. Academic and student affairs professionals must work

221

collaboratively to specify measurable student learning outcomes and systematically document what students learn in the classroom as well as outside the classroom in order to build a culture of accountability. Helfgot and Culp (2005) suggested that student affairs professionals document satisfaction with and effectiveness of programs in contributing to student learning and to supporting the college's mission. These authors (2005) concluded:

> ...data can be collected, analyzed, and used to drive both discussion and action, and community college student affairs professionals can embrace the work that needs to be done and show—with both anecdotes and evidence—that what they do really matters to their institutions, to their colleagues, and most importantly, to their students. (p. 17)

SURVEY OF BEST PRACTICES AND RECOMMENDATIONS

To determine the direction a community college may take to enhance campus collaborative efforts, the authors solicited responses to a survey from several colleges. The community colleges chosen to receive a survey are in different parts of the country, vary in size and diversity of student enrollment (including percentage of "new majority" students), and demonstrate an interest in collaboration between academic and student affairs. Nine community colleges, including a few of the League of Innovation Learning College Project institutions, were invited to participate, and seven completed the survey. The administrators who completed a survey had varying titles, including vice president of student services, student affairs, or student development; vice president of student support and success systems; executive vice president of educational programs; and vice chancellor for learning and student development. The authors are grateful for the time expended by the administrators at Austin Community College in Texas, Chandler-Gilbert Community College in Arizona, Community College of Baltimore County in Maryland, Mira Costa College in California, Moraine Valley Community College in Illinois, Napa Valley College in California, and Santa Barbara City College in California. Table 11.5 summarizes the main themes identified from the survey responses.

Table 11.5. **Summary of survey responses.**

Collaboration	Austin Community College
Student Population Profile	Headcount: 29,000; New Majority: 39.5%; FT: 25.9%
Student Learning Outcomes (SLOs)	Utilized alternative self study to identify SLOs; new joint Student Access and Success Committee dialoguing about student learning outcomes
Professional Development Activities	Professional Dev. Office provides training to all staff on student learning; AA & SA exploring areas for greater collaboration
AA/SA Collaboratively Determine the Assessment Processes to Measure Student Learning	Done in isolated pockets; Office for institutional effectiveness has online assessment; increased dialogue between units
Essential Elements of Effective Collaboration	Regular communication; shared responsibility for student learning; AA&SA at leadership table
Barriers to Forming and Sustaining Effective Collaborations	Organizational silos; lack of common language; inadequate funding and staffing
Best Practices: Effective Collaboration and How it is Assessed	Transition to College Success Course since 1997–98; assessments via student feedback; evaluated based on students' GPA, completion rate, and retention

Collaboration	Chandler–Gilbert Community College
Student Population Profile	Headcount: 13,000; New Majority: 33%; FT: 28.5 %
Student Learning Outcomes (SLOs)	Enhancing student learning success; service-learning program (14 yrs.) used to identify SLOs
Professional Development Activities	Prof. Dev. Key to success; training for all new faculty in service-learning program; travel together as a team to various local and national prof. dev. events
AA/SA Collaboratively Determine the Assessment Processes to Measure Student Learning	Regular feedback from community users; improves in-class climate
Essential Elements of Effective Collaboration	Dedicated leadership from AA & SA, pres. and board; broad-based effort; long-term joint programs; service-learning–14 years
Barriers to Forming and Sustaining Effective Collaborations	Rapid growth in enrollment and avoiding the "silo" effect; need expanded resources; reallocating funds to sustain program
Best Practices: Effective Collaboration and How it is Assessed	Service Learning Program since 1991 is Best Practice Program; ongoing assessment from community organizations, students and faculty

Collaboration	Community College of Baltimore County
Student Population Profile	Headcount: 19,972; New Majority: 37%; FT: 36%
Student Learning Outcomes (SLOs)	College-wide Learning Outcomes Assessment Advisory Board (LOAAB) est. in 2001 & reports to Vice Chancellor for Learning and Stud. Dev.; Guide for Learning Outcomes and Learning Assessment
Professional Development Activities	Learning & Teaching Excellence Ctr.; Vanguard Council for Innovation & Stud. Learning (VCISL) annual learning fair & Chats; SLO Guide; Developmental Educ. Symposium; Learning Community for New Faculty
AA/SA Collaboratively Determine the Assessment Processes to Measure Student Learning	Team up; 5 stages: 1) design and propose; 2) implement, collect & analyze data; 3) redesign the course/program 4) implement revisions and reassess learning
Essential Elements of Effective Collaboration	Understanding of: what teachers face in the classroom and of each others values; respect and belief that students will be served well in both arenas

Collaboration	Community College of Baltimore County
Barriers to Forming and Sustaining Effective Collaborations	Differing philosophies and values of what is best for students and an unwillingness to listen to each other
Best Practices: Effective Collaboration and How it is Assessed	Achieving Academic Success Course—students complete a Graduated Learning Plan; assessment of whether students completed a plan and their expression of how it would lead them to academic success

Collaboration	Mira Costa College
Student Population Profile	Headcount: 9,880; New Majority: 41%; FT: 32.2%
Student Learning Outcomes (SLOs)	Academic Senate Outcomes Assessment Comm. w/ AA & SA reps. Flex week presentations on SLOs; speakers on learning college principles
Professional Development Activities	Flex week presentations on SLOs; speakers on learning college principles
AA/SA Collaboratively Determine the Assessment Processes to Measure Student Learning	Outcome Assessment committee composed of AA & SA reps.
Essential Elements of Effective Collaboration	Commit time and resources; establish monthly joint meetings; support of president and board who require accountability are key; SA reach out to AA and listen
Barriers to Forming and Sustaining Effective Collaborations	Refusal to share resources; lack of leadership from president; estrangement between AA & SA staff
Best Practices: Effective Collaboration and How it is Assessed	Hired Director of Tutoring & Retention who reports to AA & SA VP's: set up Learning Communities project (2004–05); retained students at 84% compared to 65% in regular programs

Collaboration	Moraine Valley Community College
Student Population Profile	Headcount: 16,077; New Majority: 21.8%; FT: 41%
Student Learning Outcomes (SLOs)	Vanguard learning College (VLC); initiated org. culture change that is learning centered and innovation focused; learning outcomes published in syllabus; 7 milestones for student transition & success; SLO Primer

225

Collaboration	Moraine Valley Community College
Professional Development Activities	VLC started in 2000–01; Learning College Day open to SA/AA; new faculty orientation week; college-wide training on assessment; SLO Primer; Center for Teaching and Learning
AA/SA Collaboratively Determine the Assessment Processes to Measure Student Learning	Utilize Learning Dialogues to share info; college-wide continuous improvement—DRIVE (Define; Review; Initiate; Evaluate; Integrate);
Essential Elements of Effective Collaboration	College commitment via values, mission, vision; president leads w/ specified expectations; org'l culture focused on stud. learning; effective communication
Barriers to Forming and Sustaining Effective Collaborations	Lack of top leadership; lack of across campus communication; territorial and self-serving attitude; lack of clear expectations
Best Practices: Effective Collaboration and How it is Assessed	First-year Experience (2000) supporting student learning: course placement testing, orientation, Student. Success course; Academic Plan; evaluated regularly; students taking course have higher GPA and completion rate

Collaboration	Napa Valley College
Student Population Profile	Headcount: 6,951; New Majority: 52%; FT: 27.6%
Student Learning Outcomes (SLOs)	Joint AA/SA training on SLOs; set timeline to establish SLOs and mapping : started in 2004
Professional Development Activities	Teaching and Learning Center for all staff (est. 2003)
AA/SA Collaboratively Determine the Assessment Processes to Measure Student Learning	Process included in college program reviews
Essential Elements of Effective Collaboration	Mission, president, key joint committees, the people, SA faculty part of Academic Senate
Barriers to Forming and Sustaining Effective Collaborations	Structure prevents communication; not understanding laws governing programs; lack of funding & common language

Collaboration	Napa Valley College
Best Practices: Effective Collaboration and How it is Assessed	Matriculation Steering Committee–1987–present; evaluate via validation studies: assessment survey, orientation and advising; follow-up and research; assess via annual program evaluation

Collaboration	Santa Barbara City College
Student Population Profile	Headcount: 16,914; New Majority: 37.5% FT: 37.1%
Student Learning Outcomes (SLOs)	2nd year of SLO project; Academic Senate took lead and SA involved; organized SA/AA into a single unit– Educational Programs
Professional Development Activities	Planning joint workshops for AA/SA faculty and staff on SLOs
AA/SA Collaboratively Determine the Assessment Processes to Measure Student Learning	Plan to establish institutional SLOs and strategies for in-class assessment
Essential Elements of Effective Collaboration	AA & SA units under Executive VP; cross- functional duties; inst. priority; respect & understand each others role; goals clearly defined
Barriers to Forming and Sustaining Effective Collaborations	Due to org'l structure and commitment to holistic approach to meeting student needs, there are no barriers
Best Practices: Effective Collaboration and How it is Assessed	College Achievement Program and Gateway to Success Program are Best Practice programs; broad collaborative effort; regular assessment and research is ongoing; almost a 10–12% improvement in success rate in Best Practices over regular programs

Several main factors emerge from the survey responses that suggest guidelines to promote successful collaborative efforts at other colleges. While student learning outcomes (SLOs) seem to be a driving force in collaborative ventures between academic affairs and student affairs, the involvement of key personnel on joint committees with cross-functional roles and shared responsibilities is also an essential element. These factors come as no surprise. At Napa Valley College, the vice president of student services is an advocate of collaboration and has made it one of the hallmarks of a 30-plus-year career at the college. That the academic affairs and student affairs leaders respect each other's roles and have the desire to collaborate was noted by several responders as important to successful collaboration. Collaborative efforts must be tied to strong leadership support from the college president and the board of trustees who lead the college in setting a mission, vision, and values that form a foundation for a transformative organizational culture focused on student success. The president brings the team together and expects academic affairs and student affairs personnel to work collaboratively, whether in a model with an executive vice provost over both areas or a model with separate vice presidents.

All responders reported commitment to ongoing joint professional staff development efforts as an important factor for collaboration. Al Starr, vice chancellor for learning and student development at the Community College of Baltimore County (CCBC), noted, "Each year since the 2000–01 academic year, CCBC has dedicated a day within its operational and academic calendar for a college-wide professional conference for all faculty and staff." The emergence of teaching and learning centers as a vehicle for providing professional development also facilitates this collaborative evolution. Moraine Valley Community College and CCBC provided in-depth descriptions of their varied professional development programs to help faculty and staff understand and buy into the learning college principles and to develop a common language as they collaborate. Both of these institutions developed in-house manuals to teach faculty and staff how to write measurable student learning outcomes.

SLOs are being used as a means to bring the various units in student services and instruction together to focus on student success. Specific SLOs should drive all campus activities, especially collaborative programs in academic affairs and student affairs, and should be used as a basis for accountability by assessing effectiveness in student learning.

Long-term committees, courses, and programs comprising faculty and student personnel staff are another means of fostering collaboration. Several responders reported sharing financial resources and personnel between academic affairs and student affairs to promote student learning and success. These exemplary programs are designed to serve students in both the instructional and student service arenas. Notable best practices are Service Learning Program at Chandler–Gilbert, First-Year Experience at Moraine Valley Community College, the Gateway to Success Program at Santa Barbara City College, the Learning Communities Project at Mira Costa College, the Transition to College Success Course at Austin Community College, and the Achieving Academic Success Course at CCBC.

In every case, an assessment process was embedded in the best practices program, and responders recognized its importance in building a culture of evidence of accountability. "What is valued, gets measured," stated Nancy Bentley, vice president of student services at Moraine Valley Community College. Assessment of programs at the colleges surveyed included qualitative and quantitative methods, such as satisfaction surveys, measurement of achievement of SLOs (including effect on students' grade point average (GPA) and retention from semester to semester), focus groups of students and faculty, program reviews, and other institutional effectiveness measures. Moraine Valley Community College uses *The Milestone Approach to Student Transition and Success* to assess student services. Student services are divided into seven student milestone phases: (1) prospective students, (2) applicants, (3) first-semester registrants, (4) first-year students, (5) continuing students, (6) graduates, and (7) lifelong learners. Two major questions are used to assess outcomes: "What impact do we want to have on our students at each phase?" and "What do we want them to know and be able to do as a result of the student services and programs that we provide?" Another important area to assess might be: "To what extent do student services and academic affairs collaborate on student learning outcomes during each of these transitions?"

Besides the successes, several barriers to effective collaboration were identified. A common comment was that communication between academic affairs and student affairs personnel is paramount for effective collaboration. If communication does not exist, along with a feeling of connectedness, then collaboration will not emerge. Lack of trust, understanding, and respect for each other's roles in student learning were also noted as barriers. Organizational structures that reward silo or solo thinking as well as the lack of commitment from the president will also prevent collaborative program development. Lack of resources to support and encourage collaborative efforts is definitely considered a barrier, especially in times of declining state funding for higher education. Some respondents alluded to the fact that inadequate funding may stifle collaboration due to staffing shortages and job overload, which result in decreased energy to devote to collaborative efforts.

CONCLUSION

Lundquist and Nixon (1998) suggested that it is important to do away with compartmentalization and encourage collaborative and blended leadership roles and the sharing of resources and rewards that lead to systemic change, including a holistic response to student learning. The elimination of compartmentalization of programs and services "promotes a learner-centered focus within the college and establishes a culture that encourages collective responsibility for student success, opportunity, and achievement" (p. 46). Clements, Harvey-Smith, and James (2005) indicated that the essential elements of the institutional transformation process include leadership (student affairs and academic affairs) at the table; communication that includes multiple opportunities for stakeholders to share ideas and respond to proposed change; institutional support, including funds for professional development; integration of change into the life of the college and infusion into core competencies, strategic planning; and ongoing processes and practices (i.e., culture change). It is through this institutional transformation process that community colleges can achieve the seventh learning college principle, to "create and nurture an organization that is both open and responsive to change and learning" (Harvey-Smith, 2005, p. 113). These components are demonstrated in varying degrees at the colleges surveyed.

Kolins (2001) studied collaborative practices between academic and student affairs personnel as reported by the chief academic officer (CAO) and the chief student affairs officer (CSAO) at public two-year institutions nationwide. He mailed a questionnaire to the CAO and the CSAO at randomly selected public two-year colleges for a total sample of 1,054 possible respondents; 444 (42.1%) administrators responded to the survey. Kolins found that the perceptions were generally positive "as evidenced by the large number of collaborative practices that occur between academic and student affairs personnel at public two-year colleges" (p. 53). He also found that CAOs perceive that collaboration between the two units is important to enhancing student success, as do CSAOs, and that CAOs, more than CSAOs, tended to set the tone for collaboration. His study underscores the importance of direct communication between the unit leaders and senior-level administrator validation of collaborative practices in community colleges. Kolins recommended: (1) creating an environment in which the CAO and CSAO meet frequently to discuss areas of mutual concern; (2) support and encouragement from the president, especially for collaboration between academic and student affairs in planning, decision making, and assessing student learning; (3) allocating funds for new and existing collaborative programs; and (4) specifically having the two units work collaboratively in academic advising, advising student organizations, and helping undecided students select a major. We corroborated Kolins' findings in our survey and concur with this summary of recommendations.

As we reflect on the success of the collaborative efforts at the colleges we surveyed, we want to conclude with a summary statement made by Jack Friedlander, executive vice president of educational programs at Santa Barbara City College:

> The goals and objectives of a college's student success efforts needed to be clearly defined, included in the institution's priorities, and assessed on a periodic basis. There needs to be a recognition that multiple units of the college play a role in the progress students make on each of the learning outcome measures. Plans for increasing the percentage of students that achieve desired learning outcomes need to involve faculty and staff from instructional and student support units of the college." (personal communication, August 5, 2005)

To achieve effective collaboration and ultimately student success, resulting in a better educated citizenry, community colleges must break down historical barriers and paradigms, and acknowledge as well as celebrate the complementary roles academic affairs and student affairs play in assisting students in learning and in attaining their educational goals.

REFERENCES

Arnold, K., & Kuh, D. (1999). What matters in undergraduate education? Mental models, student learning, and student affairs. In E. J. Whitt (Ed.), *Student learning as student affairs work: Responding to our imperative* (pp. 11–34). Washington, D.C.: National Association of Student Personnel Administrators.

Blocker, E., Plummer, H., & Richardson, C., Jr. (1965). *The two year college: A social synthesis.* Englewood Cliffs, NJ: Prentice-Hall, Inc.

Boswell, K., & Wilson, C. D. (Eds.). (2004). *Keeping America's promise, A report on the future of the community college.* Denver: Education Commission of the States.

Carnevale, A. P., & Desrochers, D. M. (2004). Why learning? The value of higher education to society and the individual. In K. Boswell and C. D. Wilson (Eds.), *Keeping America's promise, A report on the future of the community college* (pp. 39–45). Denver: Education Commission of the States.

Clements, E., Harvey-Smith, A. B., & James, T. (2005). In C. J. McPhail, (Ed.), *Establishing and sustaining learning-centered community colleges.* Washington, DC: Community College Press.

De la Teja, M., & Kramer, D. (1999). Student affairs and learning in the community college. In F. K. Stage, L. W. Watson, & M. Terrell, M. (Eds.), *Enhancing student learning setting the campus context* (pp. 77–102). Lanham, MD: University Press of America, Inc.

Dowd, A. C. (2005). Data don't drive: Building a practitioner-driven culture of inquiry to assess community college performance. *Lumina Foundation for Education Research Report.*

Retrieved December 22, 2005, from http://www.luminafounda-tion.org/publications/datadontdrive2005.pdf.

Grund, N. (2004). Partnering with academic affairs: Reporting to your provost can increase opportunities. *Leadership Exchange*, *2*(4), 10–13.

Hamm, R. R. (2004). Going to college: Not what it used to be. In K. Boswell & C. D. Wilson (Eds.), *Keeping America's promise, A report on the future of the community college* (pp. 29–33). Denver: Education Commission of the States.

Harvey-Smith, A. (Ed.). (2005). *The seventh learning college principle: A framework for transformational change.* Washington, DC: National Association of Student Personnel Administrators.

Helfgot, S., & Culp, M. (Eds.). (2005, Fall). Community college student affairs: What really matters? *New Directions for Community Colleges*, *131*, 17.

Keeling, R. P. (Ed.). (2004). *Learning reconsidered: A campus-wide focus on the student experience.* Washington, DC: National Association of Student Personnel Administrators and American College Personnel Association.

Keeling, R. P. (Ed.). (2006). *Learning reconsidered 2: A practical guide to implementing a campus-wide focus on the student experience.* Washington, DC: American College Personnel Association, Association of College and University Housing Officers–International, Association of College Unions International, National Academic Advising Association, National Association for Campus Activities, National Association of Student Personnel Administrators, and National Intramural-Recreational Sports Association.

Kolins, C. A. (2001). An appraisal of collaboration: Community colleges as vanguards. *Journal of Applied Research, 9*(1), 45–56.

Lillard, J. B. (1930). Junior college growth and organization. *The Junior College Journal, 1*(2), 81–83.

Livingston, M., & Croft, L. S. (2005). Building bridges between academic affairs and student affairs. Audio conference. Madison, WI: Magna Publications, Inc.

Lundquist, S., &Nixon, J. S. (1998). The partnership paradigm: Collaboration and the community college. *New Directions for Community Colleges, 103*, 43–49.

Martinez, M. (2004). High and rising: How much higher will college enrollment go? In K. Boswell & C. D. Wilson (Eds.), *Keeping America's promise, A report on the future of the community college* (pp. 21–23). Denver: Education Commission of the States.

McClenney, K. M. (2004/2005, December/January). The promise of community colleges. *Community College Journal, 56*–61.

McClenney, K. M. (2004). Keeping America's promise: Challenges for community colleges. In K. Boswell and C. D. Wilson (Eds.), *Keeping America's promise, A report on the future of the community college* (pp. 7–19). Denver: Education Commission of the States.

McPhail, C. J. (Ed.). (2005). *Establishing and sustaining learning-centered community colleges.* Washington, DC: Community College Press.

Medsker, L. L. (1960). *The junior college: Progress and prospect.* New York: McGraw-Hill Book Company, Inc.

Milleron, M. D., & de los Santos, G. E. (2004, February). Making the most of community colleges on the road ahead. *Community College Journal of Research and Practice, 28*(2), 105–122.

Monroe, L. R. (1972). *Profile of the community college.* San Francisco: Jossey-Bass, Inc.

O'Banion, T. (1997). *A learning college for the 21ˢᵗ century.* Phoenix: Oryx Press, 1997.

Parker, L., & Vecchitto, D. (1973). A noncampus system for Vermont. In J. Lombardi (Ed.), *New directions for community colleges: Meeting the financial crisis* (pp. 27–37). San Francisco: Jossey-Bass, Inc.

Pear, R. (2005, August 12). Racial and ethnic minorities gain in the nation as a whole. *New York Times.* Retrieved August 12, 2005 from http://www.nytimes.com/2005/08/12/national/12census. html.

Phillippe, K. (Ed.). (2000). *National profile of community colleges: Trends and statistics.* Washington, DC: Community College Press.

Price, D. V. (2004). Defining the gaps: Access and success at America's community colleges. In K. Boswell & C .D. Wilson (Eds.), *Keeping America's promise, a report on the future of the community college* (pp. 35–37). Denver: Education Commission of the States.

Ruiz, A. (2002/2003, December/January). Global diversity and leadership. *Community College Journal,* 29–31.

Shenk, E. (1981). *Description of the effects of Proposition 13 on the missions of the California Community College System* (pp. 9–20). Eugene: University of Oregon.

Wilson, C. D. (2004). Coming through the open door: A student profile. In K. Boswell & C. D. Wilson (Eds.), *Keeping America's promise, A Report on the future of the community college* (pp. 25–27). Denver: Education Commission of the States.

CHAPTER TWELVE

The Once and Future Collaboration of Academic and Student Affairs

Frank P. Ardaiolo

THE ONCE

A prime reason for studying history is to avoid the mistakes of the past. For the matter at hand, it may be a small irony that the view taken herein is a revisit to the historical roots of student affairs. Our "early passage" as a profession grew in response to change and expansion among formerly small and predominately liberal arts colleges. Our "middle passage," stimulated by the tremendous

239

growth of our college populations after World War II followed by the enrollment of their baby boomer offspring, allowed our profession to grow and specialize. However, this growth and specialization inadvertently caused us to lose touch with our historical roots and philosophical underpinnings. By remembering what existed once in our then-nascent profession, we can glean insights into our "future passage." This is especially true for a future understanding of student affairs and academic affairs collaboration—for once again, we prognosticate that we will become of one mind, focused on engaging students in learning and their total development within a constant comity.

We need to recall briefly our history as part of the development of U.S. higher education that started in our colonial colleges. These colleges sought to emulate those in England, where a model devoted to total character development gained predominance. Following the English model, these early institutions were even sited away from the corrupting influences of the city so that good, moral (mostly Christian) values could be instilled in every (mostly White male) student. Moral values were considered so important that in many instances the earliest version of a capstone senior course was taught by the college president on moral and intellectual philosophy. The aims of these courses were to engage a mature mind on topics viewed essential in the development of true character, which was considered even more important than the solitary growth of the intellect (Rudolph, 1962). As former Amherst College President Stearns said in 1872, "Character...is of more consequence than intellect" (Rudolph, 1962, p. 139).

American colleges began to change intellectually with the Industrial Revolution and the superimposition of the German model of research over the English model. With the growth of colleges and the need to provide for students' disciplinary concerns and living arrangements, presidents, many of whom were the sole administrators, could no longer cope. Simultaneously, students created literary societies that morphed into fraternities, which subsequently fostered the growth of intercollegiate competition and a new extracurriculum. By the time

> the students were finished, they had planted beside the curriculum an extracurriculum of such dimensions that in time there would develop generations of college students who would not see the curriculum for the extracurriculum; who would not believe that the American college had any purpose other than those that could best be served by the vast array of machinery, organizations, and institutions known as student activities. (Rudolph, 1962, p. 137)

In response to the arrival of coeducation, deans of women were hired, soon to be followed by deans of men. Together they became the pioneers of the student affairs profession, leading to today's deans of students and the vast array of services and programs that exist to support students predominately outside the classroom. These deans naturally inherited the responsibility for character development (later called student development) in philosophical, educational, and legal ways characterized as "in loco parentis" (in place of parents). This essential relationship between students and their institutions remained mostly untouched till the 1960s and 1970s.

THE NOW

With the social upheavals that began in the 1960s and the incredible growth of the higher education industry, a dissonance has grown among stakeholders on the philosophical underpinnings of many institutions. Students may be seeking skills for paying jobs or seeking adulthood, while legislatures and businesses may intend government support of education to stimulate economic development and civic responsibility. Institutions in many ways try to be all things to all people as they give modern expression to their historical roots.

There is now usually a whole administrative structure organized for the purpose of service to students, broadly conceived. Many institutions' structures for providing student services are considered organizationally equal to the other arrangements in these complex organizations, all designed to educate students and advance knowledge. Thus, it is not uncommon for higher education institutions to have major administrative divisions devoted to student services as well as academic affairs, business affairs, and institutional advancement. In the past 35 years, the student services profession itself has also developed a significant level of sophistication about what matters for student development and success. Many scientific studies have been conducted and theories of student development constructed. While faculty routinely deliver on the promise of education within the traditional classroom for students, student affairs and student services professionals should also consider themselves educators first. Within their unique roles in American higher education, they have also evolved to be integrators (Garland, 1985) of the goals of students, faculty, and administrators.

All colleges and universities have mission statements that seek to capture and excite the imagination of students and stakeholders. Winthrop University's (2005) mission statement, for example, states that its

> students acquire and develop knowledge, skills, and values that enrich their lives and prepare them to meet the needs and challenges of the contemporary world, includ-

ing the ability to communicate effectively, appreciate diversity, work collaboratively, synthesize knowledge, and adapt to change.

However, there are conflicting if not cross-cutting societal pressures and viewpoints on what to expect from the collegiate experience, an experience that has become very costly to participate in and to provide.

These pressures and viewpoints are especially seen in the growth of modern-day American education since the introduction of the Veterans Readjustment and Assistance Act (the GI Bill) in 1944. The ultimate American dream of a better life has been promised for all since the days of the Declaration of Independence, and higher education has emerged as the vehicle best suited to achieve it for most of the nation's populace. Multiple educational vehicles have evolved, including technical colleges, community colleges, liberal arts colleges, state universities, university systems, and now online education. The faculty, too, has expectations for students that reflect their institutions' missions but more often than not reside on a personal level within the original Aristotelian premise of teaching students to find good by making meaning of new knowledge and experiences.

The historical antecedents of the philosophical underpinnings of the student affairs profession can also be traced to Aristotle, among others. Aristotle believed that education's purpose was to make people virtuous. He asserted that all people seek what they believe to be good. Ignorance, on the other hand resulted in evil, because people chose incorrectly what they mistake for good. Aristotle's solution to evil was education, because only through proper knowledge and understanding could people identify and choose what is truly good. Given its integral relationship to virtue, Aristotle argued, education was the state's highest duty (Johnson, 2004).

We have woven these classical threads of Aristotle's arguments into a rich, complex fabric shaping the relationships between students and institutions and the meaning and purposes of education. Obligations of collegiate institutions, government agencies, and boards of trustees to their students have been the topic of prodigious amounts of scholarly reflection and work. The roles and expectations of the faculty and services for students have flowed from these philosophical antecedents through historical developments. Student expectations have evolved from seeking virtue in Aristotle's days to purchasing training and seeking opportunity in today's modern global marketplace. The nexus between these classical and modern perspectives today informs the significance of the interactions among faculty, students, and student affairs educators and service providers. And they begin to form our window into the future.

> This window is initially shaped by varying perspectives, for often there is a disconnect between student expectations as consumers and institutional views of what a college education and experience should be (Miller, Bender, Schuh, & Associates, 2005). One of the disconnects that has occurred in recent years is that students as consumers come to college because they value the benefits of getting a diploma. However, many students fail to recognize the value of *learning* (Tagg, 2003). Tagg believes that students, while physically present on our campuses, are psychologically absent. He believes the fundamental challenge facing colleges today is to change the expectations, attitudes, and beliefs of incoming students about

their school setting, academic work, and their own relationship to academic institutions.

What we can say with fair confidence at this point is that most students who leave high school and enter college bring with them a set of attitudes and beliefs about schooling and their interaction with educational institutions that tend to insulate them against learning rather than to prepare them for it." (Tagg, 2003, p. 47)

Essentially, many students are not fully learning and developing because they are not engaged with their institutions. They are on campus but not engaging the campus. Engagement is both the catalyst for student responsibility and the agent of learning. Engagement is also the lens that allows us a more focused view into the future.

Cross (1996) used an analogy about lenses and vision problems that points out the criticism of higher education from legislators, media, and the public. She offered the insight that our vision problems have become serious in that many lost their focus on student learning. She suggested rather than use the stylish, expensive lenses that look good but do not do much to improve vision, institutions should concentrate on simple, serviceable ones set in sturdy, flexible frames that can bend but not break under pressure. These new prescription lenses should bring students' total learning experiences into clear view for all the stakeholders in higher education. These lenses will correct

1. Astigmatism in students, who often focus their learning on small things that appear huge and overwhelming while more important issues fade from view altogether.

2. Tunnel vision in faculty, for while they see their own discipline clearly, especially in their classrooms, their peripheral vision fails to pick up all the impacts on students' 24-hour day: course work, study, work, family, financial worries, insecurities, and uncertainties.

3. Overly powerful peripheral vision in central administrators, who overcompensate for tunnel vision by seeing threats to the academy from budget-cutting legislators, concerned alumni, avid sports fans, annoyed neighbors, and others.

4. Blurry vision in student affairs educators from using ill-fitted bifocals: the upper portion working with students as counselors and the lower portion working with them as administrators.

The American Association of Colleges and Universities (AAC&U) has been holding a series of meetings and symposia designed to conceptualize this new emphasis on learning and the research that supports this important shift. AAC&U's *Greater Expectations* (2002) initiative stated:

> Learning needs to be intentionally learning centered. Learning and teaching while related are not the same. We have relied on teaching assuming that learning would result. Learning centered education flips this relationship and begins with the learner. Teaching becomes a means for assuring the learner achieves the desired learning. Learning is recognized as occurring in multiple ways, including in less formal and non-classroom environments. It also recognizes the variety of learning styles and acknowledges the need for a variety of teaching styles. It

builds upon and appreciates the importance of an understanding of the learning process. Powerful learning
does not occur accidentally. An education that allows
all students to reach their potential must meet students
where they are and takes into account their variety of
life experiences and expectations. (p. 5)

Learning is the proper focus for our future as presented in *Learning Reconsidered* (Keeling, 2004). As the monograph stated, "Learning is
a complex, holistic, multi-centric activity that occurs throughout and
across the college experience. Student development and the adapta-
tion of learning to students' lives and needs are fundamental parts of
engaged learning and liberal education" (p. 8).

However, there is often a dissonance between the current and
potential future focus on learning and between students and their
institutions. The sources of this dissonance are depicted in Figure 12.1.
On one side of the figure are the common consumer expectations of
students. These expectations range from generally acceptable consumer
notions from the world of commerce such as full information, choice,
hearing or redress when things go wrong, safe use of the purchased
product to a desire that all personal wants and needs be immediately
satisfied through the delivery of their education. Many students pass
though the college environment with only this consumer mentality, resulting in a general lack of cognition of causality and consequence that
leads to inappropriate or insufficient expectations. These insufficient
expectations in turn result in frustrations and lost learning opportunities.

The other side of the figure depicts the engagement between students and institutions in a nonlinear (not directly causal) manner that
represents the typical expectations of faculty and student affairs staff.

These engagement activities were drawn from the National Survey of Student Engagement (NSSE) (2004). The survey "asks undergraduates about how they spend their time, what they feel they've gained from classes, their assessment of the quality of their interactions with faculty and friends, and other important activities" (p. 1). Many institutions are now encouraging these engagement activities in and outside the classroom to stimulate student learning.

The variance between students' consumer expectations and institutional learning engagement expectations results in dissonance. As Davis and Murrell (1993) pointed out, research during the last few decades has shown unambiguously that the more students put into their academic life by becoming involved and engaged in their studies and campus life, the more positive the outcomes are. Assuming students are willing to learn, good can occur through this newfound knowledge and understanding. This good is reflected in students choosing to take more responsible actions that may benefit them in the future based on learning from their poor choices in their pasts. By doing this, students gain the fuller cognition of making meaning of the causality of events, the consequences of personal actions, and the acceptance of personal responsibility. While students' consumer expectations about the college experience are important, they are not sufficient, for students fail to realize that many institutions are trying to make every activity on campus an engaging one that leads to further and fuller learning. Students who fail to become active and responsible for their own development fail to turn many experiences at their institutions into learning, meaning-making experiences.

Figure 12.1. Learning and student expectations dissonance resolution.

LEARNING ENGAGEMENT EXPECTATIONS		STUDENT CONSUMER EXPECTATIONS
Nonlinear Interactions between Institutions and Students		
Inquiring	≈	Information
Expressing	≈	Choice
Synthesizing	≈	Hearing
Working In Teams	≈	Safety
Applying Knowledge	≈	Reputation
Recreating	≈	Value
Serving Others	≈	Personal Needs Met
Appreciating Self & Others	≈	Immediate satisfaction
Building Community	≈	Growth
Supporting Success	≈	Service Delivery

Resolved By Total Engagement Leading To Cognition of Causality, Consequence, and Personal Responsibility

Students need to understand the totality of the educational experience. False expectations brought on by habit or inattention can result in educational disaster. Students must mind the gap between the rising expectations for learning at colleges and universities and their own simplistic consumer expectations. Above all, students must be willing to change, because learning always involves change. Equally important, students must take responsibility for their own development and learning (Ardaiolo, Bender, & Roberts, 2005).

Organizationally speaking, the difference between student consumer expectations and institutional learning expectations often leads to institutional dissonance. This happens at institutions where students either are not fully engaged in the educational delivery process or facul-

249

ty and student affairs personnel themselves do not properly understand student development, thus failing to engage students with their learning methods and program offerings. There is an institutional failure to understand the multiple facets of engagement that lead to learning and student growth. Educational tragedy results when students fail to realize they could have achieved more. They fail to detect the causality within all personal actions and the consequences that they could have better controlled had they chosen more wisely. They fail to take responsibility for finding the knowledge and understanding that can help them choose what is truly good, that which gives meaning to their remaining lives. Learning for all is thus lost, and the true reason for the existence of both students and institutions remains unfulfilled. High levels of activities by students and institutions are viewed as growth, but it is growth without development. Aristotle would be sad.

THE FUTURE

The future is upon us as universities and their faculties and student affairs staffs begin to work from a script that resonates with their past and seeks to resolve the current student–institutional dissonance. While this is new terrain for many, the schema on total student engagement presented in Figure 12.2 provides a map for understanding and action to encourage collaboration between academic and student affairs well into the future.

The emphasis on engagement and learning should come as no surprise to many astute student affairs professionals, as they have in recent years formulated on their own campuses missions that are express to their own institutions' relationship to student learning. As Shulman (2002) stated:

> The argument NSSE makes is that we want to know about student engagement because it serves as a proxy for learning, understanding, and post-graduation commitments that we cannot measure very well directly, or that we would have to wait 20 years to measure. As noted earlier, however, I would argue that engagement is not solely a proxy; it can also be an end in itself. Our institutions of higher education are settings where students can encounter a range of people and ideas and human experiences that they have never been exposed to before. Engagement in this sense is not just a proxy for learning but a fundamental purpose of education. (p. 40)

As early as 1996 with the publication of *The Student Learning Imperative* by the American College Personnel Association, student affairs divisions were being told they should exhibit the following characteristics:

1. The student affairs division mission complements the institution's mission, with the enhancement of student learning and personal development being the primary goal of student affairs programs and services.

2. Resources are allocated to encourage student learning and personal development.

3. Student affairs professionals collaborate with other institutions and agencies to promote student learning and personal development.

4. Staff in student affairs includes those who are experts on students, their environments, and teaching and learning processes.

5. Policies and programs of student affairs are based on promising practices from the research on student learning and institution-specific assessment data.

However, the call to become learning centered was not being heard by all student affairs professionals, and the relationships that were inherent in the concepts were not being well articulated to faculty colleagues at many institutions. This is perhaps because prior attempts to present the concept of total student development (Brown, 1972; Miller & Prince, 1976) failed to articulate the work of student affairs professionals as part of the intellectual domain of the faculty. In addition, many institutions had lost sight of their historic mission for student development, referred to in the 18th century as character development.

> The isolation of [student affairs from the rest of the institution] emerges because the model does not address the widely held understandings about the purposes of higher education or unique institutional goals. In particular, the model has failed to address the institution's mission and the centrality of the role of academic and intellectual development. This causes student development to appear anti-intellectual." (Daryl Smith, as cited in Brown, 1990, p. 247)

This anti-intellectual characterization of student affairs by many faculty members has unfortunately grown strong on many campuses. How often have student affairs professionals been shunted aside in key conversations by a joke or not even asked to participate because, "You people are only concerned with students' fun and games!" While student affairs professionals typically rail against such sentiments, many have failed to recognize they have allowed this situation because they do not understand the historic roots of their own profession or do not have mastery or understanding of the vocabulary and methodology of learning that most faculty grasp. As Brown (1990) stated:

> What is less often recognized or articulated by the student affairs profession is that the liberal education curriculum promotes student development and did so long before the student development model was created. The active learning of literature, philosophy, anthropology, psychology, history, the natural sciences—or any of the arts and sciences disciplines—contributes to the development of identity, competence, and autonomy, to the development of tolerance and appreciation of diversity, to the understanding and acceptance of interdependence, to the clarification of and commitment to values, and to the development of the whole person." (p. 255)

We must realize the potential to create a future of renewed collaboration with faculty that is being presented to us with the new emphasis on engagement and learning.

Kuh, Kinzie, Schuh, Whitt, and Associates (2005) have digested the voluminous studies of college impacts and development and concluded that "the time and energy students devote to educationally purposeful activities is the single best predictor of their learning and personal development" (p. 8). NSSE assesses student responses on various engagement activities, the agents of learning. The instrument measures engagement associated with the items listed. An example is building community; NSSE measures students working with faculty and staff members on activities other than course work (committees, orientation, student life activities, etc.); participating in co-curricular activities (organizations, campus publications, student government, social fraternity or sorority, intercollegiate or intramural sports, etc.);

253

and living in campus housing. Engagement is therefore explained as much more than just going to class; it is a multifaceted, educationally purposeful activity that occurs across varying engagement domains involving a number of campus-related populations.

Seeking to measure institutional quality, the NSSE instrument measures student views of that quality, especially (Kuh et al., 2005) the time and effort students put into their studies and other activities that lead to student success. Analyzing 20 schools' higher-than-expected NSSE results, Kuh et al. (2005, p. 24) documented six features common to such highly engaged colleges and universities:

* A "living" mission and "lived" educational philosophy

* An unshakeable focus on student learning

* Environments adopted for educational enrichment

* Clearly marked pathways to student success

* An improvement-oriented ethos

* Shared responsibility for educational quality and student success.

Concentrating on the future, the challenge remains how to depict and thus map the terrain that institutions need to traverse to foster student engagement. This is a major challenge given the complexity of our modern organizations. It is especially germane because explicit in Kuh et al. (2005) is the call to "tighten the philosophical and operational linkages between academic and student affairs" (p. 312).

An overview of the many facets of engagement that lead to learning and total student development is presented in Figure 12.2. This

254

schema, reflecting the elements more fully explored in *Learning Reconsidered* (Keeling, 2004), shows that student growth occurs within five interconnected engagement domains that institutions teach in varying degrees according to mission: intellectual/cognitive, social/interpersonal/behavioral, personal/affective, spiritual, and cultural.

The schema also presents engagement activities institutions encourage in and outside the class room to stimulate student learning within the engagement domains. These engagement activities are drawn from NSSE. A richer understanding of these engagement activities is provided when they are presented in context to varying populations involved with modern higher education: students, staff, faculty, and broader community members.

Engagement thus understood is also more than two-dimensional. The cube form graphically depicts the interrelatedness of all the components, facets, and actors associated with engagement. This is because there is a constant interplay among the campus populations: faculty, staff, broader community members, as well as students (this graphical model was stimulated by the original Student Development Model presented in Miller & Prince, 1976, p. 23). Evaluation and assessment encompasses the whole cube, signifying the importance of learning about learning and implementing change to improve functions and program delivery.

Viewing this schema, students, faculty, and staff should grasp that growth occurs in varying frequencies and in varying steps that may be sequential, synchronous, or asynchronous. Growth occurs all around the facets of the many smaller cubes within the larger cube of this complex interplay of engagement. Institutions on the leading edge are constantly assessing and evaluating their engagement activities, just as students should be.

Figure 12.2. Engagement schema that leads to learning and student development

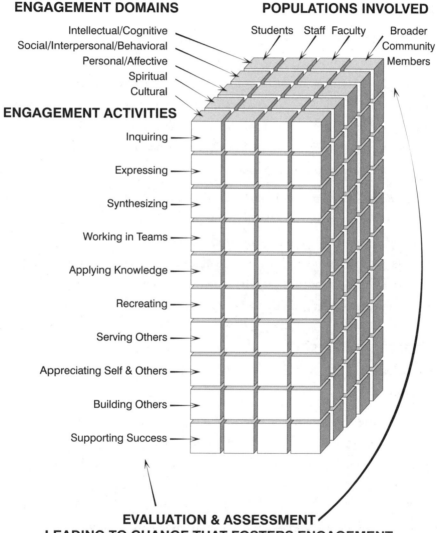

ENGAGEMENT DOMAINS

Intellectual/Cognitive
Social/Interpersonal/Behavioral
Personal/Affective
Spiritual
Cultural

POPULATIONS INVOLVED

Students Staff Faculty Broader Community Members

ENGAGEMENT ACTIVITIES

Inquiring

Expressing

Synthesizing

Working in Teams

Applying Knowledge

Recreating

Serving Others

Appreciating Self & Others

Building Others

Supporting Success

**EVALUATION & ASSESSMENT
LEADING TO CHANGE THAT FOSTERS ENGAGEMENT**

It should be noted that experience dictates the possibility for growth to occur predominately within a single domain, such as intellectual/cognitive, without corresponding growth within another domain, such as social/interpersonal/behavioral. Such a student may become remarkably cognitive of certain content matter but not able to grasp how this knowledge affects the articulation, or ethical application, of the content in the real world surrounding the student. Growth is thus truncated and the student not as fully developed as possible. The schema guards against such growth without development by providing a picture of all the engagement domains that must grow so total student development can occur.

Using the schema as a map resolves the dissonance between student consumers and their institutions because it depicts components of learning that must occur for students to be totally educated while providing a map of the terrain that academic and student affairs professionals must cross together. The power of the schema was recently demonstrated in a review of career services, service-learning, and civic engagement at Winthrop University. A task force of student affairs staff, faculty, and a community partner (populations involved) reviewed the university's organizational framework to prepare students for the world beyond the university (engagement domains) so there could be a more intentional and synchronous linkage and focus on career development and civic engagement (engagement activities). As a result of this task force's recommendations, in the summer of 2005 Winthrop University created the Center for Career Development and Service Learning by reconfiguring resources involving the Division of Student Life and faculty associated with Winthrop's University College. This center will provide visionary leadership in efforts to enhance the Winthrop experience by building a more cohesive and inclusive learning community that cultivates student engagement and committed service within the university and in the world beyond. By creating a challenging yet supportive learning environment, the center's staff will work beyond organizational boundaries to ensure that faculty, staff, and especially students recognize the links between civic engagement and establishing a meaningful career upon leaving the campus. The center provides a physical locale and a state of mind that focuses on one shared goal that is mutually supporting.

MAKING MEANING OF NEW KNOWLEDGE AND NEW EXPERIENCES: THE ONCE AND FUTURE RELATIONSHIP OF ACADEMIC AND STUDENT AFFAIRS

Some publications have discussed the future of student affairs, especially in collaboration with academic affairs, and even hazarded a guess at new organizational structures, new administrative arrangements, new responsibilities for student affairs staff, and new functional emphases (Barr, Upcraft & Associates, 1990; Keeling, 2004; Maneta, 2003). They all posit the need to overcome Hamrick, Evans, and Schuh's (2002) observation, "On most campuses, existing relationships between student affairs and academic affairs (separate and unequal) inadequately address the new way of thinking about learning as student-centered, relational, and encompassing a range of learning experiences" (p. 118).

Speaking about broader future organizational perspectives beyond just academic and student affairs, Barr and Albright (1990, p. 192) stated, "A great deal has been written about the need for strong, effective, and transforming leadership." It should be noted, however, that "to the extent the failure of a college can be attributed to a failure of leadership, it is usually not the lack of charisma but to a lack of basic organizational competence" (Bensimon, Neumann, & Birnbaum, 1989, p. 75). Given this, it is best to be cognizant of all the steps necessary to transform the future as an academic or student affairs leader.

Guskin and Marcy (2003) offered three organizing principles and seven transformative actions guiding their call for action of transforming institutions in the future rather than muddling through because of changing societal conditions:

Organizing Principles:

1. Create a clear and coherent vision of the future (focus on student learning, quality of faculty work life, and reducing cost per student).

2. Transform the educational delivery system (consistent with vision of the future).

3. Transform the organizational systems (consistent with vision of the future).

Transformative Actions:

1. Establish and assess institution-wide common student learning outcomes as a basis for the undergraduate degree.

2. Restructure the role of faculty to include faculty and other campus professionals as partners in student learning, while integrating technology.

3. Recognize and integrate student learning from all sources.

4. Audit and restructure curricula to focus on essential academic programs and curricular offerings.

5. Utilize zero-based budgeting to audit and redesign the budget allocation process involving faculty and staff as responsible partners.

6. Audit and restructure administrative and student services systems, using technology and integrated staffing arrangements to reduce costs.

7. Audit and redesign technological and staff infrastructures to support transformational change.

Future student affairs educators, in being responsible for student development and the role engagement activities can play in helping students make meaning out of new knowledge and new experiences, must understand their historic roots and the roles our pioneers played. As Pascarella and Terenzini (2005) concluded:

> In some areas of intellectual development (including critical thinking), the breadth of student involvement in the intellectual *and* social experiences of college, rather than any particular type of involvement, matters most. The greatest impact appears to stem from students' *total* level of campus engagement, particularly when academic, interpersonal, and extracurricular involvements are mutually reinforcing and relevant to a particular educational outcome." (p. 647)

Student affairs professionals coming originally from the faculty once understood this, and they must do it again in the future. They must work in partnership with faculty, with a constant flow back and forth between academic and student affairs in meaning making for students.

We need to understand that meaning making is more than cognition. Cognition (Keeling, 2004) involves the thought processes that people use to analyze and synthesize information in order to make meaning of a situation or decide how to respond to it. Cognitive development builds the capacity for reflective judgment, which describes a person's increasing ability to take information and context into account when developing judgments or making decisions. Meaning making comprises students' efforts to comprehend the essence and significance of events, relationships, and learning; to gain a richer understanding of themselves in a larger context; and to experience a sense of wholeness. Meaning making arises in a reflective connection between an individual and the wider world (Keeling, 2004, p. 17). Meaning making is also the lens through which students, faculty, and student affairs can view our collective future experiences in higher education.

Meaning making is our once and future. It is not an oversimplification to say that students are the meaningful common denominator between tomorrow's faculty and student affairs professionals in learning environments, processes, programs, and organizations where faculty generally concentrate on making meaning of new knowledge and student affairs educators generally concentrate on making meaning of new experiences. Engagement as the proxy for learning is really the fulcrum between these two meaning-making domains. Aristotle will be pleased!

REFERENCES

American College Personnel Association. (1996). *The student learning imperative: Implications for student affairs*. Retrieved August 1, 2005, from http://www.acpa.nche.edu/sli/sli.htm

Ardaiolo, F. P., Bender, B. E., & Roberts, G. (2005). Campus services: What do students expect? In T. E. Miller, B. E. Bender, J. H. Schuh, & Associates (Eds.), *Promoting reasonable expectations: Aligning students and institutional views of the college experience*. San Francisco: Jossey-Bass.

Association of American Colleges and Universities. (2002). *Greater expectations*. Washington, DC: Author.

Barr, M. J. & Albright, R. L. (1990). Rethinking the Organizational Role of Student Affairs in Barr, M. J., Upcraft, M. L., & Associates (Eds.), *New futures for student affairs*. San Francisco: Jossey-Bass.

Barr, M. J., Upcraft, M. L., & Associates. (Eds.). (1990). *New futures for student affairs*. San Francisco: Jossey-Bass.

Brown, R. D. (1972). *Tomorrow's higher education: A return to the academy*. Student Personnel Series No. 16. Washington, DC: American Personnel and Guidance Association.

Brown, S. S. (1990). Strengthening ties to academic affairs. In M. J. Barr, M. L. Upcraft, & Associates (Eds.), *New futures for student affairs*. San Francisco: Jossey-Bass.

Cross, K. P. (1996, March–April). New lenses on learning. *About Campus*, 4–9.

Davis, T. M., & Murrell, P. H. (1993). *Turning learning into teaching: The role of student responsibility in the collegiate experience*. ASHE-ERIC Higher Education Report No. 8. Washington, DC:

The George Washington University, School of Education and Human Development. (ERIC Documentation Reproduction Service No. ED347921).

Garland, P. (1985). *Serving more than students*. Washington, DC: Association for the Study of Higher Education.

Guskin, A. E., & Marcy, M. B. (2003, July/August). Dealing with the future now—Principles for creating a vital campus in a climate of restricted resources. *Change*, 10–21.

Johnson, D. F. (2004). Toward a philosophy of online education. Tomorrow's Professor Listserve Msg.#520, Stanford Center for Teaching and Learning. Retrieved January 11, 2004, from http://ctl.stanford.edu/Tomprof/postings/520.html

Hamrick, F. A., Evans, N. J., & Schuh, J. H. (2002). *Foundations of student affairs practice*. San Francisco: Jossey-Bass.

Keeling, R. P. (Ed.). (2004). *Learning reconsidered: A campus-wide focus on the student experience*. Washington, DC: National Association of Student Personnel Administrators and American College Personnel Association.

Kuh, G. D., Schuh, J. H., Whitt, E. J., & Associates. (2005). *Student success: Creating conditions that matter*. San Francisco: Jossey-Bass.

Maneta, L. (2003). Future trends and challenges for student affairs. *The Leadership Exchange, 1*(1) 6–9.

Miller, T. E., Bender, B. E., Schuh, J. H., & Associates. (2005). *Promoting reasonable expectations: Aligning students and institutional views of the college experience*. San Francisco: Jossey-Bass.

Miller, T. K., & Prince, J. S. (1976). *The future of student affairs*. San Francisco: Jossey-Bass.

National Survey of Student Engagement, Indiana University, Center for Postsecondary Research. (2004). Retrieved January 20, 2004, from http://www.iub.edu/~nsse/html/brochure_2004.shtml

Rudolph, F. (1962). *The American college and university—A history.* New York: Vintage Books.

Pacarella, E. T., & Terenzini, P. T. (2005). *How college affects students. Vol. 2. A third decade of research.* San Francisco: Jossey-Bass.

Schulman, L. S. (2002, November–December). Making differences—A table of learning. *Change,* 36–44.

Tagg, J. (2003). *The learning paradigm college.* Bolton, MA: Anker Publishing Company.

Winthrop University. (2005). *Mission statement.* Retrieved August 7, 2005, from http://www.winthrop.edu/president/mission.htm

CHAPTER THIRTEEN
Developing Effective Collaborations

Alma R. Clayton-Pedersen
and Gwendolyn J. Dungy

T he overarching message of this book is that collaboration, especially between academic and student affairs, is critical to achieve essential student learning outcomes—a core educational mission of colleges and universities. The chapters in this book address the advantages of collaboration and focus on specific efforts that ensure effective partnerships to foster student achievement. These calls for collaboration are not new; rather, they represent a return to earlier practices that ensured that students achieved the learning outcomes both institutions and students desired.

265

When college attendance was reserved for the elite, institutions were structured so that faculty roles and responsibilities were approached holistically. Faculty instilled in students different ways of knowing through study in the disciplines; they simultaneously nurtured students' character and leadership development through mentoring and personal engagement. In addition, faculty members interacted much more with each other across disciplines. The academy was a tightly knit community. As a result of the level of specialization and separation within the academy today, faculty members often interact more with members of their own disciplines in other states and around the world than with their colleagues on campus. Given the modern intellectual divide between academic disciplines, this lack of collaboration within institutions is not surprising.

Changes in the student population have further impacted faculty and administrators' roles. For example, growing numbers of students are first-generation college-goers, many of whom have been under-served by the U.S. education system and are not prepared for college-level work. Furthermore, many campuses are not prepared to foster these students' academic development. Because of these dynamics and near-universal access to higher education, faculty often voice frustrations about the difficulties of teaching students with such broad ranges of ability. These frustrations serve as incentive for institutions to focus on attracting more academically able students. Quite often this focus results in institutions neglecting to examine institutional structures that may fail to foster all students' success.

Current educational, political, and economic conditions are prompting calls for educators to redesign campus environments to improve student learning. Although some may argue that the current plans accommodate the efficient management of this constantly changing environment, few can argue that these discrete designs fully achieve the goals of developing students intellectually, socially, emotionally, and spiritually. These isolated designs cannot be sustained. They are less effective in serving all students, less efficient due to unnecessary program duplication, and less economical because of resourcing redundancies. Designs that are more coherent, comprehensive, and collaborative will better serve students and the nation, particularly during a time when resources devoted to higher education are shrinking.

The first three chapters of this book provided background information about student and academic affairs collaboration efforts and the difficulties involved. These chapters also underscored student and academic affairs constituents' mutual desire to improve student learning through increased collaboration. Chapters 4 through 10 described eight necessary elements—or circles—for effective collaboration. The chapters detailed promising practices that were uncovered in the national survey of student and academic affairs collaboration conducted by NASPA's Student Affairs Professionals Working In and With Academic Affairs Knowledge Community. These practices outline the elements of a positive working culture between student affairs and academic affairs, with examples throughout of institutions where collaboration is taking place successfully. Chapter 11 explored the specific case of collaboration in community colleges. Chapter 12 highlighted the development of the field of student affairs and reminded us to recognize and draw on the strength of the field's purpose as collaboration efforts are approached.

This last chapter, devoted to developing effective collaboration, serves as the ninth circle in the blueprint for effective collaboration between student and academic affairs. It provides a conceptual framework for collaboration that may help student affairs practitioners organize their approaches to the practices in order to ensure effective campus action and assessment. The framework is rooted in *inter-organizational* collaboration research that identifies conditions necessary for "true" collaboration to occur. In light of the totality of the interventions, supports, and actions needed to improve students' achievement of essential learning outcomes, student affairs practitioners can consider their work as an *intra-organizational* collaboration. This work can be informed by inter-organizational collaboration because the structure of our institutions involves multiple work units with different primary goals. This chapter first provides an overview of this collaboration framework and then links each condition to the promising practices discussed in the previous chapters in order to increase the likelihood that collaboration efforts will be established on campuses.

A newcomer to collaboration efforts may review the barriers outlined in Chapter 1 and those alluded to throughout the book and conclude that these challenges are exclusive to student and academic affairs collaboration efforts. In fact, these barriers are common to many types of collaboration in education—including those across academic units (e.g., interdisciplinary studies initiatives), across academic programs (e.g., integrative learning initiatives and ethnic studies programs), and across academic institutions (e.g., consortia of colleges and universities within a region), as well as in collaborations between K–12 and higher education. The framework that follows gives practitioners an important guide to understanding the general nature of collaboration.

Overview of the Collaboration Conceptual Framework

Four critical conditions are characteristic of inter-organizational collaboration that can inform our intra-organizational work. The involved entities must

1. Recognize the external and internal **forces** for change, and intentionally pursue collaboration as a viable response;

2. Identify and agree on the common **goals** that the collaboration will work to achieve;

3. Identify and commit **resources** to achieve the common goals; and

4. Develop the **capacity** to carry out the work of the collaboration at individual, unit, and collaborative levels (Clayton-Pedersen, 1992; Rein, 1983; Weiss, 1981, 1986, 1987).

These conditions have sequential qualities in that the conditions build on one another; they have simultaneous qualities in that leaders and constituents can work to improve the conditions without the previous conditions being developed fully.

Although these conditions are believed essential for collaboration, their presence does not automatically guarantee success. Rather, the determinants of success are related more to (a) the degree to which the conditions exist individually and as a whole, (b) the quality of the leaders and constituents' efforts to ensure that each condition is present at the highest levels, and (c) whether intra-organizational collaboration becomes part of an institution's culture—institutionalized.

External and Internal Forces for Change

External forces can be brought to bear on organizations and push leaders to satisfy "demands" for change, resulting in a need for greater collaboration. In the case of higher education, several common forces create these enabling conditions for change. The changing demography of the college-going population and the limited resources devoted to higher education—especially in the public sector—are two external forces. Federal and state legislative bodies and advocacy groups seeking reforms, like the U.S. Secretary of Education's Commission on the Future of Higher Education's calls for greater accountability (U.S. Department of Education, 2006), are external forces acting on higher education institutions and the community as a whole. Individual champions and national organizations advocating the end of inequitable educational outcomes for underserved students are external forces.

Among the common internal forces that drive campus leaders and constituents toward collaboration are senior administrators' desire to address disparities in graduation rates among various student groups; leaders' recognition of the need to attract more diverse student bodies for institutional viability—both educationally and financially; and traditionally underrepresented students' challenges to the administration to offer a curriculum that is relevant to their experiences.

It is natural for organizations to turn inward initially to develop responses to these forces. Their first instincts tend to be to respond alone. Agendas, messages, and resources are generally better controlled that way—or so they think. Yet effective leaders turn to collaboration for a variety of reasons, including (a) they cannot envision garnering the necessary resources to address an issue alone, (b) they are convinced that others have some expertise that can assist them in addressing the issue, and/or (c) they believe that working with others is not simply additive but synergistic.

Organizations should consider three questions when deciding

whether to reach across traditional boundaries: (1) Can they find or forge commonality across their individual units' primary goals? (2) Do they have the resources to achieve the identified goals as well as to mount the collaboration effort? (3) Do they have or can they develop the capacity to achieve their individual *and* collective organizational goals?

Goals. By choosing to collaborate, organizations accept that they can accomplish certain goals more effectively by working with others outside of their units, or that synergy among units will achieve better outcomes. When collaboration is mandated, such awareness among team members cannot be assumed, but it can be continually worked on. Even though all units are ostensibly focused on achieving their overall missions, there is a reason that they are separate—they perform different functions, and thus their primary goals may differ greatly. A key to successful collaboration is for each unit to understand how others' goals are related to their own and how they can work together to achieve mutual goals.

Resources. All endeavors require resources, including human, time, space, and financial resources. Identifying and securing these resources is an essential aspect of successful collaboration. Resources must be devoted to collaboration at two levels—the effort of individuals to work across traditional boundaries and the act of achieving mutual goals.

Capacity. Even if all units understand clearly the relationships between their goals and adequate resources are devoted to the entire enterprise, unless individual units develop the capacity to carry out collaboration, it cannot be established meaningfully. These capacity-building elements include constituents' working knowledge of the goals of the collaboration and the available resources; information, communication, and structural systems that work across boundaries; implementers' abilities to carry out the tasks; and leadership to help guide the process at different organizational levels.

These conditions are not completely discrete, which we alluded to when addressing the sequential qualities of the framework. Yet they are discrete enough to provide a guiding framework for campus constituents to approach collaborative efforts effectively.

THE CORNERSTONE OF COLLABORATION

Throughout this book, authors offer strategies on how to overcome barriers to effective collaborations, which range from finding a common language to team teaching. Common aspects of these strategies are working together to determine mutual goals, retaining a focus on desired outcomes, and committing to shared responsibilities. This section highlights the cornerstone of effective collaboration: a common vision.

Student affairs professionals have often expressed frustration over efforts to collaborate with faculty. An aspect of the endeavor that is often overlooked in failed attempts is the nature of the ongoing roles and responsibilities of faculty beyond classroom interaction with students. Faculty must prepare for classes as well as grade papers and exams; assist students with coursework; advise students; prepare reports for and attend departmental and institution-wide committee meetings; conduct research; and maintain currency in their disciplines through professional development and reading. These are but a few of the activities common to all faculty. Faculty are often frustrated by calls for greater collaboration with student affairs because they feel that their workload is already overwhelming. They have minimal time to collaborate even with their academic colleagues. Given these time constraints, any effort to collaborate will need to address a compelling interest of faculty and be consistent with their existing roles and responsibilities.

Senior leaders can foster collaboration in a number of ways, as discussed in Chapter 5. Perhaps most important, they can promote the idea that all campus constituents are responsible for advancing learning. They can also create formal structures that reinforce and support the collaborative efforts of faculty and student affairs professionals. Furthermore, it is imperative that all parties understand that effective collaboration is built on a common vision of what the goals or outcomes of collaboration will yield. Senior leaders set these expectations and hold the parties mutually responsible for achieving them.

Chapter 6 provided examples of how student affairs can appeal to the self-interest of faculty and initiate structures that facilitate collaboration focused on what each constituent group contributes to student learning. Beginning with the premise that faculty members want to be successful in teaching, and the measure of success is how well students achieve course outcomes, student affairs members need to initiate conversations with faculty, showing that they want to know the specific nature of what students are expected to learn in the classroom. Faculty will be more than willing to work with their colleagues in student affairs to determine the most effective ways for students to apply what they learn in the classroom in their programs and activities outside of class. As the authors of *Learning Reconsidered* (Keeling, 2004) pointed out, "Transformative learning always occurs in the active context of students' lives" (p. 13). This same point of view is reiterated in *Learning Reconsidered 2*, (Keeling, 2006), which notes that "it is impossible to separate learning, development, and context" (p. 5). Assisting students with integrating their learning is a powerful goal for faculty and student affairs. Faculty members are interested in deepening student

273

learning through the practice of applying the theories learned in class to real-world settings. Student affairs educators are interested in having students demonstrate in class how their out-of-class experiences are integrated with their subject matter learning. As individual faculty members gain familiarity with the complementary nature of in- and out-of-class learning, they are more likely to see student affairs educators as partners in achieving the desired learning outcomes.

Resources—Collaborate by What Means?

Chapter 5 addresses the impact of resources on efforts to collaborate. Using Kuh's (1996) work, the author notes the "importance of leveraging the human and fiscal resources needed to create an effective learning environment." The suggestion here is that requests for resources from *both* academic and student affairs will have more impact than separate requests. If the senior team is committed to the goals of the collaboration and willing to forgo individual needs for the good of the whole, as is suggested in Chapter 5, this strategy will be effective in securing the needed resources.

Following the theme of integrated learning, Chapter 6 notes that resources may be saved by making faculty appointments in student affairs for periods of time and calling on the knowledge found within academic units rather than outside consultants for student affairs consultations and vice versa. Finding "diamonds in our own backyard" saves money and lays the foundation for future collaborations.

For collaboration to succeed, institutions must be committed to providing the resources needed to support mutual goals between academic and student affairs. The key to making resource requests compelling is to have the goals and plans intentionally and unequivocally address student learning outcomes that will be measured and assessed as part of the process. If senior leaders are committed to the mission of the institution and support collaborative efforts, it will be difficult for them to deny such requests.

To become funding priorities, project goals must be tied to the institution's mission and its president's aims. Also, academic and student affairs professionals must be courageous and vocal advocates for student success; they must make sure that senior leaders understand that the absence of funds for collaborative efforts to achieve student learning outcomes sends the message that such efforts are not a campus priority. In addition, student and academic affairs need to pool their existing resources to implement evidence-based strategies that support learning and degree attainment, as well as to identify alternative funding sources. This is when it is important to think about the needs of constituents beyond the campus. Corporations, foundations, communities, and federal, state, and local governments all have a stake in developing well-educated workers and responsible citizens. These entities are likely supporters of efforts that are aligned with their goals and address their specific needs.

CAPACITY—COLLABORATE BY WHAT PROCESSES?

Thus far this chapter has focused on establishing the following among leaders and constituents in student and academic affairs:

* A clear understanding of the forces influencing action and determining that collaborative action is an appropriate response

275

* An agreement on the goals common to the involved parties that the collaborative response is intended to address

* A sufficient level of resources to work on achieving the goals collaboratively

Many are convinced that if they have established these three elements, all that is left is to work together. Leaders and constituents alike often overlook the processes by which work gets done and the underlying values and beliefs that drive the units and individuals doing the work, which can either foster or hinder collaborative behavior.

Then, still left to examine and establish are the systems and structures needed to support a collaboration effort and the influence of leadership and culture on those systems and structures. These resources will determine the institution's capacity for collaboration. Such resources include, but are not limited to, communication; reporting and managerial structures; systems of sanctions, incentives, and accountability; and professional development. Examining these systems and structures will enable leaders to ascertain whether their campuses are ready to take up the challenges of collaboration. They may determine that establishing effective collaboration structures and systems requires redefining and/or enlarging individuals' and units' roles and responsibilities, and being particularly attentive to the cultural values and beliefs that can undermine these efforts.

ASSESSMENT—HOW WILL WE KNOW COLLABORATION WORKS?

Establishing a collaborative effort is but one aspect of a larger process of educational change whose goal is to improve learning outcomes for all students. Another aspect is establishing monitoring processes

276

to sustain and evolve the educational change effort over time. Student and academic affairs collaboration is thus a part of this larger institutional change that leaders would be wise to pursue if their campuses are to achieve the goals outlined in the *Greater Expectations* report (Association of American Colleges and Universities, 2002), *Learning Reconsidered* (Keeling, 2004), and *Learning Reconsidered 2* (Keeling, 2006)—those of developing intentional students and institutions. Creating a manageable monitoring system will enable campus leaders to alter ineffective efforts and sustain effective ones.

Chapter 11 on collaboration in the community college, the collaboration framework outlined in this chapter, and the collaborative work done by the Association of American Colleges and Universities and Claremont Graduate University in the Campus Diversity Initiative Evaluation Project form the basis of the discussion in this section. General and ideal conditions are outlined that may help campus leaders construct benchmarks against which they can ascertain if their collaboration efforts are working.

The literature concerning organizational change—and change in higher education in particular—highlights analysis frameworks that have been useful. A study conducted by the American Council on Education proposed using a depth and breadth analysis to capture the level of change on a particular campus (Eckel, Green, & Hill, 2001). In addition, a review of diversity efforts (Smith, 1997) and the results of the national evaluation study of diversity (Musil, Garcia, Hudgins, Nettles, Sedlacek, & Smith, 1999) suggest that depth, breadth, and institutionalization can be reflected by a number of indicators. When changes become a permanent part of an organization's functioning, they can be considered to have been institutionalized, and "when a change is not institutionalized, it is likely to be terminated" (Curry, 1992, p. iii).

Both faculty and student affairs professionals value achievement and therefore should assess the quality of their collaborations. One way to assess how collaborations have contributed to the attainment of learning outcomes is to "gather information about favorable conditions for learning" (Council for Higher Education Accreditation, 2003, p. 6). Chapter 11 described aspects of well-coordinated assessment, such as a "conceptual mapping of institutional opportunities that support and supplement learning objectives." The chapter suggested using "multiple assessment methods within and outside the classroom." Student surveys, focus groups, and observations of student engagement will produce useful data for assessing the effectiveness of collaboration and will provide information on how to improve the environment for learning.

CONCLUSION

It seems altogether fitting that the executive director of the nation's largest association for student affairs administrators and a vice president of the nation's leading voice for quality undergraduate liberal education write this final chapter of a book about student affairs–academic affairs collaborations. In so doing, we model what we hope the book will contribute to the higher education community: a mutual respect for what each brings to the act of collaboration and equal responsibility for the outcomes they produce. We hope that our work reflects why we collaborate—so that we accomplish together something much richer than we could accomplish alone.

Many of the issues discussed in this chapter apply to a whole institution's transformation toward a more collaborative culture that fosters students achieving the essential learning outcomes. Even if campus leaders using this guide focus only on developing student and academic affairs collaborations, it is at least a start toward mobilizing the *entire* campus toward all students' success.

REFERENCES

Association of American Colleges and Universities. (2002). *Greater expectations: A new vision for learning as a nation goes to college.* Washington, DC: Author.

Clayton-Pedersen, A. R. (1992). *The elements of success: An implementation analysis of the Job Opportunities and Basics Skills (JOBS) program in Tennessee.* Unpublished doctoral dissertation, Vanderbilt University, Nashville, TN.

Council for Higher Education Accreditation. (2003). *Statement of mutual responsibilities for student learning outcomes: Accreditation, institutions, and programs.* Washington, DC: Author. Available at http://www.chea.org/pdf/StmntStudentLearningOutcomes9-03.pdf

Curry, B. K. (1992). *Instituting enduring innovations: Achieving continuity of change in higher education.* ASHE-ERIC Higher Education Report No. 7. Washington, DC: The George Washington University, School of Education and Human Development. (ERIC Digest No. ED358811, HE026562).

Eckel, P., M. Green, & B. Hill. (2001). *Riding the waves of change: Insights from transforming institutions.* Washington, DC: American Council on Education.

Keeling, R. P. (Ed.). (2004). *Learning reconsidered: A campus-wide focus on the student experience.* Washington, DC: American College Personnel Association and National Association of Student Personnel Administrators.

Keeling, R. P. (Ed.). (2006). *Learning reconsidered 2: A practical guide to implementing a campus-wide focus on the student experience.* Washington, DC: American College Personnel Association, Association of College and University Housing Officers–International, Association of College Unions International, National Academic Advising Association, National Association for Campus Activities, National Association of Student Personnel Administrators, and National Intramural-Recreational Sports Association.

Kuh, G. D. (1996). Guiding Principles for creating seamless learning environments for undergraduates. *Journal of College Student Development, 37*(2), 135–146.

Musil, C. M., M. Garcia, C. A. Hudgins, M. T. Nettles, W. E. Sedlacek, and D. G. Smith. (1999). *To form a more perfect union: Campus diversity initiatives.* Washington, DC: Association of American Colleges and Universities.

Rein, M. (1983). *From policy to practice.* Armonk, NY: M.E. Sharpe, Inc.

Smith, D. G. (1997). *The progress of a decade: An imperative for the future.* San Francisco: The James Irvine Foundation.

U.S. Department of Education. (2006). A Test of Leadership: Charting the Future of U.S. Higher Education. Washington, DC: Author.

Weiss, J. A. (1981). Symbol vs. substance in administrative reform: The case of human services coordination. *Policy Analysis 7,* 21–45.

Weiss, C. I. (1986). Agency "domain" and mental health care for the aged: A case study of services integration planning. *Human Organization, 45*(3), 239–245.

Weiss, J. A. (1987). Pathways to cooperation among public agencies. *Journal of Policy Analysis and Management, 7,* 94–117.

APPENDIX A

University of Cincinnati
A Statement of Shared Responsibility
"Creating a Learning Oriented Campus"

Academic affairs and student affairs should forge a partnership to create and sustain a campus committed to learning.

Increasingly, we know that student growth and learning takes place in all dimensions of the student experience—in the classroom, in the laboratory, in study groups, through work and volunteer activities, and all kinds of interactions with peers, staff and faculty. The traditional barriers that have separated students' formal instruction from their life outside the classroom are increasingly blurred. With the advent of instructional technology and a richer understanding of what constitutes good teaching, faculty have more choices, tools and resources to affect learning. Commensurate with this diverse educational landscape, students are expected to take more responsibility for their own learning.

It is no longer a static, one-dimensional activity of an expert imparting knowledge to a novice. Learning occurs in varying contexts, relationships and interactions. Therefore, traditional roles and structures that have divided the formal and informal are increasingly irrelevant in the new learning-oriented university. Academic roles are assuming far more responsibility for affecting the whole student. Student affairs professionals view their role as educators and less as administrators. The goals and strategies used to achieve our goals are parallel and in some instances overlapping.

Although we may start at different places to understand what works to improve retention, this clearly is a priority shared by both units. Using the academic lens, retention is no longer about lowering standards and pleasing students. It really is about the methodologies that constitute good teaching and establishing high expectations. Using the student affairs lens, improved retention is no longer simply advocating for students; it is far more about creating structured opportunities for students to be engaged in campus life applying many of the same techniques that define good teaching practice. Improved retention is a positive byproduct of our collective efforts in creating an opportunity-rich, engaging, learning environment—a shared responsibility of student affairs and academic affairs.

Beyond our collective efforts to improve retention, this shared responsibility is clearly evident when you examine the array of initiatives or activities that both units are actively pursuing:

* Enhancing the first-year experience

* Creating learning communities

* Developing the whole student

* Promoting institutional values

* Expanding opportunities for civic engagement (service-learning and volunteer activities)

* Encouraging global awareness and cultural diversity

* Improving the quality of support services

* Eliminating intra-university barriers

* Marketing and recruitment

It is very apparent that we must strengthen this partnership to accomplish these important institutional responsibilities. Creating a learning-oriented university is a collective responsibility of student and academic affairs.

APPENDIX B
A Service and Learning Typology

A Service and Learning Typology

service-LEARNING	*LEARNING goals primary; service outcomes secondary*
SERVICE-learning	*SERVICE outcomes primary; learning goals secondary*
service learning	*Service and learning goals completely separate*
SERVICE–LEARNING	*SERVICE and LEARNING goals of equal weight and each enhances the other for all participants*

Source: R. L. Sigmon, *Linking service with learning in liberal arts education.* Washington, DC: Council of Independent Colleges, 1994.

APPENDIX C

What Students Participating in Service-learning Develop

* Increased ability to apply material learned in class to real problems

* Greater self-knowledge

* A reduction of negative stereotypes and an increase in tolerance for diversity

* Greater spiritual growth

* Increased ability to work with others

* Increased feeling of being connected to a community

* Increased leadership skills

* Increased connection to the college experience through closer ties to students and faculty

* Increased reported learning and motivation to learn

* Deeper understanding of subject matter

* Deeper understanding of the complexity of social issues

Source: J. Eyler, & D. E. Giles, Jr., *Where's the learning in service-learning?* San Francisco: Jossey-Bass, 1999.

APPENDIX D

Questions to Ask
About Service-learning Partnerships

How do student affairs and academic affairs professionals work to:

* Develop shared, mutually agreed-upon vision and goals to ground service-learning initiatives?

* Forge a heightened understanding and appreciation about one another's work?

* Challenge their "mental maps" and consider cross-divisional and interdisciplinary perspectives based on shared learning goals?

* Invest the time and energy necessary to engage in ongoing, regular communication?

* Value, solicit, and learn from the diverse expertise, perspectives, and knowledge of individual partners?

* Develop a "seamless curriculum" and support pedagogies that integrate social, intellectual, and affective domains of learning and view in- and out-of-class distinctions as artificial and permeable?

* Create and implement shared, inclusive, facilitative decision-making structures that promote work toward the shared vision?

* Feel comfortable with and value the increasing ambiguity and fluidity in each others' roles and responsibilities?

* Support each other's personal growth and development and create structures that promote reciprocal learning?

* Reinforce the fact that they are working together over time rather than for a one-time experience?

* Create relationships based on respect, trust, and mutual understanding?

* Recognize conflict as a source of learning and resolve difficult issues through conversations based on candor, honesty, and empathy?

* Create a safe environment to take risks, make mistakes, and share vulnerabilities?

* Develop a belief that each participant's involvement makes a significant, positive difference in the lives of students, the institution, and the community?

* Stimulate creativity and entrepreneurialism in each other's work?

* Share resources such as staff, funds, and facilities?

* Engage in joint scholarship, assessment, and evaluation regarding service-learning?

* Celebrate shared accomplishments together?

* Demonstrate courageous leadership by consistently advocating for one another and communicating publicly about the contributions each partner makes to student learning?

* Identify and challenge organizational structures and systems that hinder efforts between faculty and student affairs to work toward designing innovative, seamless learning experiences?

Source: C. M. Engstrom, Developing collaborative student affairs–academic affairs partnerships for service-learning. In B. Jacoby, (Ed.), *Building partnerships in service-learning* (pp. 65–84). San Francisco: Jossey-Bass, 2003.

APPENDIX E

Student Affairs and Academic Affairs Collaborative Examples

Learning Link	Collaborative Project	Academic/Student Affairs Partners	Source
Residence Hall	Learning community	Provost/VPSA Faculty/RA	Troy University University of South Carolina Middle Tenn State So. Methodist University
Course Development	Leadership Counseling Honors seminar	Deans, dept. chairs, student affairs	University West Florida Elon College Western Carolina
Career Development Portfolio	Online course delivery	Deans, dept. chairs, student affairs	Kennesaw State University
Adventure Learning	Ropes course Confidence building	Student activities outreach to academics	Lynchburg College
Summer Reading Program	Fall new student convocation	VPSA also member of council of deans	Middle Tenn State Clemson
First-Year Task Forces	Bridge builders for new concepts and retention	Combined academic and student services leadership	Troy University So. Methodist University UNC-Charlotte No. Kentucky University
International programs/study abroad	International center with residence hall	Director, International program with residence hall directors	University of Florida
Shared research projects	Various research projects	Faculty with housing staff	University of Florida
Mentoring/advising	Engage faculty in process	Joint Deans Council/ office Student Success	Elon College Georgia Tech
Service-learning	Enhance community service projects	Faculty fellow with service-learning component	Western Carolina

APPENDIX F

Weatherford Residential College
in Entrepreneurship Curriculum Map

FALL TERM

FALL TERM DELIVERY: Faculty in Residence Seminar		
Week	**Topic**	**Competency**
1	Relationship Building and Orientation	
2	"Introduction to Entrepreneurship"	
3	Opportunity Recognition	Knowledge (Entrepreneurial)
4	"Market Research/Analysis"	Knowledge (Entrepreneurial)
5	"Business Planning"	
6	Resource Acquisition	Knowledge (Entrepreneurial)
7	Legal Issues	Knowledge (Entrepreneurial)
8	Harvest	Knowledge (Entrepreneurial)

FALL TERM DELIVERY: Visiting Fellow		
Week	**Topic**	**Competency**
1	Relationship Building and Orientation	
2		
3	Self Assessment	Team
4	Impression Management	Individual
5		
6	Team Evolution	Team
7	"Similarity/Complimentary Skills"	Team
8	Company Structure	Team

FALL TERM DELIVERY: Programmed Event 1

Week	Topic	Competency
1	Relationship Building and Orientation	
2	Civic Engagement	Community
3	Collaboration	Community
4	Socio-Cultural Awareness	Community
5	"Persuasion and Influence"	Individual
6	Social Confidence	Community
7	"Socio-Cultural Awareness"	Community
8	"Social Adaptability"	Individual

FALL TERM DELIVERY: Programmed Event 2

Week	Topic	Competency
1	Relationship Building and Orientation	
2	Impression Management	
3	Self Assessment	Team
4	"Introduction to Entrepreneurship"	
5	Opportunity Recognition	Knowledge (Entrepreneurial)
6	"Similarity/Complimentary Skills"	Team
7	Self Assessment	Team
8	Company Structure	Team

FALL TERM DELIVERY: Programmed Event 3

Week	Topic	Competency
1	Relationship Building and Orientation	
2	"Introduction to Entrepreneurship"	
3	Opportunity Recognition	Knowledge (Entrepreneurial)
4	Team Evolution	Team
5	"Market Research/Analysis"	Knowledge (Entrepreneurial)
6	"Similarity/Complimentary Skills"	Team

FALL TERM DELIVERY: Programmed Event 3

Week	Topic	Competency
7	"Finance and Harvest"	Knowledge (Entrepreneurial)
8	"Socio-Cultural Awareness"	Community

FALL TERM DELIVERY: Personal Experience 1

Week	Topic	Competency
1	Relationship Building and Orientation	
2	Impression Management	Individual
3	Social Perception	Individual
4	Collaboration	Community
5	Impression Management	Individual
6	Expressiveness	Individual
7	"Social Adaptability"	Individual
8	Self Efficacy	Community

FALL TERM DELIVERY: Personal Experience 2

Week	Topic	Competency
1	Relationship Building and Orientation	
2	Social Confidence	Community
3	Impression Management	Individual
4	Team Evolution	Team
5	Social Confidence	Community
6	Self Assessment	Team
7	Collaboration	Community
8	Impression Management	Individual

FALL TERM DELIVERY: Personal Experience 3

Week	Topic	Competency
1	Relationship Building and Orientation	
2	"Social Adaptability"	Individual
3	Collaboration	Community

299

FALL TERM DELIVERY: Personal Experience 3		
Week	**Topic**	**Competency**
4	Expressiveness	Individual
5	Collaboration	Community
6	Social Perception	Individual
7	"Social Adaptability"	Individual
8	Opportunity Recognition	Knowledge (Entrepreneurial)

FALL TERM: Competencies		
	Term Opportunity	**Year Required**
Team	12	
Self Assessment	4	1
Team Evolution	3	1
Similarity/Complimentary Skills	3	1
Company Structure	2	1
Individual	14	
Social Perception	2	1
Expressiveness	2	1
Impression Management	4	1
Persuasion and Influence	1	1
Social Adaptability	3	1
Community	13	
Civic Engagement	2	1
Self Efficacy	1	1
Socio-Cultural Awareness	2	1
Social Confidence	3	1
Collaboration	5	1
Knowledge (Entrepreneurial)	10	
Opportunity Recognition	4	1

FALL TERM: Competencies		
	Term Opportunity	**Year Required**
Resource Acquisition	1	1
Market Research and Analysis	1	1
Legal Issues	2	1
Finance and Harvest	2	1

FALL TERM: Delivery Method Examples	
Faculty in Residence	
	Seminar Series - Topic Specific
	Drop-in Coffee Discussions
Visiting Fellow	
	Industry leader - Topic Specific
Programmed Event	
	Odyssey
	RA Program
	Campus Program
	Class
Personal Experience	
	Reflection on an interaction
	Roommate/Community discussion
	Addressing a Conflict
	Reading and Reflection

BA 199 Credit: *Assigned Spring Term, resident must have successfully "Achieved" minimum of 500,000 points.*
Portfolio - Year 1: *Each competency must be "Achieved" to be eligible for portfolio. Curriculum offers multiple opportunities to develop competency. Successful "Achievement" will be evaluated, and then points will be assigned.*
Certificate - Year 2: *Each competency must be "Achieved." Second year, resident must "Achieve" additional 500,000 points, and successfully complete a feasibility plan to be eligible for Certificate*

WINTER TERM

WINTER TERM DELIVERY: Faculty in Residence Seminar		
Week	**Topic**	**Competency**
1	Relationship Building and Orientation	
2	Opportunity Recognition	
3	Introduction to Entrepreneurship	Knowledge (Entrepreneurial)
4	Market Research/Analysis	Knowledge (Entrepreneurial)
5	Business Planning	
6	Resource Acquisition	Knowledge (Entrepreneurial)
7	Legal Issues	Knowledge (Entrepreneurial)
8	Harvest	Knowledge (Entrepreneurial)

WINTER TERM DELIVERY: Visiting Fellow		
Week	**Topic**	**Competency**
1	Relationship Building and Orientation	
2		
3	Self Assessment	Team
4	Impression Management	Individual
5		
6	Team Evolution	Team
7	Similarity/Complimentary Skills	Team
8	Company Structure	Team

WINTER TERM DELIVERY: Programmed Event 1		
Week	**Topic**	**Competency**
1	Relationship Building and Orientation	
2	Civic Engagement	Community
3	Collaboration	Community

WINTER TERM DELIVERY: Programmed Event 1

Week	Topic	Competency
4	Socio-Cultural Awareness	Community
5	Persuasion and Influence	Individual
6	Social Confidence	Community
7	Socio-Cultural Awareness	Community
8	Social Adaptability	Individual

WINTER TERM DELIVERY: Programmed Event 2

Week	Topic	Competency
1	Relationship Building and Orientation	
2	Impression Management	Individual
3	Company Structure	Team
4	Introduction to Entrepreneurship	
5	Resource Acquisition	Knowledge (Entrepreneurial)
6	Similarity/Complimentary Skills	Team
7	Self Assessment	Team
8	Team Evolution	Team

WINTER TERM DELIVERY: Programmed Event 3

Week	Topic	Competency
1	Relationship Building and Orientation	
2	Introduction to Entrepreneurship	
3	Finance and Harvest	Knowledge (Entrepreneurial)
4	Team Evolution	Team
5	Market Research/Analysis	Knowledge (Entrepreneurial)
6	Company Structure	Team
7	Finance and Harvest	Knowledge (Entrepreneurial)
8	Socio-Cultural Awareness	Community

WINTER TERM DELIVERY: Personal Experience 1		
Week	Topic	Competency
1	Relationship Building and Orientation	
2	Social Perception	Individual
3	Social Adaptability	Individual
4	Civic Engagement	Community
5	Social Perception	Individual
6	Expressiveness	Individual
7	Persuasion and Influence	Individual
8	Self Efficacy	Community

WINTER TERM DELIVERY: Personal Experience 2		
Week	Topic	Competency
1	Relationship Building and Orientation	
2	Social Confidence	Community
3	Impression Management	Individual
4	Team Evolution	Team
5	Social Confidence	Community
6	Self Assessment	Team
7	Collaboration	Community
8	Impression Management	Individual

WINTER TERM DELIVERY: Personal Experience 3		
Week	Topic	Competency
1	Relationship Building and Orientation	
2	Social Adaptability	Individual
3	Collaboration	Community
4	Expressiveness	Individual
5	Collaboration	Community
6	Social Perception	Individual
7	Persuasion and Influence	Individual
8	Legal Issues	Knowledge (Entrepreneurial)

WINTER TERM: Competencies		
	Term Opportunity	Year Required
Team	**12**	
Self Assessment	2	1
Team Evolution	4	1
Similarity/Complimentary Skills	3	1
Company Structure	3	1
Individual	**14**	
Social Perception	3	1
Expressiveness	2	1
Impression Management	3	1
Persuasion and Influence	3	1
Social Adaptability	3	1
Community	**13**	
Civic Engagement	3	1
Self Efficacy	1	1
Socio-Cultural Awareness	2	1
Social Confidence	3	1
Collaboration	4	1
Knowledge (Entrepreneurial)	**10**	
Opportunity Recognition	1	1
Resource Acquisition	2	1
Market Research and Analysis	2	1
Legal Issues	2	1
Finance and Harvest	3	1

WINTER TERM: Delivery Method Examples	
Faculty in Residence	
	Seminar Series - Topic Specific
	Drop-in Coffee Discussions

WINTER TERM: Delivery Method Examples	
Visiting Fellow	
	Industry leader - Topic Specific
Programmed Event	
	Odyssey
	RA Program
	Campus Program
	Class
Personal Experience	
	Reflection on an interaction
	Roommate/Community discussion
	Addressing a Conflict
	Reading and Reflection

BA 199 Credit: *Assigned Spring Term, resident must have successfully "Achieved" minimum of 500,000 points.*

Portfolio - Year 1: *Each competency must be "Achieved" to be eligible for portfolio. Curriculum offers multiple opportunities to develop competency. Successful "Achievement" will be evaluated, and then points will be assigned.*

Certificate - Year 2: *Each competency must be "Achieved." Second year, resident must "Achieve" additional 500,000 points, and successfully complete a feasibility plan to be eligible for Certificate*

SPRING TERM

SPRING TERM DELIVERY: Faculty in Residence Seminar		
Week	**Topic**	**Competency**
1	Relationship Building and Orientation	
2	Introduction to Entrepreneurship	
3	Opportunity Recognition	Knowledge (Entrepreneurial)
4	Market Research/Analysis	Knowledge (Entrepreneurial)
5	Business Planning	
6	Resource Acquisition	Knowledge (Entrepreneurial)
7	Legal Issues	Knowledge (Entrepreneurial)
8	Harvest	Knowledge (Entrepreneurial)

SPRING TERM DELIVERY: Visiting Fellow		
Week	**Topic**	**Competency**
1	Relationship Building and Orientation	
2		
3	Self Assessment	Team
4	Impression Management	Individual
5		
6	Team Evolution	Team
7	Similarity/Complimentary Skills	Team
8	Company Structure	Team

SPRING TERM DELIVERY: Programmed Event 1		
Week	**Topic**	**Competency**
1	Relationship Building and Orientation	
2	Civic Engagement	

SPRING TERM DELIVERY: Programmed Event 1		
Week	Topic	Competency
3	Self Efficacy	Community
4	Socio-CulturalAwareness	Community
5	Persuasion and Influence	Individual
6	Social Confidence	Community
7	Socio-CulturalAwareness	Community
8	Social Adaptability	Individual

SPRING TERM DELIVERY: Programmed Event 2		
Week	Topic	Competency
1	Relationship Building and Orientation	
2	Impression Management	Individual
3	Company Structure	Team
4	Introduction to Entrepreneurship	
5	Resource Acquisition	Knowledge (Entrepreneurial)
6	Similarity/Complimentary Skills	Team
7	Team Evolution	Team
8	Similarity/Complimentary Skills	Team

SPRING TERM DELIVERY: Programmed Event 3		
Week	Topic	Competency
1	Relationship Building and Orientation	
2	Introduction to Entrepreneurship	
3	Finance and Harvest	Knowledge (Entrepreneurial)
4	Team Evolution	Team
5	Market Research/Analysis	Knowledge (Entrepreneurial)
6	Company Structure	Team
7	Finance and Harvest	Knowledge (Entrepreneurial)
8	Socio-Cultural Awareness	Community

SPRING TERM DELIVERY: Personal Experience 1

Week	Topic	Competency
1	Relationship Building and Orientation	
2	Expressiveness	Individual
3	Social Adaptability	Individual
4	Civic Engagement	Community
5	Social Perception	Individual
6	Expressiveness	Individual
7	Persuasion and Influence	Individual
8	Self Efficacy	Community

SPRING TERM DELIVERY: Personal Experience 2

Week	Topic	Competency
1	Relationship Building and Orientation	
2	Self Efficacy	Community
3	Impression Management	Individual
4	Company Structure	Team
5	Social Confidence	Community
6	Self Assessment	Team
7	Collaboration	Community
8	Impression Management	Individual

SPRING TERM DELIVERY: Personal Experience 3

Week	Topic	Competency
1	Relationship Building and Orientation	
2	Social Adaptability	Individual
3	Civic Engagement	Community
4	Expressiveness	Individual
5	Self Efficacy	Community
6	Social Perception	Individual
7	Persuasion and Influence	Individual
8	Legal Issues	Knowledge (Entrepreneurial)

309

SPRING TERM: Competencies		
	Term Opportunity	Year Required
Team	**12**	
Self Assessment	1	1
Team Evolution	3	1
Similarity/Complimentary Skills	4	1
Company Structure	4	1
Individual	**14**	
Social Perception	2	1
Expressiveness	3	1
Impression Management	3	1
Persuasion and Influence	3	1
Social Adaptability	3	1
Community	**13**	
Civic Engagement	3	1
Self Efficacy	4	1
Socio-Cultural Awareness	3	1
Social Confidence	2	1
Collaboration	1	1
Knowledge (Entrepreneurial)	**10**	
Opportunity Recognition	1	1
Resource Acquisition	2	1
Market Research and Analysis	2	1
Legal Issues	2	1
Finance and Harvest	3	1

SPRING TERM: Delivery Method Examples	
Faculty in Residence	
	Seminar Series - Topic Specific
	Drop-in Coffee Discussions

SPRING TERM: Delivery Method Examples	
Visiting Fellow	
	Industry leader - Topic Specific
Programmed Event	
	Odyssey
	RA Program
	Campus Program
	Class
Personal Experience	
	Reflection on an interaction
	Roommate/Community discussion
	Addressing a Conflict
	Reading and Reflection

BA 199 Credit: *Assigned Spring Term, resident must have successfully "Achieved" minimum of 500,000 points.*

Portfolio - Year 1: *Each competency must be "Achieved" to be eligible for portfolio. Curriculum offers multiple opportunities to develop competency. Successful "Achievement" will be evaluated, and then points will be assigned.*

Certificate - Year 2: *Each competency must be "Achieved." Second year, resident must "Achieve" additional 500,000 points, and successfully complete a feasibility plan to be eligible for Certificate*

APPENDIX G

Contact Information for Institutions with Promising Practices

ANNE ARUNDEL COMMUNITY COLLEGE

Terry Clay

Assistant Dean for Student Development and Success

101 College Parkway

Student Union Building #224

Arnold, MD 21012

Phone: (410) 777-2305

tmclay@aacc.edu

CARROLL COMMUNITY COLLEGE

Michele Lenhart

Student Life

1601 Washington Road

Westminster, MD 21157

Phone: (410) 386-8408

mlenhart@carrollcc.edu

CENTRAL MICHIGAN UNIVERSITY

Dyke Heinze

Director, Leadership Institute

130 Powers HallMount Pleasant, MI 48859

Phone: (989) 774-1211
heinz1dj@cmich.edu

CLEMSON UNIVERSITY

Casey Berkshire
Director of Freshman Academic Programs
Office of Undergraduate Studies
E-101 Martin Hall
Clemson, SC 29634
Phone: (864) 656-6902
clberks@clemson.edu

ELON UNIVERSITY

Smith Jackson
Vice President for Student Life
Elon, NC 27244
Phone: (336) 278-7220

DEPAUL UNIVERSITY

Ellen Meents-DeCaigny
Student Affairs Assessment and Research Coordinator
Division of Student Affairs
25 E. Jackson Bld., Suite 1400
Chicago, IL 60604
Phone: (312) 362-7298
emeentsd@depaul.edu

FURMAN UNIVERSITY

Harry B. Shucker
Vice President
Student Services
3300 Poinsett Highway
Greenville, SC 29613
Phone: (864) 294-2202

INDIANA UNIVERSITY–PURDUE UNIVERSITY INDIANAPOLIS (IUPUI)

Frank E. Ross
Associate Vice Chancellor for Student Affairs
Student Life and Diversity
355 North Lansing Street
Indianapolis, IN 46202
Phone: (317) 274-8990
frross@iupui.edu

KENNESAW STATE UNIVERSITY

Karen B. Andrews
Director of Career Services
1000 Chastain Road #0118
Kennesaw, GA 30144
Phone: (770) 423-6555
kandrews@kennesaw.edu

LYNCHBURG COLLEGE

Paul Stern

Coordinator
Hundley Hall, Terrace Level
1501 Lakeside Drive
Lynchburg, VA 24501
Phone: (434) 544-8224
newhorizons@lynchburg.edu

MANSFIELD UNIVERSITY OF PENNSYLVANIA
Shari J. Clarke
Vice President for Student Affairs
Mansfield, PA 16933
Phone: (570) 662-4000

MINNESOTA STATE UNIVERSITY, MANKATO
Kelly S. Meier
Director
Student Leadership Development & Service-Learning
CSU 173
Mankato, MN 56001
Kelly.meier@mnsu.edu

NORTHERN KENTUCKY UNIVERSITY
Mark Shanley
Vice President for Student Affairs
Nunn Drive
Highland Heights, KY 41099
Phone: (859) 572-6447
mshanley@nku.edu

316

SLIPPERY ROCK UNIVERSITY

Paula Olivero

Assistant Vice President for Student Development

302 Old Main

1 Morrow Way

Slippery Rock, PA 16057

Phone: (724) 738-2683

paula.olivero@sru.edu

STONY BROOK UNIVERSITY

Dallas W. Bauman III

Assistant Vice President for Campus Residences

Division of Campus Residences

Stony Brook, NY 11794-4444

Phone: (631) 632-6974

dbauman@notes.cc.sunysb.edu

SYRACUSE UNIVERSITY

Barry L. Wells

Senior Vice President and Dean

Student Affairs

306 Steele Hall

Syracuse University

Syracuse, NY 13244

blwells@syr.edu

UNIVERSITY OF ARIZONA

Carol Funckes

Associate Director
Disability Resource Center
1224 East Lowell Street
Tucson, AZ 85721
Phone: (520) 621-3274
carolf@email.arizona.edu

UNIVERSITY OF FLORIDA

Wayne Wallace
Director, Career Resource Center
JWRU PO Box 118507
Gainesville, FL 32611-8507
Phone: (352) 392-1601
WayneWallace@crc.ufl.edu

UNIVERSITY OF KENTUCKY

Rebecca Jordan
Associate Dean of Students
518 Patterson Office Tower 0027
Lexington, KY 40506
Phone: (859) 257-6597
rjordan@email.uky.edu

UNIVERSITY OF RICHMOND

28 Westhampton Way
University of Richmond, VA 23173
Phone: (804) 289-8000

University of South Carolina

Gene Luna
Associate Vice President for Student Affairs
Columbia, SC 29208
Phone: (803) 777-6911
genel@sc.edu

Western Carolina University

Robert Caruso
Vice Chancellor for Student Affairs
Interim Coordinator, College Student Personnel Program
Cullowhee, NC 28723
Phone: (828) 227-7147

CONTRIBUTORS

Frank P. Ardaiolo, EdD, has been the vice president for student life and an associate professor at Winthrop University in Rock Hill, South Carolina, for the past 18 years where he oversees a broad portfolio of student-related areas at this public comprehensive institution. He has been instrumental in moving his institution's focus more on student learning while creating cross-functional structures to bridge the efforts between academic and student affairs. He earned his doctoral degree from Indiana University in higher education, student affairs, political science, and African studies and his bachelor's from Assumption College.

Robert Caruso, PhD, is currently vice chancellor for student affairs at Western Carolina University and Interim Program Director for the graduate program in College Student Personnel. His professional interests include: student development, minority student achievement, collaboration with academic affairs, teaching student affairs courses, enrollment management, and theory-to-practice applications in student affairs.

Alma R. Clayton-Pedersen, PhD, is the vice president of the Office of Education and Institutional Renewal at the Association of American Colleges and Universities (AAC&U). Her work at AAC&U concentrates on developing collaborative campus leadership to enhance student and organizational learning. She served as an administrator in both student and academic affairs positions during her 15 years at Vanderbilt University. Her publications include *Enacting Diverse Learning*

321

Environments: Improving the Climate for Racial/Ethnic Diversity in Higher Education and several publications that resulted from a six year project designed to assist 28 California campuses in building their internal capacity to evaluate their diversity initiatives funded by the James Irvine Foundation.

James H. Cook, EdD, is dean of enrollment management at Tarleton State University in Stephenville, Texas. He has 17 years of experience as a student affairs and academic affairs administrator, having held positions ranging from associate vice president of student affairs to his current position in academic affairs. He also has 14 years of experience teaching in a college of business. His bachelor's and master's degrees are in business administration and his doctorate is in higher education administration with an emphasis in student personnel administration.

Gwendolyn J. Dungy, PhD, has been executive director of NASPA–Student Affairs Administrators in Higher Education since 1995, after serving as the associate director of the Curriculum and Faculty Development Network for the Association of American Colleges and Universities. Her campus experience includes being a senior academic and student affairs administrator at the County College of Morris in New Jersey, Montgomery College in Maryland, Catonsville Community College in Maryland, and St. Louis Community College in the Department of Counseling. She has served on the ACE Commission on Government Relations and as a trustee at several colleges and universities. She earned BS and MS degrees from Eastern Illinois University, an MA degree from Drew University in New Jersey, and a PhD from Washington University in St. Louis.

Robert E. Eaker, EdD, is a professor of education at Middle Tennessee State University. Prior to his current position, he served as dean of the College of Education and also as the interim executive vice-president and provost. He holds a BS from the University of Chattanooga; an MEd from the University of Tennessee, Chattanooga; and an EdD from the University of Tennessee. He has authored and co-authored numerous books and articles and regularly consults throughout North America.

Abby M. Ghering, MA, is currently the assistant dean/associate director of academic support and enrichment at Denison University in Granville, Ohio. She earned her master's degree in higher education administration from Indiana University Bloomington.

Christopher A. Lewis, EdD, is the assistant dean for student services at the University of Wisconsin–Manitowoc where he oversees all aspects of student services and enrollment management. Chris has 10 years of experience as a student affairs and academic affairs administrator and is the co-founder and past national chair of NASPA's Student Affairs Professionals Working In and With Academic Affairs (SAPAA) Knowledge Community. He earned his doctoral degree from Eastern Michigan University in educational leadership, his master's degree in college student personnel administration from Miami University, and his bachelor's degree from Western Michigan University.

Tomás D. Morales, PhD, is the provost and vice president for academic affairs at California State Polytechnic University, Pomona. He also retains the position of professor of education in the College of Education and Integrated Studies. He holds a PhD in educational administration and policy studies from the State University of New York in Albany, New York. He has served as an administrative leader and educator in higher education for more than 28 years.

Kim C. O'Halloran, PhD, is the associate dean of the Graduate School at Montclair State University in New Jersey. She is also an assistant professor in the Department of Counseling, Human Development and Educational Leadership, where her research focuses on student retention and persistence in graduate programs and student and academic affairs collaboration. She has 15 years of experience as a student affairs and academic affairs administrator, having held positions in the areas of student activities, greek life, student leadership programs, community service and service-learning, student health and graduate education. She has a BA in English and an EdM in education administration from Rutgers University in New Jersey and a PhD in higher education administration from New York University.

Sandi N. Osters, PhD, has been the director of student life studies at Texas A&M University for the last nine. Her 20 years in student affairs spans positions in administration, judicial affairs, and student activities. She has a BA in political science from Miami University (Ohio), an MA in education from The Ohio State University, and a doctorate in higher education administration from Texas A&M University.

John W. Schmidt, EdD, is the senior vice chancellor for student services at Troy University. He formerly served as the executive assistant to the chancellor and vice president for advancement. He is a retired U.S. Marine Corps colonel.

Debra K. Sells, EdD, serves as the associate vice provost for academic services at Middle Tennessee State University (MTSU). She came to MTSU in 1996, after having worked in the division of student affairs at Arizona State University, California Polytechnic State University in San Luis Obispo, and Grinnell College. She holds a BA from Hope College; an MSW from the University of Michigan; and an EdD from Arizona State University. Her doctoral work focused on the creation of student affairs–academic affairs partnerships to retain first-year students.

Edward J. Shenk, EdD, is an associate professor and program director in the Graduate School of Education at Alliant International University. He is also the editor of the *iJournal* for the statewide Chief Student Service Administrators Association. He retired from Napa Valley College after 31 years where he was the vice president of student services. He was active state-wide in the community college system for more than 36 years. He is a former national chair for NASPA's Community and Two-Year Colleges Knowledge Community.

Jeff P. Stein, MFA, is assistant dean of students for service-learning and residence life at Elon University and serves as assistant professor in the English department. He earned his MFA in creative writing from Colorado State University and has published poems in *New Delta Review, Phoebe, Many Mountains Moving* and others.

Magdalena H. de la Teja, JD, PhD, is dean of student services at Austin Community College and has 17 years community college experience. She graduated with a PhD and JD from The University of Texas at Austin; served for eight years in various administrative positions at UT Austin and three years as an attorney with the Texas Legislature. She is a published author on student retention and success issues, and serves as the chair of NASPA's Community and Two-Year Colleges Advisory Board.